WOMEN, FAMILI
A Sociological Perspective

Women make up 16 percent of total AIDS cases in the U.S. today, and the number of women with HIV disease is now growing at a faster rate than that of men. Women are contracting HIV through heterosexual transmission faster than by any other means of transmission, including injection drug use. How did female cases in the United States grow from 43 in 1983 to over 2,000 times that number 14 years later? What factors have influenced the course of the epidemic for women? What has been the impact of this disease on women and on families? This book offers the first comprehensive sociological explanation.

Carole Campbell examines the position of women in this epidemic (women living with HIV and the growing number of women who must care for HIV-infected family members) in a sociocultural context. The early male profile of the AIDS epidemic has given rise to education and prevention programs based upon the needs of men. Campbell draws a clear connection between women's risk of getting AIDS, gender roles (particularly gender role socialization in adolescence), and the sexual behavior of men. She demonstrates that no effort to contain the spread of the disease to women can succeed without also targeting the male behavior that puts women at risk.

Campbell concludes that, compared with men, HIV-infected women face unequal access to care and unequal quality of care, which affects not only these women and their children but also the women who care for HIV-infected family members. Campbell argues compellingly that social institutions such as health care and the media have created barriers for women because they fail to take account of the differences between men and women in social roles, status, and power. Informed by the moving, personal accounts of eleven HIV-infected men and women, this book offers a rare, broad picture of the sociocultural causes of AIDS among women and the impact of the disease on American society.

Carole Campbell, professor of sociology at California State University, Long Beach, has been researching and publishing on the subject of women and AIDS for the past 12 years.

WOMEN, FAMILIES, AND HIV/AIDS

A Sociological Perspective on the Epidemic in America

CAROLE A. CAMPBELL

//

CAMBRIDGE
UNIVERSITY PRESS

PUBLISHED BY THE PRESS SYNDICATE OF THE UNIVERSITY OF CAMBRIDGE
The Pitt Building, Trumpington Street, Cambridge, United Kingdom

CAMBRIDGE UNIVERSITY PRESS
The Edinburgh Building, Cambridge, CB2 2RU, UK   http://www.cup.cam.ac.uk
40 West 20th Street, New York, NY 10011-4211, USA   http://www.cup.org
10 Stamford Road, Oakleigh, Melbourne 3166, Australia

First published 1999

Printed in the United States of America

Typeface Adobe Garamond 10/13 pt.   *System* QuarkXPress™   [TW]

*A catalog record for this book is avilable from
the British Library*

Library of Congress Cataloging-in-Publication Data
Campbell, Carole A.
Women, families, and HIV/AIDS : a sociological perspective
on the epidemic in America / Carole A. Campbell.
p. cm.
Includes bibliographical references and index.
ISBN 0-521-56211-2 (hardbound)
ISBN 0-521-56679-7 (paperback)
1. AIDS (Disease) – Social aspects – United States. 2. HIV
infections – Social aspects – United States. I. Title.
RA644.A25C3627 1999
362.1′969792′00973 – dc21   98 – 29607
CIP

ISBN 0 521 56211 2   hardback
ISBN 0 521 56679 7   paperback

CONTENTS

PREFACE

Using data from epidemiological and other biomedical sources, *Women, Families, and HIV/AIDS* describes women at risk for AIDS. This book, which is based on a conceptual framework combining descriptive epidemiological methods and sociological theory, offers a sociological analysis of how women's social and economic positions in relation to men affect their sexual decisions as well as their health practices. In addition, the book analyzes how the generally stronger position men have in society and the behaviors of men place women at elevated risk for AIDS. Finally, this book explores the emotional and social consequences of an AIDS illness on children and other family members.

This book is the culmination of my work in the field of women and AIDS for the last 12 years. My first formal research in this field was as a collaborator in a multicenter study of female prostitutes (Project 72) conducted by the Center for Disease Control and Prevention in 1985. Working with Rick Reich of the Clark County (Nevada) Health Department, I collected data at a legal brothel outside of Las Vegas. I am grateful to Rick for his encouragement and support in that research endeavor as well as in my subsequent work on AIDS.

In 1987 I developed the course "AIDS and Society" for the Sociology Department at California State University, Long Beach (CSULB), where I teach. I am indebted to my students in that course who have continuously challenged and inspired me. Teaching a course on AIDS is among the most difficult, yet inspiring, ventures of my professional career. My hope is that this book will be useful to other faculty and students in AIDS courses.

In the early years of the AIDS epidemic, most research attention was directed toward gay men. Women's issues related to HIV were being overlooked. In particular, the role that gender played in determining women's risk for HIV and their access to care was not being addressed. In 1990 I published "Women and AIDS" in *Social Science and Medicine*. In that work, I examined the implications of gender roles and gender stratification for women's HIV/AIDS risk and prevention. That publication was followed, in 1991, by "Prostitution, AIDS, and Preventive Health Behavior," also in *Social Science and Medicine*, which dealt with the work lives of prostitutes in relation to their risk for HIV. In writing that article I also drew upon data collected in the 1985 multicenter study.

After focusing for several years on women's vulnerability to HIV, I realized that the role of heterosexual men in determining this vulnerability was not being given sufficient attention. Gender role socialization and gender power relations needed to be studied more closely. This line of thinking led me to write "Male Gender Roles and Sexuality: Implications for Women's AIDS Risk and Prevention," published in *Social Science and Medicine* in 1995. This article emphasized the gender role socialization and sexuality of heterosexual men in determining women's risk for HIV and examined the conflict between masculine identity and HIV/AIDS prevention goals.

By now it is well recognized that women do not have control over condom use (e.g., Wermuth, 1992; Worth, 1989). Acknowledging women's vulnerability, however, is not enough. Men's behavior, particularly that behavior that is formed during adolescence and increases women's risk for AIDS, should be closely scrutinized in the context of gender power relations. That is one of my goals in this book.

I have had the fortunate opportunity to present some of the ideas from my work on heterosexual men and AIDS at several professional conferences. These meetings of practitioners in AIDS prevention and service delivery have included HIV/AIDS Epidemiology and Prevention Information Exchange, sponsored by the State Office of AIDS in 1994 and held in Fresno, California; Women and HIV: A Call to Action, sponsored by the University of California, Santa Cruz, in 1995; and the 1997 conference, Safer Communities: Rethinking HIV Intervention Strategies, sponsored by the HIV Epidemiology Program of Los Angeles.

My thoughts on the need to further examine the role played by men in prevention and service delivery were well received and reinforced at those meetings. Several health service providers commented that my perspective was refreshing and long overdue. It is gratifying to know that my ideas are relevant to those working in the trenches of AIDS prevention and service delivery. I appreciate their comments, insights, and support, and their enthusiastic response has encouraged me to continue in this line of advocacy. I also want to express my admiration for their tireless dedication to AIDS prevention and service delivery.

From a focus on heterosexual men, my work has expanded to include research on families with HIV/AIDS. Interviews with infected caregivers showed me the extent to which entire families were affected by the disease. Another goal of this book, therefore, is to examine the impact of HIV disease on all family members.

I am extremely indebted to Project AHEAD and the CARE Program, both of which are community-based organizations in Long Beach, California. For the last few years I have been involved with these agencies as a collaborator and consultant, which has taught me a great deal about the realities of AIDS service delivery to families dealing with HIV disease. I wish to thank these programs for facilitating the interviews for this book.

As part of my teaching at CSULB, I serve as field placement coordinator for the Sociology Internship Program. In this role, I work with a number of other community-based AIDS organizations in addition to Project AHEAD and the CARE Program. My ongoing contact with service providers at these agencies has sensitized me to the tremendous barriers to AIDS service delivery, some of which are described in the last two chapters of this book. I hope that what I have gained from my involvement with the community is reciprocal, that is, that this book will contribute to better AIDS prevention and service delivery and that service providers will benefit from reading it.

I am greatly indebted to the individuals who willingly shared with me their personal accounts of living with HIV disease. Their descriptions of how the disease has changed their lives are indeed sobering. I am deeply grateful for their enthusiastic response to and interest in this book. Their contribution is immeasurable.

Many persons helped make this book possible. Dr. Raymond M. Berger helped revise several chapters. Two CSULB students, Lourdes Vidal and Gail Libbee, provided painstaking assistance with the interviews.

Preface

I am grateful to my colleagues in the Sociology Department at CSULB for their support of this project. Professor Douglas A. Parker deserves special acknowledgment for his guidance and support. The Sociology Department's secretary, Lily Monji, performed numerous tasks in the production of the manuscript.

Research support to conduct and transcribe the interviews was provided by CSULB. I am most grateful to Joy Thomas, librarian, who compiled the index for the book. Her careful work and attention to detail are appreciated. The CSULB library, particularly the Interlibrary Loan Deparment, assisted by obtaining many books and articles.

I also wish to acknowledge the anonymous reviewers of this manuscript and its earlier prospectus. Their comments and suggestions were most helpful. In addition, I am grateful to Elizabeth Neal and Mary Child, social sciences editors at Cambridge University Press, for their guidance and support. Their editorial comments were especially useful.

I also wish to recognize William F. Wagner, my undergraduate mentor at the University of Albuquerque and now on the faculty of Mankato State University, for his support during the early years of my academic career in sociology. My graduate school mentors, Professor Richard H. Ogles and Professor Edward L. Rose, at the University of Colorado (Denver and Boulder, respectively), also deserve recognition for their support throughout my academic career. Both have contributed much to my growth as a professional sociologist and to them I express my deepest gratitude.

Family members also provided much help. My mother, Dorothy Baumgardner, and sister, Marie Rosales, sent numerous helpful articles. And my three-year-old grandson, Malik Jameel Campbell, helped by taking naps while under my care, which allowed me to work on this book. I am grateful to all those persons who gave me encouragement and a sense that I could make a contribution to (and possibly a difference in) people's lives.

Portions of some chapters in the book appeared in the three articles in *Social Science and Medicine*: "Women and AIDS," vol. 30, pp. 407–415, 1990; "Prostitution, AIDS, and Preventive Health Behavior," vol. 32, pp. 1367–1378, 1991; and, "Male Gender Roles and Sexuality: Implications for Women's AIDS Risk and Prevention," vol. 41, pp. 197–210, 1995. Some content also derived from two coauthored publications: with M. D. Peck, "Issues in HIV/AIDS Service Delivery to High Risk

Youth," *Journal of Gay and Lesbian Social Services,* vol. 2, pp. 159–177, 1995; and, with P. DiCarlo, "How Are Heterosexual Men Reached in HIV Prevention?" *HIV Prevention: Looking Back, Looking Ahead,* Center for AIDS Prevention (CAPS), University of California and Harvard AIDS Institute, 1996.

INTRODUCTION:
WOMEN AT RISK

From the beginning of the AIDS epidemic in the United States, cases of the disease in men have outnumbered cases in women, and this disparity has played a powerful role in constructing the epidemic's male profile. Early cases of acquired immunodeficiency syndrome (AIDS) among male homosexuals, injection drug users (IDUs), and hemophiliacs reinforced this profile. Table 1 in Chapter 1, which breaks down transmission categories by gender, demonstrates this male profile of the disease.

As a result of the male profile of AIDS, the impact of the epidemic on women in America has often been underemphasized and even overlooked. To understand the magnitude of this epidemic, there is a need to construct a female profile for it. The aim of this book is to create such a profile by describing the sociological impact of the epidemic on women, including women who are caregivers. The figures cited in this book will be for the United States only, unless otherwise stated.

Women's risk of infection from the human immunodeficiency virus (HIV) cannot be understood without closely examining gender roles and gender stratification. Toward this end, this book documents the relationship between poverty and HIV disease. In particular, this book will show that the concept of the "feminization of poverty" is vital to understanding the position of women in this epidemic.

Although the control and containment of the epidemic of AIDS among heterosexuals depends on male behavior, few studies have focused on the role of men in elevating women's risk patterns. Another aim of this book is, therefore, to thoroughly examine the behavior of heterosexual men as a determinant of women's elevated risk for HIV/AIDS.

AIDS education and prevention efforts have often targeted women without considering their male partners or the role of men in sexual decision making. This book will examine women's risk vis-à-vis the behavior of their male partners, especially the vulnerability of female adolescents to HIV disease.

The first case of AIDS in a woman was reported in 1981, the same year in which AIDS was identified in homosexual men (CDC, 1981). The female case was hidden in a table listing cases of Kaposi's sarcoma (KS) and pneumocystis pneumonia (PCP) by gender and diagnosis (KS and/or PCP). Mortality rates were given for both KS and PCP and for the 108 total (107 male and 1 female) cases. The table also broke down the male cases by race and sexual identity. The only information given about the female case, however, was that the woman had PCP. The female case was not remarked on in the report itself, which simply stated that most cases of KS and PCP had occurred in white men. Two earlier issues of *Morbidity and Mortality Weekly Report* (*MMWR*), one of which documented the first five AIDS cases in the United States, had included only male cases. The issue that had in it the table listing the female case was about KS and PCP.

By the end of 1981, 6 cases of AIDS among women had been identified in surveillance figures, representing 3% of total number. Yet these cases were largely unrecognized in the scientific literature, an indication of how women would be treated in the years to come. By January 1983, 43 cases of AIDS among women had been reported (CDC, 1983a). In most of these the infected women were either drug users themselves or the sex partner of drug users. Many of the women who did not use drugs themselves had had no idea that their sex partners did. Thus, these women were unaware of the risk that they faced through heterosexual transmission. These early cases portended the epidemic of AIDS among heterosexuals in the United States.

The transmission categories of these early female AIDS cases were difficult to determine. It was thought that they had become infected through injection drug use. Moreover, the injection drug and heterosexual categories were not distinct. It soon became apparent, however, that some infected women who were sex partners of IDUs had been infected through heterosexual intercourse. The injection drug use and heterosexual transmission categories have remained intricately intertwined throughout the epidemic.

As soon as cases of AIDS were identified among heterosexuals, attention focused on women for their role in infecting others. For example, in media accounts women were portrayed as "infectors" rather than as "infectees" (Wofsy, 1987). Research and policy agendas also reflected concern about women's role in infection (Patton, 1994). Women were seen as presenting a risk to others, and as a result, far more alarm was expressed about women's role in transmission than about the very real risk that women themselves faced. The media portrayed women as "vectors" or "reservoirs" of infection, either to their male partners or to their unborn children (Caravano, 1991; Patton, 1994; Treichler, 1988). Female prostitutes were targeted because of the risk they represented to their clients, and prenatal women, for the risk to their unborn children. Public concern about AIDS prevention had more to do with the health of men and children than with the health of women (Caravano, 1991).

The intertwined transmission categories used in surveillance reports through 1983 also obscured female cases. As already mentioned, heterosexual transmission did not exist as a separate category; significantly the next highest transmission category for women after "injection drug use" was "none/unknown." At the end of 1983, 36% of female cases – compared to 4% of male cases – were in this category (CDC, 1983b). However, the nearly 200 female cases remained overshadowed by the male cases, which were more than 10 times that number.

The potential magnitude of the female epidemic continued largely unremarked. The small number of reported female cases were especially deceiving because of the long latency of the disease from the time of infection to the onset of symptoms. Women who were just beginning to exhibit symptoms had been infected years earlier. But many more women were infected with the virus and would be identified as having AIDS in the years to come.

Early in the epidemic, seropositivity for the AIDS virus could not be determined because the antibody test did not become available until 1985. Even when the test did become available, however, infected women continued to be overlooked. Many women did not recognize their own risk and did not ask to be tested. Likewise, physicians often did not think to test women because of the disease's powerful male profile.

Physicians were slow to recognize the symptoms of HIV disease in women. In many women, the disease was detected only after a long process of exclusion of other diseases. AIDS-defining conditions had a male profile, and women were experiencing different symptoms compared to men. Physicians often failed to connect recurrent vaginal candidiasis, or yeast infections, an early symptom in women, to HIV disease. As a result, many women were in the advanced stages of the illness before receiving an AIDS diagnosis, and some women died before receiving such a diagnosis. Because of late detection and diagnosis, female cases were seriously undercounted.

Today, female cases comprise 16% of the total AIDS cases (CDC, 1997a). The incidence of AIDS cases is increasing more rapidly among women than men (CDC, 1995). The injection drug transmission category, the largest category for women, represents almost half of the female cases. The second largest category for women, heterosexual transmission, represents over one-third of female cases. Heterosexual transmission has continued to increase for women and is currently the fastest growing transmission category (CDC, 1995).

These figures raise perplexing issues: How did female cases in the United States grow over 2,000 times in 14 years, from 43 in 1983 to 98,468 at the end of 1987? And, what factors in particularly have influenced the course of the epidemic for women? This book will offer a sociological explanation.

Although the epidemiologic impact of AIDS has been evident for some time, the sociological impact has not yet been fully described. We need to address the gap between the advances made in biomedicine and the lingering sociological issues. An examination of the sociocultural context of the AIDS epidemic among women is long overdue and is the focus of this book.

Chapter 1 reviews the epidemiology, risk/transmission, and natural history of HIV disease in women and children. A profile of female cases will show that HIV disease affects women differently, depending on their age, race, geographic location, and sexual orientation. This profile will also show that transmission and disease presentation and diagnosis are different for women and for men. The chapter includes a discussion of HIV disease in children and adolescents.

Chapter 2 discusses the complex sociological issues that HIV disease creates for women's reproductive health. Reproductive rights and sexual discrimination are critical issues facing many infected women. The chapter covers approaches to perinatal risk reduction and examines women's reproductive choices and sexual decision making. Adolescent sexuality is given special attention in this chapter.

Chapter 3 deals with two special populations of women – drug users and prostitutes – and examines the roles of gender and culture in drug use and sexual behavior. The important influence of male behavior on female drug use and sexual behavior will be shown. The chapter investigates the intricate tie between drug use and prostitution and reveals the problems created for women by a legal system that criminalizes both of these behaviors.

As soon as AIDS cases were identified among heterosexuals, concern was expressed about prostitutes, who were seen as vectors for heterosexual transmission. Chapter 3 examines this attention to prostitutes and especially to the behavior of their partners, both paying and nonpaying, and reviews policies on the mandatory testing of prostitutes.

An understanding of women's risk for HIV disease cannot be achieved without examining gender and cultural roles. Development of effective HIV prevention strategies requires a close examination of these roles. Chapter 4 covers the intersection of gender, culture, race, and class in the epidemic. It will show that women's position in the epidemic, compared with that of men, has been one of both unequal access to care and unequal quality of care. The male profile of the epidemic has resulted in education and prevention programs based on the needs of men. This chapter reveals how the media and social institutions involved with health care have created barriers for women by failing to take account of differences between men and women in social roles, social status, and power. Particular attention is given to adolescent socialization in shaping power relations based upon gender.

The gender role and sexuality of men also must be understood if successful AIDS prevention and control strategies are to be developed. Toward this goal, Chapter 5 closely examines male sexuality in the heterosexual context and male-female gender dynamics. The socialization of adolescent males and the importance of altering male behavior as factors in controlling the heterosexual epidemic are stressed.

It has been evident for some time that HIV disease is a family-based disease. Women, as mothers, grandmothers, sisters, and aunts, have assumed informal, caregiving roles in the family for both adult members with HIV and the children of infected women. The impact of the disease on family life and the caregiving role of kin are discussed in

Chapter 6. The women who have had to become caregivers have many unmet needs themselves. This chapter also examines the barriers to service delivery to families with HIV disease and stresses the need for family-based services.

Women have played an important and heartening role in AIDS service delivery throughout the AIDS epidemic. Chapter 7 looks at women's other roles in the epidemic, including those they have taken as either professional or volunteer caregivers, and underscores the importance of informal caregiving. This final chapter presents a critical evaluation of the policies affecting families dealing with HIV disease, particularly those policies that affect children and youth.

Each chapter opens with excerpts from either the interview transcripts or diaries of the women and men (eleven in all) who kindly provided accounts of their experiences living with HIV disease. These vignettes give an important human dimension to the book, one not always achievable in a scholarly treatment; their direct accounts document daily realities and enable readers to understand the challenges for and constraints upon persons living with HIV disease. Biographies of these individuals as well as a description of how the interviews and diaries were obtained are found in the appendices.

Women, Families, and HIV/AIDS is organized around the theme of gender. The material presented here will show how gender dynamics permeate the AIDS epidemic and how gender roles and expectations affect AIDS transmission, prevention, and care.

1

EPIDEMIOLOGY, RISK/TRANSMISSION, AND NATURAL HISTORY OF HIV DISEASE IN WOMEN AND CHILDREN

When I first found out I had HIV, I was living on the streets of downtown L.A. I was addicted to heroin, cocaine, and alcohol. I had careless sex, shared needles, and ignored all precautions. I got it from sharing needles.

I'm still alive, living with HIV and dealing with it in the most positive way I possibly can. HIV is not death but a situation that I got myself into by my own actions.

– Loretta

I have an 11-year-old son who has AIDS. He was infected through a blood transfusion in 1986 when he was 14 months old. I didn't find out his diagnosis until 2 ½ years ago. He is really doing good right now. He has regular colds and ear infections like regular kids. He's never been hospitalized.

It's rough. It's really hard but we just take one day at a time. I don't know if it would be any easier if it were an adult you were dealing with. I guess it hurts to everyone in their own little way. But it's real hard when it's a kid. It's real hard but I just cope with it day to day.

– Mariana

The doctors that diagnosed me told me that my daughter wasn't born infected. Because I breastfed her for 8 months, that's what harmed her.

And up to this point we haven't had problems which have required hospitalization, thank God. I thank God that in the six years of her life, my daughter has remained stable, so her doctors say. I ask God that he always keeps us this way.

– Juana

I started turning tricks. I kept on doing it 'cause the money was good and I was so strung out. I didn't care – didn't never bleach no needle.

– Eunice

I'm from Central America – Guatemala. My husband, Bobby, was from Puerto Rico. He was recovering from drug addition in a rehabilitation place in New Hampshire. He was admitted in the hospital and because of his drug history was found HIV positive. I was told I should go and get tested for HIV. I got the diagnosis of HIV in 1988. Our son, Marvin, passed away in 1993, and Bobby passed away three years later in 1996.

– Leticia

EPIDEMIOLOGY

Experts consider HIV seroprevalence estimates of childbearing women to be a good measure of the rate of infection in women because most women with HIV disease are in their childbearing years. One way seroprevalence of HIV infection in childbearing women has been estimated is through anonymous HIV antibody testing of blood specimens routinely collected from newborns for metabolic screening. A seroprevalance study of childbearing women conducted by the Centers for Disease Control and Prevention (CDC) since 1988 has used data from anonymous newborn serosurveys. This nationwide blind serosurvey, the Survey of Childbearing Women, has found that 7,000 HIV-infected women have given birth each year since 1990 (Rogers, 1997a).

Currently, there are 633,000 adult and adolescent (> 13 years) AIDS cases in the United States. Males comprise 534,532 and females, 98,468 of total cases (Table 1). From the beginning of the AIDS epidemic, the number of male cases has exceeded the number of female cases. However, the number of female cases continued to increase at a rapid rate. In 1981, the year in which HIV disease was first identified in women, women comprised 3% of total adult AIDS cases. Today, women comprise 16% of total cases (CDC, 1997a).

A majority (68%) of female AIDS cases have been reported in the four years between 1993 and 1997 (Stine, 1998). In 1997 women comprised 22% of new cases. Table 2 shows how the percentage of female cases has increased yearly since 1981. The increase has been especially

8

Table 1. *U.S. adult/adolescent[a] AIDS cases by exposure category and gender*

	Males		Females		Total	
Exposure Category	No.	(%)	No.	(%)	No.	(%)
Men who have sex w/men	309,247	(58)	–	–	309,247	(49)
Injection drug use	118,658	(22)	43,214	(44)	161,872	(26)
Men who have sex w/men & inject drugs	40,534	(8)	–	–	40,534	(6)
Hemophililia/coagulation	4,483	(1)	206	(0)	4,689	(1)
Heterosexual contact	20,493	(4)	38,391	(39)	58,884	(9)
Transfusion	4,705	(1)	3,509	(4)	8,214	(1)
Other/undetermined	36,412	(7)	13,148	(13)	49,560	(8)
Total (% of cases)	534,532	(100)	98,468	(100)	633,000	(100)

[a] >13 years.
Source: HIV/AIDS Surveillance Report, cases through December 1997, Centers for Disease Control and Prevention.

significant since 1985 when women accounted for about 7% of total AIDS cases.

Age. A large majority (74%) of women with AIDS are between 25 and 44 years old, and their median age is 35 years old (CDC, 1997a). The mean age at diagnosis with AIDS for women is 36 (Sabo & Carwein, 1994). Women who are IDUs and sexual partners of IDUs make up the largest number of HIV-infected women of childbearing age. Although most of the women with AIDS are between 25 and 44, 13% are between 45 and 59 (CDC, 1997a). In recent years, for both men and women aged 50 and over, cases attributed to injection drug use and heterosexual transmission increased whereas cases caused by transfusion declined (CDC, 1998).

Female cases are similar to male cases in that a majority of the infected women and men, 74% and 76%, respectively, are in the 25–44-year-old age category. The modal age category for each is 30–39 years old (CDC, 1997a). Female cases differ from male cases in that the women are slightly younger: Although the average age of women at diagnosis is 36, the average age for men is 38 (Sabo & Carwein, 1994). Male cases outnumber female cases in every age category.

Women, Families, and HIV/AIDS

Table 2. *Adult and adolescent female AIDS cases, United States, 1981–1997*

Year	Female Percentage of Total Cases
1981[a]	3.0
1982	6.9
1983	6.8
1984	6.4
1985	6.6
1986	7.4
1987	8.0
1988	10.4
1989	10.5
1990	11.5
1991	12.8
1992	13.5
1993	15.9
1994	17.7
1995	18.8
1996	20.2
1997	21.8

[a] Reporting began in late spring.
Source: HIV/AIDS Surveillance Reports, year-end figures, 1981–1997, Centers for Disease Control and Prevention.

In 1993 when the surveillance definition of AIDS was expanded, the largest increases in cases were among persons 13–19 and 20–24 years old. In these age groups, a greater proportion of cases was reported among women (35% and 28%, respectively), and was due to heterosexual transmission (CDC, 1994). Overall, the expanded definition resulted in a greater proportional rise in cases for women than for men (128% vs. 113%, respectively) (Ibid.). This disproportionate increase was predominantly due to the inclusion of individuals with CD4 T-cell counts below 200 or with pulmonary tuberculosis. Further implications of the expanded definition are dealt with later in this chapter.

Today, one in four new infections occurs among youth under the age of 22 (Rotheram-Borus, 1997a). Adolescents are at increasing risk for HIV infection from sexual transmission. HIV infection is growing at an alarming rate among young women particularly, and the highest rate of increase is found among those 15–19 years old (Stine, 1998).

10

There is a greater proportion of female adolescent cases (13–19 years) compared with female cases (20–24 years). Female adolescents comprise over one-third (38%) of the total cases in the 13–19-year-old age category whereas females 20–24 years comprise slightly over one-fourth (26%) of the total cases in that age group (CDC, 1997a). Unlike HIV-infection patterns among adults, adolescent females are being infected through heterosexual transmission at a rate almost equal to gay and bisexual adolescents (Rotheram-Borus, 1997a). Statistics sometimes cross age categories, and it should be noted that, unless otherwise stated, the term "adolescent" applies to young people 13 to 19 years old.

Certain groups of adolescent females have high numbers of AIDS cases. African American teenagers account for 39% of adolescent AIDS cases. In 1992, the highest AIDS rate was among African American female adolescents, who had a rate of 2.6 per 100,000 (Chadwick, 1995). Among female students entering Job Corps programs for disadvantaged youth aged 16–21, seroprevalence was 3.2 per 1,000 (St. Louis et al., 1991). Since 1990, HIV prevalence among female Job Corps applicants has been higher than among male applicants (as cited in Wortley, Chu, & Berkelman, 1997). Most of the increase between 1988 and 1990 in seroprevalence rates among female applicants can be explained by increasing rates among African American women (Ibid.). This situation demonstrates the increased risk for HIV infection faced by socioeconomically disadvantaged young women.

Mortality. HIV/AIDS has become a prevalent threat to women's health in the United States, pushing upward the spectrum of AIDS-related illnesses and female mortality rates. Since 1985, the proportional yearly increase in death rates attributed to HIV/AIDS for women has surpassed that of men (CDC, 1993a). As of the end of 1997, 55% of the women with HIV/AIDS had died compared to 63% of infected men (CDC, 1997a).

Death rates from AIDS decreased by 19% during 1996 (Cimons, 1997). The biggest decline was among men, for whom death rates declined by 22%. Although death rates among women dropped by only 7%, this was the first time a decrease in mortality rates for women was reported. The decline in overall death rates was attributed to effective new combination drug therapies and increased resources for treatment and prevention (Ibid.).

Since 1992, HIV/AIDS has been the fourth leading cause of death for women between the ages of 25 and 44 nationwide. It is the leading cause of death for African American women nationwide and for all women in New York City in that age group. In 1992, HIV/AIDS became the leading cause of death among women between the ages of 25 and 44 in 15 cities with populations of more than 100,000 (as cited in Wortley, Chu, & Berkelman, 1997). All of the cities are located in eight east coast states with the exception of Oakland, California.

Race/Ethnicity. A majority (76%) of women with AIDS are African American and Hispanic/Latino. African American women comprise 56% of total females cases and Hispanic/Latino women, 20% (CDC, 1997a). These women are overrepresented in AIDS cases, because they are only around 21% of the total female population in the United States. Minority women are primarily at risk from their own drug use and/or the drug use of their sexual partners.

The ethnic/racial profile of women with AIDS also differs from that of men with AIDS, the majority of whom are white. Whereas African American women comprise over half (56%) of female AIDS cases, African American men comprise almost one-third (32%) of the male cases. The proportion of Hispanic/Latino female AIDS cases is roughly the same as that of Hispanic/Latino male cases (20% and 18%, respectively) (CDC, 1997a). The injection drug use and heterosexual transmission categories are similar in that these categories for both men and women are disproportionately African American and Hispanic/Latino.

Region. The AIDS epidemic for both women and men is based in urban areas. The epidemic resembles other epidemics of STDs in that in these urban areas it is concentrated among minorities.

Cases of AIDS in women have been reported in all 50 states and territories (Stine, 1998). A majority of infected women live in New York, New Jersey, Florida, California, and Puerto Rico. The largest percentages of female AIDS cases are found in northeast and southern regions of the United States. Cases are heavily localized (CDC, 1994), with highest rates in urban areas primarily on the east coast. In New York, cases are concentrated in New York City; in Florida, Miami; and in New Jersey, Newark and Jersey City. In the South, however, high rates are found in some nonurban areas (Wasser, Gwinn, & Fleming, 1993), and the heterosexual epidemic is growing faster in rural areas than in other parts of the country (Stine, 1998).

In contrast to the HIV/AIDS epidemic among men, the epidemic among women is concentrated in inner-city areas of the Northeast and Southeast (Wortley, Chu, & Berkelman, 1997). The geographic distribution of female AIDS cases is similar to that of male IDUs because of the interaction between these two groups.

RISK/TRANSMISSION

Women are at risk for AIDS and become infected through three routes of transmission. These routes, parenteral, sexual, and perinatal, can be found within the injection drug use and heterosexual transmission categories. A discussion of these transmission categories follows.

Injection Drug Use Transmission

From the beginning of the AIDS epidemic injection drug use has been the principal route by which the disease is transmitted to women. Today this transmission route accounts for 44% of female cases (Table 1). Injection drug use is the main link to adults through heterosexual transmission and to children through perinatal transmission.

A majority of women with AIDS are either injection drug users (IDUs) or the sex partners of IDUs. In the last decade, however, the proportion of women infected through their own drug use has been declining so that in 1997, among women, the number of AIDS cases caused by heterosexual transmission exceeded the number of cases caused by injection drug use (CDC, 1997a). Nevertheless, drug use continues to be the driving force behind the epidemic among heterosexuals. Most heterosexual transmission occurs among women, whether drug users themselves or not, whose sex partners engage in injection drug use. For women who do use drugs, the injection drug transmission category is clouded by the heterosexual transmission category because these women often have sex partners who also use drugs. Thus most women are at risk for AIDS from both injection drug use and sexual transmission.

Injection drug use is the second largest transmission category for men (22%) following the men-who-have-sex-with-men (MSM) category

(58%) (Table 1). The injection drug transmission category includes only heterosexual men. There is a separate category for MSM who also engage in injection drug use. For surveillance purposes, it would be helpful to have an additional category for heterosexual men who are at risk from both injection drug use and sexual transmission, as there is for MSM. Such a category could provide much clarification on risk behavior.

Changes in patterns of drug use have affected the epidemiology of AIDS in women. In many localities, heroin has become less popular, and other drugs, such as cocaine and amphetamines, are increasingly used intravenously. These drugs are injected more frequently than is heroin and are associated with increased needle sharing (Wortley, Chu, & Berkelman, 1997). The form of cocaine known as crack also became popular in inner-city communities in the United States in the mid-1980s. In recent years, crack cocaine has emerged as the drug of choice for many individuals, especially for women (Weissman, Sowder, & Young, 1990). Indeed, most users of crack are women (Stine, 1998).

Initially, AIDS prevention focused on the risk of sharing injection equipment during injection drug use. Because crack is smoked rather than injected, risk from crack use was overlooked. The risk that crack presents for HIV transmission does not have to do with its route of administration like injection drugs. Rather, the risk from crack is due to the effects it produces. Crack, which is highly addictive, lowers inhibitions (Inciardi, Lockwood, & Pottieger, 1993). Thus crack use has been associated with the spread of HIV disease because users frequently have unprotected sex with multiple partners. Increased rates of STDs have also been associated with crack use (Ibid.). Crack users often have coexisting untreated STDs, particularly genital ulceration, which heighten vulnerability to HIV infection.

Heterosexual Transmission

In the United States, heterosexual transmission is the second most common type of sexual transmission, after homosexual transmission. (The MSM transmission category has been the largest one from the beginning of the epidemic.) Therefore, the U.S. epidemic differs from the epidemic in Africa and in developing countries worldwide where heterosexual transmission is the most common type of sexual transmission.

Nine percent of total AIDS cases in the United States are the result of heterosexual transmission (Table 1). Heterosexual transmission is the fastest growing type of transmission, increasing by 15% to 20% annually (Cimons, 1997). Although it is the third largest transmission category of AIDS cases overall, it is the second largest for women. In 1997, female cases of AIDS resulting from heterosexual transmission outnumbered those resulting from injection drug use (38% compared to 32%) (CDC, 1997a). Today 39% of female cases are from heterosexual transmission. This compares to only 4% of male cases (Table 1).

Women comprise 65% of total heterosexual cases (CDC, 1997a). There is a striking gender difference in the heterosexual category, as it is the only category in which the number of female cases exceeds that of male cases. This has been true since the beginning of the epidemic. For example, in 1982, 14% of female cases were from heterosexual contact with an infected male. That figure compared to 0.2% of male cases (Table 3). Since 1985, the number of cases from heterosexual contact has increased more rapidly for women than for men (Figure 1).

The larger number of female heterosexual cases compared to male cases in the United States is linked to injection drug use patterns. This is in contrast to Africa where injection drug use does not play a role in transmission. The male-to-female ratio among African AIDS cases is 1:1 with a slight preponderance of females. Heterosexual transmission appears to be linked to the high number of sexual partners among African males.

In the United States, 44% of female heterosexual AIDS cases are the result of sexual contact with an IDU (Table 4). Compared to men, women are at more risk of sexual transmission from an injection drug user because there are more male than female IDUs. Thus, in areas where prevalence of injection drug use is high, women are more likely than men to encounter an infected partner.

The heterosexual transmission category can also include women's sexual contact with bisexual men, referred to as men who have sex with men and women (MSMW), and with men infected by tainted blood products. Sexual contact with an infected person of unknown risk comprises 46% of female heterosexual cases and is the most common type of sexual contact (Table 4).

Sex with an infected person of unknown risk is the most common type of heterosexual contact resulting in AIDS in men as well as in

Table 3. *Trends in heterosexual contact, 1982–1997*

	Percentage of Cases	
Year	Males	Females
1982	0.2	14
1983	0.1	14
1984	0.3	17
1985	0.3	20
1986	0.4	26
1987	2.0	29
1988	2.0	29
1989	3.0	32
1990	3.0	35
1991	3.0	37
1992	4.0	39
1993	4.0	37
1994	4.0	38
1995	5.0	38
1996	6.0	40
1997	7.0	38

Source: HIV/AIDS Surveillance Reports, year-end figures, 1982–1997, Centers for Disease Control and Prevention.

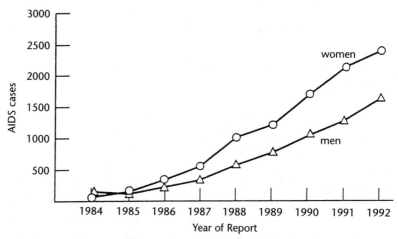

Figure 1. Women with AIDS. Number of AIDS cases due to heterosexual contact by gender, U.S., 1984–1992.
Source: Centers for Disease Control and Prevention. Reprinted with permission from *Social Science and Medicine*, Vol. 41, No. 2, p. 199, 1995.

Table 4. *Heterosexual AIDS cases by type of sexual exposure and gender*

| | Gender | | | | | |
| | Males | | Females | | Total | |
Exposure Category	No.	(%)	No.	(%)	No.	(%)
Heterosexual contact						
Sex with IDU	7,328	(36)	16,800	(44)	24,128	(41)
Sex with hemophiliac	43	(0)	358	(1)	401	(1)
Sex with bisexual male	–	–	2,887	(8)	2,887	(5)
Sex with transfusion recipient	356	(2)	537	(1)	893	(2)
Sex with HIV-infected						
person – risk not specified	12,766	(62)	17,809	(46)	30,575	(52)
Total (% of cases)	20,493	(100)	38,391	(100)	58,884	(100)

Source: HIV/AIDS Surveillance Report, cases through December 1997, Centers for Disease Control and Prevention.

women (Table 4). This type of sexual contact represents 62% of male heterosexual cases followed by sex with an IDU (36%). It is clear from the data in Table 4 that both men and women do not always know about the risk behaviors of their sexual partners.

More than it is for older women, heterosexual transmission is particularly risky for young women. A higher proportion of adolescent females are infected from heterosexual transmission than adult females (CDC, 1997a).

Gender is a significant factor in the profile of heterosexual contact among adolescents (13–24 years); a much larger percentage of adolescent girls than boys contract AIDS through this route. Fifty-four percent of female adolescent cases are from heterosexual contact, compared with 4 percent of adolescent male cases (CDC, 1997a). Heterosexual transmission represents the largest transmission category for adolescent females. In comparison, MSM is the largest category for adolescent males.

The higher number of women with AIDS from heterosexual contact is due to several factors. Women have a greater risk of coming in contact with an infected partner. There is a larger pool of infected men. Most IDUs and hemophiliacs are men, and, in addition, some men who acquired HIV disease from sexual contact with men also have sex with women. Women are more likely than men to have sex partners who are IDUs or who themselves have had multiple partners. Women in areas of high injection drug use are at greatest risk of becoming infected through heterosexual contact. The spread of the epidemic through heterosexual transmission depends on such variables as the rate of sexual partner exchange, type of sexual contact, and type of sexual partner.

Sexually transmitted disease has a role in the heterosexual spread of HIV, either as a co-factor for HIV transmission and/or as a marker for HIV risk behavior. In the latter case, STD may portend the future trend of he AIDS epidemic. Increased incidence of STDs in general, and in syphilis, gonorrhea, and trichomonas specifically, are cause for concern. This incidence has been associated with the use of crack cocaine and the related practice of sex in exchange for drugs. These practices are most prevalent among young black women in urban areas (Wofsy et al., 1992). A history of genital sores and infections has been identified as a co-factor in heterosexual transmission (Padian, 1991). These infections would increase the infectiousness in the infected individual and the susceptibility in the partner. Susceptibility would then depend on factors such as genetic variation and immune competence of the sexual partner.

Male-to-Female Transmission. The higher rate of male-to-female HIV transmission is also a result of biological and physiological factors. There is a higher concentration of HIV (referred to as viral load) in semen than in vaginal secretions (Williams, 1992a; Laga, 1993). There is also variation in viral strain, some strains being more infectious than others. In addition, there is a greater amount of mucosal area in the vagina, adding to women's risk. Ordinary vaginal intercourse can result in microscopic tears in the vagina. The vaginal area can be exposed to HIV for long periods because it serves as a receptacle for semen after unprotected intercourse. In contrast, the exposure to HIV of a male involves briefer contact and a smaller vulnerable area.

Generally, women are at increased risk because the efficiency of male-to-female transmission is greater than female-to-male. This has been determined in studies of discordant couples (European Study Group, 1992; Haverkos & Battjes, 1992; Padian, 1987; Padian, Marquis et al., 1987). Cross-sectional studies of couples in which one partner is HIV infected have reported a fairly consistent transmission rate of 20%

from infected men to female partners (Padian, 1991). In studies of discordant couples the infected partner is used as an index case. These studies are valuable in examining true seroconversion because the couples are monitored over time. But findings from these studies are complicated by the fact that the couples are encouraged during the study to adopt safer sex practices. If the accompanying educational component in the study is effective, no seroconversions will occur. For example, the Heterosexual Partners Study, conducted at the University of California, San Francisco, since 1985, has had no recent seroconversions because of the couples' uniform adoption of safer sex practices (Padian, 1995).

Unprotected vaginal intercourse is the most common risk factor for heterosexual transmission in women. The number of a woman's sexual contacts with an infected partner is an additional risk factor, as is anal intercourse (Padian, Shiboski, & Jewel, 1989; Padian, 1991). Anal sex can cause mucosal lesions in the rectum, thereby facilitating entry of the virus. There is also an abundance of lymphocytes in the area surrounding the rectum. The practice of anal sex is more common among women who are partners of bisexual men than among women who are partners of men from other risk groups. The European Study Group, which examined 563 couples, also found anal sex to be a risk (European Study Group, 1992).

Additionally, although women are at greater risk from men who are in advanced stages of disease, laboratory studies have indicated that men receiving zidovudine therapy (AZT) are less likely to shed HIV and present less risk (Wofsy et al., 1992). Men on AZT are therefore less likely to transmit the virus to women because of the temporary effect of decreased viral load.

Women are not at increased risk of becoming infected with HIV by heterosexual transmission during menses. Women over the age of 45 (perimenopausal women), however, are at more risk than younger women because of increased fragility of genital mucosa (European Study Group, 1992; Haverkos & Battjes, 1992). Defloration may cause a similar fragility (European Study Group, 1992). In general, all factors, including traumatic, infectious, and hormonal ones, that are able to impair genital mucosa may increase the risk of HIV transmission (Ibid.).

Evidence for the role of the cervix in HIV transmission is provided by the presence of HIV-infected lymphocytes in the cervix of infected women, particularly in women with cervical ectopy. Cervical ectopy, a condition in which the cervix is eroded, increases women's risk. Cervical ectopy refers to the displacement of the cervical squamocolumnar junction distally. This condition leads to increased cervical secretions and has been associated with increased risk of transmission.

Cervical ectopy is more common in adolescent women who have a larger zone of ectopy, thereby heightening their vulnerability to HIV infection. Age-related differences in younger women's cervical tissue can also facilitate infection with human papilloma virus (HPV), which in turn can heighten risk for HIV infection.

Cervical ectopy demonstrates the importance of the cervix as the portal of entry for HIV. The high rates of HIV infection among adolescent females in sub-Saharan Africa were at first thought to be the result of sociodemographic factors. However, these rates are now thought to be explained in part by the immaturity of the cervix of adolescent females in whom the epithelium is ectopic and exposed (Stein, 1995). The cervix in mature women, in contrast, is covered and protected by the squamous epithelium of the vagina.

The genital tract of adolescent females is not fully mature. As a result, during intercourse an adolescent's vaginal lining is more likely to suffer physical trauma and lacerations than that of a woman with a more mature genital tract (Sabo & Carwein, 1994). Even if lacerations do not occur, the immature genital tract is not an efficient barrier to HIV. Vaginal secretions, which are a physical barrier to harmful organisms, are not fully developed or functional in adolescent females. This physiologic immaturity may play a role in heightening young women's risk (Ibid.).

Other forms of contraception may also increase women's risk. Women who take oral contraceptives also have a larger zone of ectopy and are therefore at increased risk. Oral contraceptives may affect the thickness of the cervical mucous and thus its efficiency as a barrier to infection. Women who use oral contraceptives are also at greater risk from chlamydia and candida infections. The use of an intrauterine device (IUD) has also been identified as a possible risk factor (Padian, 1991). These devices create a stable local inflammation of the uterine mucosa. This inflammation may make women vulnerable to various infections because chronic inflammation of the uterus increases the number of lymphocytes that are ready targets for HIV.

Female-to-Male Transmission. Studies of female-to-male transmission have been far less consistent than studies of male-to-female. There are reports of equally efficient bidirectional transmission, but there are also findings that range from no transmission at all to only one-half the infection rate of male-to-female transmission. Clearly, much work still must be done in sorting out the factors in female-to-male transmission.

Unlike women in male-to-female transmission, who remain un-affected, men are at increased risk from women if sex occurs during menses. Anal sex, however, does not appear to be a risk for men. In contrast, in both kinds of heterosexual transmission the risk is increased if either sexual partner is in an advanced stage of infection (European Study Group, 1992).

Two early studies found that men who were not circumcised were at greater risk of infection than men who had undergone the procedure (Cameron et al., 1989; Fischl, Fayne, & Flancga, 1988). Most reports on the risk of remaining uncircumcised are based on studies of men attending STD clinics in Africa. A history of genital ulceration was found to be a factor in transmission. Just why uncircumcised males appear to be at greater risk is not clear. It is speculated that the foreskin of uncircumcised males increases their susceptibility to HIV by trapping infected vaginal secretions and providing an environment for the virus to survive. It is also possible that the intact foreskin provides a larger surface area for contact with infected secretions and may be more vulnerable to trauma during sexual intercourse. Women do not appear to be at risk from sex with an uncircumcised man. Table 5 summarizes factors associated with heterosexual transmission.

Other Routes of Transmission

Although injection drug use and heterosexual transmission are the main route of HIV infection in women, there are other transmission categories for women as well. These additional routes include artificial insemination, blood products, and female-to-female transmission.

Artificial Insemination. Women have been infected through artificial insemination with semen from an infected donor. In the first such cases, reported in Australia in 1985, four of eight women became infected from a single donor (Stewart et al., 1985). In the United States,

Table 5. *Factors associated with heterosexual transmission of HIV*

Factor	Male-to-Female	Female-to-Male
Lack of condoms	yes	yes
Anal intercourse	yes	no
Sex during menses	no	yes
Number of sexual contacts	yes	yes
Advanced disease state	yes	yes
AZT[a]	possibly	unknown
Genital sores or infections	yes	yes
Oral contraceptives[b]	yes	unknown
IUD use	possibly	unknown
Cervical ectopy	yes	unknown

[a] Possibly protective by decreased viral load.
[b] Whether oral contraceptives are protective or increase likelihood of transmission is controversial.
Source: "Epidemiology of AIDS and Heterosexually Transmitted HIV in Women," in *AIDSFILE*, Vol. 3, pp. 1–2, 1991, by N. Padian. Reproduced from AIDSFILE with permission. Copyright © 1993 The Regents of the University of California.

two cases of transmission through artificial insemination have been reported. One involved a woman in New York City who was inseminated with semen from five infected donors between 1984 and 1985 (Chaisson, Stoneburner, & Joseph, 1990). The other case was a woman who was inseminated with processed semen from her husband who was a hemophiliac (CDC, 1990).

For women who undergo artificial insemination, pregnancy is often foremost on their minds, and risk of HIV is usually not even considered in this context. Also, some couples with HIV so strongly desire to become parents that they purposely have unprotected sex in order to conceive. To reduce this risk through unprotected sex, one obstetric clinic, in Milan, Italy, offers an artificial insemination service for discordant couples in which the man is infected (Semprini, 1993; Semprini et al., 1992). This relatively large program has developed semen-processing techniques that reduce the risk of transmission.

Undetermined Risk. The undetermined risk category includes persons for whom no specific risk is identified. It also includes persons for whom risk information is incomplete because of death, refusal to be interviewed, or the loss of data in follow-up efforts. This category should be distinguished from that of sex with an infected person of unknown risk in the heterosexual category. More information is known about the sexual contact in the heterosexual category. For example, it is known that the sex partner is infected. This information is not known in the undetermined category.

Thirteen percent of female AIDS cases are due to undetermined risk. This figure compares to 7% of male cases (Table 1). As indicated in Table 6, women have always had a larger percentage than men of cases due to undetermined risk. Women are more likely than men to be reported with heterosexual undetermined risk because the women are less likely to know about the risk behavior of their partners (CDC, 1995). In addition, health care providers may not recognize risk behaviors of women and their partners. Many women do not see themselves at risk for HIV and, upon learning that they are seropositive, experience a stronger denial reaction than men who engage in risk-related behavior (as cited in Stuntzner-Gibson, 1991).

Blood Products. Four percent of AIDS cases in women are the result of transfusions with contaminated blood products. This figure is larger than that for men (1%). In contrast, whereas the hemophilia/coagulation category also comprises 1% of men with AIDS (Table 1), it does not account for a large enough number of female cases to make up a percentage for women.

Female-to-Female Transmission. Female-to-female transmission of HIV has been reported but appears to be lower than either same gender sex between men or opposite gender sex between men and women. As discussed earlier, female-to-male transmission of HIV indicates that vaginal secretions and menstrual blood are potentially infectious and that mucous membrane exposure to these secretions can lead to HIV infection. Thus the potential for female-to-female transmission exists.

One possible case of female-to-female transmission that involved sex during menses and traumatic sexual activity has been reported (Marmor, 1986). Two other possible cases involved oral sex (Monzon & Capellan, 1987; Perry, Jacobsberg, & Fogel, 1989). Through December 1996, women in 1,648 out of 85,500 female AIDS cases reported having had sex with women (CDC, 1997b). However, a majority of these

Table 6. *Trends in undetermined risk, 1982–1997*

	Percentage of Cases	
Year	Males	Females
1982	2	14
1983	3	12
1984	2	12
1985	2	11
1986	3	11
1987	3	9
1988	4	8
1989	5	9
1990	4	8
1991	6	11
1992	5	9
1993	7	13
1994	11	19
1995	13	22
1996	15	24
1997	20	28

Source: HIV/AIDS Surveillance Reports, year-end figures, 1982–1997, Centers for Disease Control and Prevention.

women had other risks as well, such as injection drug use, sex with high-risk men, or receipt of blood or blood products. Three hundred thirty-three of the 1,648 women reported having had sex only with women, but 97% of these women also had another risk, in most cases, injection drug use.

In a CDC review of 79 AIDS cases among women who reported sex only with women, 95% of the women reported a history of IDU. The remaining 5% had become infected through contaminated blood products (Chu, Birchler, Fleming, & Berkelman, 1990). Another study conducted by the CDC found tht the main route of infection among lesbian and bisexual women was heterosexual sex with male IDUs (McCombs et al., 1992). In both studies, injection drug use played an important role in transmission among lesbian and bisexual women.

The low incidence of female-to-female transmission may have to do with the classification system used by the CDC. Surveillance data do not include a category for female-to-female transmission. As a result, these cases are included in the undetermined risk category or in other categories when there is a confounding risk. A woman who self-identifies as a lesbian but who has a single heterosexual contact will be included in the heterosexual category. In the same way, a woman who self-identifies as a lesbian but who uses injection drugs will be included in the IDU category. This classification system may actually mask cases of female-to-female transmission. That the CDC has a separate transmission category encompassing men who have sex with men and who also engage in injection drug use is another indication of just how underdeveloped AIDS surveillance for women remains.

It should be noted that lesbian women sometimes have unprotected vaginal and anal sex with gay and bisexual men. Adolescent lesbians, particularly, will sometimes act out heterosexually by having sexual experiences with men (Martin, 1988). Young gay men will sometimes serve as sex partners for these women because of the greater acceptance of this type of relationship by gay men, compared to heterosexual men. These men may be more sensitive to lesbians' needs to act out heterosexually. Because the sexual relationship involves mutual acceptance and belonging, it is not seen by those involved as carrying a risk for HIV. The risk that lesbians face through sexual transmission should therefore not be overlooked. The issue of HIV diagnosis in lesbian women is given more attention in Chapter 4.

NATURAL HISTORY

Arriving at an understanding of whether or how the clinical progression of HIV disease in women differs from that in men has been difficult. Most information comes from small studies on disease progression after an AIDS diagnosis. Initial natural history studies of HIV disease were based on male cohorts, with the implicit assumption that HIV behaved the same in women as it did in men and that any differences in disease progression were due to factors other than gender. At that time, the focus was on routes of transmission and region as the causes of differences.

Several longitudinal studies of gay men and IDUs contributed data about the disease's progression in men. From the early years of the epidemic, there were large groups of infected men to study. But no really comparable longitudinal study was done on women, and it was therefore not possible to identify gender-related factors in disease progression. However, HIV disease is a relatively recent disease in women, and their small numbers in comparison to men did not allow for the same level of analysis. Therefore, how gender affected opportunistic infections (OIs) and treatment effectiveness could not be determined.

Surveillance Definition of AIDS

The original surveillance definition of AIDS was criticized for omitting disorders of women's reproductive systems (Cf. Burkett, 1995; Corea, 1992; Patton, 1994). This clinical definition of AIDS for reporting purposes was based on AIDS-related illnesses found in men, first in MSM and then in IDUs.

The CDC expanded its surveillance definition of AIDS in 1993 to include invasive cervical cancer as an indicator illness (CDC, 1993b). The organization added other indicator illnesses at that time, but invasive cervical cancer was the first indicator illness specific to women to be included. The 1993 definition was based on either 26 indicator illnesses *or* a CD4 (T-cell) count $\leq$ 200. The expanded definition resulted in a significant rise in the number of AIDS cases in women, a consequence of including not only cervical cancer but also tuberculosis and low CD4 counts. The increase in number of cases was 151% for women and only 105% for men (CDC, 1994). In 1994, 59% of AIDS cases among women were reported according to this expanded definition (CDC, 1995).

The revised CDC classification also included poorly responsive candida vulvovaginitis, moderate or severe cervical dysplasia, and cervical carcinoma as symptomatic HIV-related conditions (CDC, 1993b). This revision was significant in that it recognized gynecological symptoms as early signs of HIV disease in women. The change in the surveillance definition was the result of great pressure placed on the CDC by women (Cf. Burkett, 1995; Corea, 1992; Patton, 1994).

Female-Specific Clinical Conditions. In general, women are subject to more organ-specific diseases and conditions than are men. These diseases include pelvic infections, vaginal candidiasis, and cervical cancer. Women also have a higher incidence of urinary tract infections, human papilloma virus (HPV) infection, and breast cancer. In addition, women tend to have more complications from STDs such as chlamydia and gonorrhea and to suffer more frequent and severe consequences from STDs than men (Aral & Wasserheit, 1995). This background is important for understanding the clinical course of HIV disease in women.

Gynecological diseases occur more frequently and are more aggressive in women who are HIV infected than in uninfected women (Kaplan, 1997). Recurrent vaginal candidiasis (yeast infection) is often the initial clinical manifestation of HIV disease in women (Sabo & Carwein, 1994). Yet its occurrence usually does not prompt women to have themselves tested for HIV. Because vaginal candidiasis occurs even in women who are not HIV infected, many women, as well as their physicians, are unaware of the relationship between chronic vaginal candidiasis and HIV disease. Frequency of vaginal candidiasis in a woman is considered to be increased if the condition occurs four times per year. Although vaginal candidiasis generally responds well to standard treatment during the early stages of HIV disease, it does not respond as well in the advanced stages.

Herpes simplex virus (HSV), or genital herpes, occurs more often in women with HIV infection than in uninfected women (Ibid.). Genital lesions associated with HSV may serve as an entry for the virus. In HIV-infected women, the lesions become more resistant to treatment as immune system dysfunction progresses.

A number of studies have found a high rate of HIV infection among women with pelvic inflammatory disease (PID) (Hoegsberg et al., 1990; Safrin et al., 1990; Sperling et al., 1991). The first study just cited examined the impact of HIV on the clinical course of PID and found that HIV-positive women with PID have a more severe clinical course than those who are HIV negative.

Women with HIV disease are also at high risk for cervical dysplasia, a precursor lesion for cervical cancer. Infected women have higher rates of cervical dysplasia than do women who are HIV-negative controls (Feingold et al., 1990; Provencher et al., 1988; Schraeger et al., 1989). Moreover, human papillomavirus has been linked to cervical dysplasia. Immunosuppressed HIV-infected women appear to be at greater risk for acquisition, progression, and recurrence of HPV-related cervical lesions. The more severe the HIV-induced immunosuppression, the greater the rate of HPV infection. HPV is more likely to be detected in symptomatic HIV-positive women than in women who are asymptomatic or HIV-negative controls (Feingold et al., 1990; Vermund et al., 1991).

Cervical cancer is the most dangerous gender-specific condition threatening HIV-infected women (Sabo & Carwein, 1994). It should also be noted that cervical cancer is not familial as is breast cancer. Rather, it is caused by a STD and is therefore treatable with early intervention.

Gender Differences in Morbidity and Mortality

Many manifestations of HIV disease are similar in men and women. For both HIV-infected men and women, the most common OI is pneumocystis carinii pneumonia (PCP) (NIAID, 1997a). But women are more likely than men to have bacterial pneumonia (Kaplan, 1997; NIAID, 1997a). This distribution may be explained by a woman's tendency to delay in seeking care and/or by her having less access than a man to anti-HIV therapies or preventive therapies for PCP. Some studies have found that women have higher rates of esophageal candidiasis (yeast infection of the windpipe) and herpes simplex infection than men (Ibid.).

The Women Interagency HIV Study (WIHS), sponsored by the National Institute of Allergy and Infectious Diseases (NIAID), is a multicenter prospective cohort study that began in 1993. This study aims to find out more about the natural history of HIV infection in women, particularly about aspects of HIV infection such as genital infections and conditions leading to cervical cancer that are specific to women. The WIHS includes six U.S. sites and has enrolled 2,080 HIV-infected women and 575 HIV-uninfected women at risk for HIV infection (NIAID, 1997b). The WIHS is collaborating with a companion multicenter prospective cohort study of women, the HIV Epidemiology Research Study (HERS), which is sponsored by the CDC and NIAID. This study includes 920 HIV-infected women and 460 HIV-uninfected women in four U.S. sites (Ibid.).

Early studies of disease progression in women indicated that women had both a more rapid disease progression and a shorter survival time after diagnosis than did men (Rothenburg et al., 1987; Stoneburner et al., 1988). In recent studies, women appeared to be iller than men and to have a more severe and rapid disease course (Williams, 1992b). However, it is not clear from these studies if the gender differences resulted more from biology or from socioeconomic factors.

The differences in survival noted in studies of disease progression were difficult to control for and could have been caused by differences in duration of infection before an AIDS diagnosis was made. Women with HIV disease had later presentation at medical facilities and correspondingly later diagnosis and more advanced disease (Brettle & Leen, 1991). Furthermore, women generally experience more and longer-lasting symptoms than do men (Siegel, Raveis, & Gorey, 1997). These factors are inextricably related to poverty and poor access to care. As will be discussed in Chapter 4, women often have competing economic, medical, and social needs that result in barriers to their receiving optimal care (Hirschhorn, 1995).

Additional variables accounting for differences in survival include age, transmission category, and lack of AZT therapy (Legg, 1993). About the latter, women with HIV disease have been less likely to receive AZT therapy than men (Ibid.). This lack of access extends to more recent combination therapies with protease inhibitors (Wolfe, 1997). Furthermore, women historically have not had the same opportunity as have men throughout the epidemic to participate in clinical trials (Ibid.). The issue of unequal access to care is also covered more thoroughly in Chapter 4.

CHILDREN AND ADOLESCENTS
Epidemiology

Children in the United States comprise 1% of the nation's total AIDS cases (CDC, 1997a). Perinatal transmission, accounting for 91% of pediatric cases under 13, comprises a disproportionate amount of HIV disease in children. Nevertheless, after having peaked in 1992, the number of cases caused by perinatal transmission has declined (Mofenson, 1997; Rogers, 1997b). Reasons for this decrease are covered in the next chapter, which takes up perinatal transmission.

As shown in the table on transmission categories in children under 13 (Table 7), the remaining pediatric cases are distributed among the blood transfusion category (5%), the hemophilia transmission category (3%), and the undetermined risk category (2%). Table 8 shows a

Table 7. *U.S. pediatric*[a] *AIDS cases*

Exposure Category	Cumulative No.	Total (%)
Hemophilia/coagulation disorder	233	(3)
Mother with/at risk for HIV infection	7,335	(91)
Recipient of blood transfusion, blood components, or tissue	374	(5)
Undetermined risk	144	(2)
Total	8,086	(100)

[a] < 13 years old.

Source: HIV/AIDS Surveillance Report, cases through December 1997, Centers for Disease Control and Prevention.

breakdown of mothers' exposure categories for perinatal cases. Most (58%) cases of perinatal transmission have a tie to injection drug use. Of infants infected perinatally, 40% are born to mothers who were themselves infected from IDU. An additional 18% are born to mothers who are sex partners of IDUs. It is significant that in the second highest category (23%) the mother has HIV infection from unknown risk.

Because most AIDS in children is the result of perinatal transmission from infected mothers, pediatric AIDS cases tend to follow racial and ethnic distributions similar to that of women. Most of the infected mothers are either IDUs or the sex partners of IDUs, and it follows, therefore, that a disproportionate number of children with AIDS are African American or Hispanic/Latino.

Also pediatric AIDS cases tend to follow a similar geographic distribution to that of women because of perinatal transmission. Since most perinatal transmission is due to a mother's drug use, there is a strong overlap between geographic areas of injection drug use among women and HIV seroprevalence among infants.

In the early years of the epidemic, a large proportion of the AIDS cases in children had been caused by their receiving contaminated blood or blood products. In recent years, the number of these cases has subsided in the wake of effective blood screening. Perinatal transmission differs from transmission through contaminated blood in that in the latter the child's health is independent of the health of the mother.

Epidemiology, Risk, and Natural History

Table 8. *U.S. perinatal cases by mother's exposure category*

Mother's Exposure Category	Perinatal No.	Cases (%)
Injection drug use	2,936	(40)
Sex with a/an:		
injection drug user	1,340	(18)
bisexual male	159	(2)
hemophiliac	28	(0)
transfusion recipient	24	(0)
HIV-infected person, unknown risk	1,033	(14)
Recipient of blood transfusion, blood		
components, or tissue	154	(2)
Has HIV infection, unknown risk	1,661	(23)
Total	7,335	(100)

Source: HIV/AIDS Surveillance Report, cases through December 1997, Centers for Disease Control and Prevention.

Perinatal transmission necessarily means that the mother is infected and the father perhaps as well. The consequences for children of these two kinds of transmission are quite different.

Finally, AIDS has had a substantial impact on childhood mortality in the United States. It is now the seventh leading cause of death for children who are one to four years of age (Rogers, 1997a).

Risk

Adolescents are at risk for HIV disease primarily from their sexual activity. First intercourse occurs at an increasingly younger age, and adolescents are inconsistent in their use of condoms (Chadwick, 1995; Rotheram-Borus, 1997a). From 1985 to 1990, growing numbers of adolescents became sexually active at younger ages, and during this time, the number of teenage mothers aged 13–15 rose by 26% (Rotheram-Borus, 1997a). Adolescents, particularly girls, often have sexual experiences with older persons who currently have a higher prevalence of HIV infection.

Adolescence can be a confusing time for the young people who are forming their sexual identity. Peer pressure also can be a powerful

31

influence on an adolescent's risk behavior. These factors, combined with the perception of invulnerability to disease and consequent immortality that is common among young people, are often compelling in HIV risk behavior.

Alcohol and drug use, which are risk factors for HIV disease, are also common among the adolescent population. Most early drug use among adolescents does not involve injection drugs. However, drug use among adolescents is sometimes experimental and may grow to become poly-drug use, including injection drugs. Moreover, the increased use of methamphetamines (which are sometimes injected) has been noted among young people (Rotheram-Borus, 1997b). This increase has been most evident among gay and bisexual men living on the west coast, particularly in Southern California where methamphetamines have become the preferred drug (Reback, 1997). A recent rise in crack use resulting in an increase in STDs among adolescents has also been reported (Guinan & Leviton, 1995).

Female adolescents are at particular risk for HIV disease because of sexually transmitted diseases. The rate of STD infection, including syphilis and gonorrhea, among 10–14-year-old girls is 3 to 4 times higher than the rate among 10–14-year-old boys (Males, 1996). The rate among girls 15 to 19 years old is also higher than the rate among boys 15 to 19 years old, but not as pronounced. However, among males > 20 years the rate is higher than the rate among females > 20 years. From these data, it appears that young women infected with STDs may have had male partners who are older.

A study of age cohorts that examined AIDS incidence rate ratios found that rates were highest for heterosexually infected women who were born between 1970 and 1974 and who were 14 to 18 years old in 1988 (Wortley & Fleming, 1997). AIDS incidence rates are intricately tied to age-based behavior because this age cohort was initiated into sex and drug use during the AIDS era. These trends suggest that successive cohorts of young women may become at risk for HIV infection as they reach adolescence and early adulthood.

Their age is also significant for adolescents because of the specific clinical course of HIV disease. Because of the long latency of the disease many adolescents with AIDS became infected years earlier than their diagnosis, and many young adults with AIDS actually became infected when they were in their teens. Assuming a 10-year latency,

15% of all adults with AIDS became infected during adolescence, and 25% of all persons acquiring infection through heterosexual contact were infected as teenagers (Chadwick, 1995). Almost one-fourth (22%) of women with AIDS were diagnosed between the ages of 20 and 29 years (CDC, 1997a). These findings indicate that a substantial amount of HIV transmission occurs in adolescence and the early twenties. Seropositive youth may be sexually active for many years before becoming symptomatic and may infect other persons during this time.

Not all sex between adolescents, however, takes place among persons from the same age cohort. The idea that adolescents are engaging in reckless sex and spreading HIV/AIDS and other STDs among themselves is actually misleading (Males, 1996). As stated earlier, many adolescents, particularly females, have sex with older partners (Ibid.). In other words, different age cohorts can interact. The risk that this interaction presents to young women is discussed in more depth in Chapter 4.

Disease Progression

Unlike infected adults, children with AIDS become symptomatic quickly. Infants are exposed to primary infection with opportunistic organisms, whereas adults experience reactivation of these infections. An infant's survival time after an AIDS-defining condition, compared to that of an adult, is also shorter. About 70% of children develop symptoms by one year of age, and 17% die within the first year (Forsyth, 1995). However, more than half of children infected at birth live to seven years of age, and some even live to adolescence.

Long-term survival for children has not been given as much attention as it has for adults, and relatively little information on the health of perinatally infected older children exists. Based on available data, long-term survival with true nonprogression of disease is unusual among perinatally infected children (Kline, 1995). HIV RNA levels are high in perinatally infected infants and decline slowly during the first two years of life. Infants who have very high viral loads in the first few months of life are at increased risk for rapid progression of disease (Shearer et al., 1997), suggesting that these infants could possibly benefit from antiretroviral therapy.

Little age-specific information is available on the natural history of HIV disease in both adolescents infected perinatally and those infected through other routes of transmission. Specifically, the impact of puberty on the course of HIV infection has not been determined (Office of National AIDS Policy, 1996). The limited information available on the course of HIV disease is on hemophiliacs who are overwhelmingly male (Barnhart, 1997). Like their adult counterparts, those young women recruited for perinatal studies were enlisted more out of interest in the infants than in the women. More information on adolescents is especially needed because treatment approaches for adolescents may differ from those used for adults and infants.

Thus far, long-term survival has been defined only on the basis of age. Yet children of similar ages may differ in a number of important ways, such as immunologic status and history of AIDS-defining illnesses. Total emphasis on age may obscure other critical factors in studies of long-term survivors of perinatally infected children. The existence of these children does offer some optimism. However, that optimism is tempered by the fact that one or sometimes both parents may not survive the duration of the child's life. The societal impact of perinatal HIV disease on children is far-reaching. In many major cities, HIV disease is increasingly associated with orphanhood. HIV, as the newest chronic disease of childhood, will continue to present challenges to personal and professional caregivers.

The facts of HIV disease – that Hispanic/Latino and African American families, and particularly the young women in these families, that the sex partners of IDUs, and that the children of people in these categories are disproportionately affected – help frame the sociological issues discussed in the book. This section was designed to give readers an understanding of the background and progression of HIV/AIDS among the population, male and female, young and old, in the United States, so that they can better understand how women and families are affected.

2

FEMALE REPRODUCTIVE
HEALTH AND SEXUALITY

Out of that relationship a daughter was born. Flora was sick. So she was tested. The results were positive for HIV. The most painful thing was that on that same day, a beautiful girl was born who was also positive. For me it was very hard to receive such bad news.

In December 1993, she [Flora] spent Christmas and New Year's with her mother and son in Honduras. I thought I would see her again but that was not possible. I received a letter which notified me that she had died. To me this news was the most difficult, having a daughter ill with HIV and being ill myself. My daughter was only 10 months old when her mother died.

– Jose

We were being careful using preventatives but I became pregnant with the baby. When we had relations, the condom was broken and we didn't notice. I was convinced that I was sick and that the baby was going to be born sick. And I became depressed, really depressed. I would think of how hard it would be to deal with a sick baby.

Then the same thing happened again. I got pregnant. Imagine, my baby was only 7 months old. It wasn't like I got pregnant and who cares what happens. One person asked me and said, "Well, if you knew he was sick why did you let yourself get pregnant?" And I told her, "It's not that I wanted to get pregnant, it's just that it happened. It's not like I can say I'll just get an abortion."

– Rosemary

They took the three of us to a room and informed us that we had tested HIV positive. I felt really awful listening to these words. We went home, my husband, my daughter, and myself, without saying a single word.

35

I had to tell my parents and he told me not until we went to Mexico to tell them personally since my parents would always ask me why Alfonso was always ill. But my conscience was not at peace until one day I couldn't hold back anymore and I told my sister. I didn't have the words to explain what was happening. The whole time I was crying and crying. Finally I told her the truth about Alfonso's test being HIV positive and that both my little girl and I had tested positive. My sister and I both cried together and we have cried a lot since then.

– Juana

Bobby came back. I wasn't taking any precautions not to get pregnant because I wasn't dating anyone. My health was going down because I was working too many hours and so much pressure. So I went to the clinic to pick up the results and I was positive. And the first thing that came to my mind was my other two children have it because they were so young – 5 months and a year and a half. I got worried because I didn't know much about this disease. All I knew was that it was a terminal illness. I didn't say anything at home. I just kept working. I had to work overtime about 12 hours because I was raising my children.

I just decided that I wanted to have the baby because it would help my Christian beliefs. It would have been worse to go through an abortion because I would probably feel guilty all my life. I had the baby but I felt guilty. I'm the mom. I gave it to my child directly.

As a mom, I just kept dreaming of the time the doctor would say my child was going to be discharged but I had the feeling this time was more terrible than the other times. I would just hold him next to me. I was so broken hearted. I didn't do anything but hold him and sing to him and read the Bible to him. His health was going down. His body was just too worn down. When he turned 19 months he passed away. It was a terrible day.

– Leticia

It was hard when I was in prison. I found out I was positive at the same time. I didn't want to live. I wanted to die. I tried to commit suicide. And it was like God didn't want me to die. There'a a purpose for me somewhere.

In prison we didn't have an HIV doctor. We actually were treating ourselves. We were giving each other medication. We were actually medicating each other to keep each other strong. I found out I had cervical cancer too because of the HIV.

– Naomi

FEMALE REPRODUCTIVE HEALTH

As already discussed, women are often not aware that they are at risk for HIV. Therefore, having access to information about HIV and being tested for the disease are critical to women's health status.

Testing and Disclosure

HIV-antibody testing is often a component of education and prevention in HIV/AIDS services. But its inclusion in prevention is actually misguided, because testing is actually a measure of risk behavior *after* that behavior has taken place. If the test turns out to be positive, education and prevention are unfortunately too late for the infected individual. This issue is relevant to women because a woman's discovery of her positive serostatus often precedes the realization that she may be at risk. Testing can mean early detection of infection, however, which then makes possible early intervention with drug therapy (Rotheram-Borus, 1997). In addition, the person who the test reveals to be infected can take precautions to avoid infecting others.

Most women with HIV disease learn of their infection during antenatal care or after a male partner tests positive (Patton, 1994). Both situations are significant because the women would otherwise remain ignorant of their infection. In this way, women's knowledge of their own serostatus is intricately tied either to their being pregnant or to their male partner's being tested.

Rates of perinatal transmission have declined in recent years. Nevertheless, children continue to be infected perinatally today. Delivery of HIV uninfected infants requires that infected women be identified and treated during pregnancy. Factors associated with the lack of testing among women include inadequate services, poor training of health care providers, and inadequate prenatal care for women at risk (Rogers, 1997). The way most women learn of their serostatus also suggests that they are not making use of HIV testing services not associated with prenatal care. If HIV testing and counseling were more often a part of routine health care for women not only would women's own health benefit but that of their children as well.

Antenatal screening for HIV in women has another important implication. A major strategy for preventing perinatal transmission has been HIV antibody testing of women in prenatal and family planning clinics (Wagner & Cohen, 1993). The fallacy underlying testing as a prevention approach was noted earlier. And it is also relevant that this strategy aims to get women tested but not their male partners (Sherr, 1993a). If a man is positive, he is capable of transmitting the virus to his female partner and then, she to her unborn child. Although this potential would seem to be a strong reason to test the father also, it has not been made part of the strategy for reducing perinatal transmission (Ibid.). Fathers are rarely consulted or tested at the same time as the mother (Sherr, 1996). This omission of men in family planning programs is examined in depth in Chapter 5.

Although lower rates of HIV infection are found among women compared to men, women have higher rates of getting tested (Sherr & Quinn, 1993). In addition, behavior changes related to testing are found more often among women than among men (Ibid.).

Disclosure of test results is also an important issue for women. Many women choose not to know their HIV status for fear that their drug use will be discovered and/or that their children will be taken from them. For more on the problem this choice creates for women, see Chapter 3. Some women believe that if they are found to be HIV positive, they may be coerced into terminating a pregnancy. Other women who discover they are HIV positive may be at risk for domestic violence or abandonment if they disclose their seropositivity to their partners (Denenberg, 1995).

Women are more likely to disclose their serostatus to their male partners than their partners are to them (Sherr, 1993b). In one study, a majority (95%) of the women informed their partners that they were seropositive whereas only 74% of the men did so (De Bertolini et al., 1996). Men have also been shown to be more likely to abandon an infected female partner than the reverse (Sherr, 1993b). Strategies for testing thus must take account of the entire social context in which women live.

Perinatal Transmission

Perinatal transmission includes transmission to a fetus during pregnancy, to a newborn during labor and delivery, and to an infant through breast-feeding. As stated in Chapter 1, a majority (91%) of infants with AIDS are infected through perinatal transmission (CDC, 1997). The perinatal transmission category of HIV disease in infants shares an intricate relationship with the IDU and heterosexual transmission categories.

In the United States, the first four infant AIDS cases through perinatal transmission were reported in December 1982, one year after the first AIDS cases among women had been identified (CDC, 1982). One of these infants was a baby girl. Of the four infants, two had been born to mothers who used injection drugs, and the other two to Haitian parents living here. Some of the early documented heterosexual cases in the United States were also among persons from Haiti where heterosexual transmission is the predominant mode of transmission.

Perinatal transmission can occur during pregnancy through transplacental transmission, during labor and delivery through exposure to blood or to vaginal secretions, or after delivery through breast milk. Rates of perinatal transmission have varied throughout the epidemic. In recent years the rates have steadily declined. Studies of perinatal HIV transmission in the United States have noted a decrease in perinatal transmission rates of from 20–25% in 1994 to just 10% or lower in 1996 (Rogers, 1997). This decline in transmission rates is attributed to the increased use of AZT among pregnant women, improved obstetric practices, and the avoidance of breast-feeding.

Transmission of HIV can occur during all stages of pregnancy. Evidence for intrauterine transmission, as opposed to intrapartum transmission, comes from cases in which infected mothers gave birth to infected children through caesarean delivery. Isolation of the virus from cord blood and fetal tissues provides additional evidence. Evidence of fetal infection has been found as early as the 13th week of pregnancy. Transmission in early stages of pregnancy has been documented in both first- and second-trimester fetuses (Sprecher, Soumenkoff, Puissant, & Deguelde, 1986; Mano & Chermann, 1991; Soeiro, Rubenstein, Rashbaum, & Lyman, 1992). In one study of 100 fetuses with a mean age of 22.4 weeks, no HIV was detected in 92 fetuses from elective midtrimester terminations (Brossard et al., 1995). Facial malformations indicating infection with HIV were evident in the other 8 fetuses from spontaneous intrauterine deaths and miscarriages. The actual frequency of in utero HIV infection appears to be low compared to peripartum rates, suggesting that most transmission occurs through exposure to blood and vaginal secretions at or near delivery.

Early intrauterine transmission has been documented by positive viral cultures and polymerase chain reaction (PCR) tests of newborns. Positive tests indicate that transmission occurred before labor and delivery. A majority of infants, however, do not show immunologic or virologic indicators of infection until after the first few days of life (Simonds & Oxtoby, 1995). This also suggests either that a substantial number of infected infants are infected close to or during labor and delivery or that infection may be detectable only after birth, or both. Indirect evidence supporting the acquisition of HIV around the time of delivery includes the absence of HIV-related congenital abnormalities, the lack of a birth weight effect, the finding that the virus can be detected in the first few days of life in less than half of infected children, and the association between vertical transmission and certain delivery types, including caesarean section.

Viral cultures and PCR tests have greater sensitivity in adults than in children. Only half of neonates later found to be infected are originally identified in these tests (Kuhn et al., 1994). However, perinatal HIV infection can be diagnosed during the first two to six months of life through viral culture or PCR (Kline et al., 1994; Krivine et al., 1992). Thus the inability to detect HIV infection at birth in a majority of cases suggests that active HIV replication occurs during the first few weeks of life.

Risk of Transmission. Major factors that have been associated with an increased risk of perinatal transmission include a mother's immunity and high viral load, decreased T4-cell counts, lack of HIV neutralizing antibody, and advanced clinical illness (Bryson, 1996). In addition, placental conditions and duration of membrane rupture play a role in HIV transmission risk. Nevertheless, significant gaps remain in our knowledge about variables in transmission, including the answer to why a majority of infants born to infected mothers escape infection. Mothers who previously gave birth to an infected child can have uninfected children. The subsequent children born to an infected mother do not appear to be at a higher risk of infection if the first child was infected. There is considerable variation in outcomes. One mother gave birth to an HIV-infected child followed by an uninfected child who was followed by an infected child.

Perinatal transmission is associated with advanced clinical illness in the mother because in the advanced stages of AIDS there is a greater presence of virus and/or a decline in immune function. It follows that the risk may be less for women who are beyond the window period but who have few or no symptoms and relatively high T4-cell counts. The European Collaborative Study (1992) found the rate of transmission to infants from women with T4-cell counts above 700 to be 6% and from women with T4-cell counts below 700 to be 19–22%. The association of rates of vertical transmission and maternal T4-cell counts has been found to be consistent across studies (Mayaux et al., 1995; St. Louis et al., 1993).

If the mother becomes infected during pregnancy or near the time when her child is to be born, the risk of transmission may be increased. More virus is present in the mother just after infection occurs and before she produces antibodies. The risk may also be greater if the infant is not carried to term, particularly if birth occurs before 34 to 37 weeks of gestation. Prematurity in an infant may indicate that infection has occurred. Another possibility is that the infant became infected in the birth canal because its prematurity made it more vulnerable (Mitchell, 1993).

Delivery type may play a role in transmission. Caesarean section may reduce risk of transmission because the newborn would not pass through the birth canal and would therefore not be exposed to blood and vaginal secretions. However, there is a potential for exposure to maternal blood through microbreaks in the placental barrier during labor. This suggests that delivery prior to both rupture of membranes and onset of labor may be required for the full benefit from caesarean section to be realized.

Twins born to HIV-infected mothers provide a unique situation illustrating the epidemiology and natural history of HIV disease, including the role of delivery type. A prospective study of 115 twin pairs born to infected mothers found a higher rate of transmission among the first-born twins than among the second born (Duliege et al., 1995). HIV infection was concordant in 80% of the 115 prospectively followed twin pairs. The strongest risk factor was infection of the co-twin. Moreover, infection with HIV occurred in 35% of the vaginally delivered and 16% of the caesarean delivered first-born twins and in 15% of the vaginally delivered and 8% of the caesarean delivered second-born twins. This study concluded that HIV infection of first-born twins occurs predominantly intrapartum whereas infection in second-born twins occurs predominantly in utero and that most vertical transmission occurs intrapartum. Thus, reducing exposure to HIV in the birth canal may reduce transmission of the virus from mother to infant.

Evidence for the benefits of caesarean section is not conclusive enough to warrant recommendation of routine caesarean section for infected women (Dunn et al., 1994; European Collaborative Study, 1994). Additionally, one study found that HIV-positive women who have caesarean sections are at increased risk of postoperative complications and that the risk of complications is even higher in women who are severely immunodepressed (Semprini et al., 1995). The actual benefit of caesarean section for the mother is therefore compromised due to increased risk of maternal morbidity.

In addition to intrapartum and antepartum, transmission has also been documented postpartum through breast-feeding. In these cases, the women were negative at the time of delivery and then seroconverted because they became infected through blood transfusions, IDU, or sexual transmission. A review of four published studies in which mothers acquired HIV postnatally found that the estimated risk of transmission to their infants was 29% (Dunn, Newell, Ades, & Peckham, 1992). The high rate associated with breast-feeding may be due to a confounding influence of a peak in viral load asssociated with primary infection rather than with breast-feeding (Kuhn & Stein, 1995).

There is evidence that HIV can be transmitted through breast-feeding by mothers who are already infected at the time of delivery (Dunn et al., 1992; European Collaborative Study, 1992). For such women, the additional risk to their infants from breast-feeding is around 15% (Peckham, 1993).

Breast-feeding has been a more frequent transmission route in developing countries where the practice is more common than in the United States. Indeed, breast-feeding may be responsible for more cases of maternal-infant transmission than are apparent. Thus the higher rate of perinatal transmission in developing countries may be because more infants born in them are breast-fed.

Breast-feeding benefits the infant because a mother's antibodies against infection are passed through her breast milk. In this way, unlike formula, breast milk protects infants from gastrointestinal, respiratory, and other diseases. For children already infected with HIV at birth, breast-feeding could also have beneficial effects, because the practice supports maternal health, contributes to child spacing, and is important in mother-infant bonding (Mitchell, 1993).

Despite breast-feeding's benefits the risk from it is seen in the United States, where there is ready access to formula, as being too great. For this reason, it is recommended that infected women not breast-feed their infants. In developing countries, however, because of their high infant mortality rates from infection and malnutrition and their lack of clean water to mix formula, breast-feeding is viewed as the best way in which children can be fed. Accordingly, the World Health Organization (WHO) has recommended that mothers breast-feed their infants in these countries (WHO, 1992).

Reducing the Risk of Perinatal Transmission. An important part of the reproductive health of infected women's concerns reducing the risk of transmission to their unborn children. Various approaches to perinatal transmission risk reduction at different stages of pregnancy, labor, and delivery have been suggested. For example, during pregnancy, avoidance of invasive diagnostic procedures, such as amniocentesis and chorionic villi sampling, would help reduce the risk of transmission to the fetus. Table 9 summarizes the approaches that will be discussed in this section.

The risk to newborns of vaginal delivery and the possible benefit of caesarean delivery were discussed earlier. Additional circumstances of delivery can increase potential for transmission. Any complications, regardless of delivery type, that either increase or prolong exposure to maternal blood and fluids can heighten risk. Invasive procedures during labor, including fetal scalp electrodes, scalp clips, and episiotomy, may increase risk of transmission because of the possibility of inoculating the fetus or newborn with virus.

Some types of vaginal antiseptic or virucidal agent may reduce the risk of transmission that occurs late in pregnancy or during birth. The cleansing of the birth canal prior to vaginal delivery as well as the decontamination of the surface of the infant may serve as a less invasive and a less costly strategy to reduce transmission (Siena Consensus Workshop II, 1995). But if a significant amount of virus transmission occurs transplacentally, this procedure may not be as beneficial, and thus the actual benefit of vaginal lavage becomes inconclusive.

Table 9. *Approaches to reducing the transmission of HIV
from mother to child*

Avoidance of breast-feeding
Antiretroviral therapy (for the mother during pregnancy and delivery and for the
　　infant after birth)
　　Zidovudine
　　Other antiretroviral agents
Reduction in peripartum exposure
　　Caesarean section
　　Avoidance of intrapartum invasive procedures
　　Vaginal disinfection
　　Treatment of sexually transmitted diseases
Immunotherapy for the mother or infant (or both)
　　Passive therapy
　　Active immunization

Source: "Mother-to-Child Transmission of the Human Immunodeficiency Virus," Vol. 33, pp. 298–302, by C. Peckham and D. Gibb. Reprinted by permission of *The New England Journal of Medicine.* Copyright 1995, Massachusetts Medical Society.

Antiretroviral therapy has been recommended for pregnant women to reduce risk of perinatal transmission. A study of pregnant women conducted by the Pediatric AIDS Clincial Trials Group (ACTG 076) from 1991 to 1993 indicated that AZT therapy was effective in reducing maternal-infant transmission (Connor et al., 1994).

The case-controlled study included 180 infants who were given AZT and 183 who were given a placebo. Each woman who participated had a T-cell count > 200, only mild symptoms of disease, and no prior treatment with antiretroviral drugs. Zidovudine was given antepartum and intrapartum to the mother beginning in the 14th week of pregnancy and to the neonate for 6 weeks.

The National Institutes of Health (NIH) announced the results of the study in February 1994. The risk of maternal-infant transmission had been reduced by two-thirds (Ibid.). Zidovudine appears to have had a preventive effect by reducing maternal HIV RNA levels prior to delivery (Dickover et al., 1996). Although some infants did become infected, despite treatment with AZT, this study provided promising evidence for the benefits of the drug in reducing risk of maternal-infant transmission. In fact, the study was stopped because the results were so significant and it was felt that it would be unethical to let the study proceed without giving all participants access to AZT treatment.

Based on the results of this research, the U.S. Public Health Service (PHS) recommended routine voluntary HIV counseling and testing for all pregnant women (CDC, 1995). It also recommended that infected pregnant women be informed not only of the potential benefits but also of the unknown long-term risks of preventive therapy with zidovudine (Ibid.). The 076 study demonstrated the importance of early access to care and AZT therapy for pregnant women.

In studies such as the one just discussed, zidovudine was shown to lessen the risk of HIV transmission to infants and thereby to improve the chances of an infant's survival. These findings have had an important impact on pregnant women as well as on health care providers. This impact can be seen in the increased rates of testing among women after the 076 findings were released (Rogers, 1997). When zidovudine has been offered to women they have accepted it (Ibid.). By making their chances of having uninfected children seem more likely, findings from the 076 study have influenced women's reproductive decision making. Other factors that influence women's decision making are covered later in the chapter.

Follow-up studies with AZT have produced even better results and are even more encouraging (Mofenson, 1997). Findings from the Twelfth World Conference on AIDS held in Geneva in 1998 showed promising results from AZT therapy combined with caesarean delivery (Maugh, 1998). AZT presumably reduced maternal viral load and caesarean delivery, the infant's exposure to HIV during delivery, thereby reducing transmission of HIV to less than 1%. Yet some infants still become infected, despite AZT therapy. Factors responsible for infection may include the mother's drug resistance and nonadherence to the treatment regimen as well as poor timing in administration of the drug (Rogers, 1997). Since most transmission is believed to occur at or near delivery, the feasibility of short-term AZT therapy is being examined. There is a great interest in short-term therapy in developing countries where health care budgets are severely limited. Promising results with short-term therapy from a study in Thailand, Uganda, and Tanzania were reported at the Twelfth World Conference on AIDS (Maugh, 1998). Twice-daily dosages of AZT were administered beginning in the 36th week of pregnancy and continuing through delivery. This regimen reduced transmission from 19% in the group not getting AZT to 9% in the group that did.

Studies involving combinations of recently developed drugs known as protease inhibitors are now being conducted on pregnant women (Haney, 1997). Some of these drugs are being used in combination with AZT. The idea here is that monotherapy is suboptimal – that patients can benefit most from drug combinations. Thus far, however, only 3 of the 11 antiretroviral drugs approved to treat HIV disease have been pharmacokinetically evaluated in human pregnancy (Pediatric AIDS Foundation, 1997). These include two nucleoside reverse transcriptase inhibitors – AZT and 3TC – and one nonnucleoside HIV reverse transcriptase inhibitor – nevirapine. Only AZT has been approved by the Food and Drug Administration (FDA) for use in human pregnancy (Ibid.).

Nevirapine is also being used as a monotherapy and is given in pill form to the mother and to the baby after birth (Haney, 1997). Studies are also being conducted on the use of nevirapine in HIV-infected children, including adolescents (Luzuriaga, Bryson, McSherry, Robinson, et al., 1996). AIDS trials in children are typically conducted long after a drug has been approved for adults. Children have a developing and immature immune system which makes evaluating the drug's efficacy more difficult. In addition, children metabolize drugs at different rates as compared to adults. This difference has to be taken into account in determining effective dosages. An additional compounding factor is that there are many psychosocial issues that may interfere with a family's ability to carry out complex medical regimens associated with these drugs.

The relative proportion of perinatal infections attributable to transmission during each stage of pregnancy and postpartum is not known. However, this information is critical for the design of appropriate interventions to prevent perinatal transmission, as some interventions may be effective for only certain stages of pregnancy. For example, infections that occur early in pregnancy might be prevented by immunizing the mother with a protective vaccine before she becomes pregnant (Andiman, 1995). This technique is currently used to prevent congenital defects associated with rubella. Infections transmitted at the time of delivery could be prevented by providing the neonate with both a hyperimmune globulin product and a series of vaccinations within 24 hours of birth (Ibid.). This type of strategy has been used successfully to prevent perinatal transmission of hepatitis B. An ideal preventive intervention would be inexpensive, nontoxic to the mother and fetus, simple to administer, and effective in preventing perinatal transmission (Mofenson, 1997). These goals are indeed difficult to achieve. Of course, the most effective way to eliminate perinatal transmission is to eliminate HIV infection in women. That goal is even more daunting.

Pregnancy and HIV Disease

Studies of disease progression in HIV-infected women have had a disproportionate focus on pregnancy. Thus, existing knowledge about HIV-disease progression has come largely from pregnant women and mothers. Study participants are usually recruited after their HIV disease has been determined in prenatal tests or in tests of their infants or children. It is usually not possible, therefore, to know the actual duration of HIV infection in these women.

Assessing the role of pregnancy in HIV disease is difficult because many infected pregnant women have additional risk factors for poor pregnancy outcomes. These risks include substance abuse, other concurrent illnesses, poor nutrition, low socioeconomic status, and limited access to health care. Indeed, in assessing the impact of pregnancy on HIV disease it appears that these factors have a more adverse effect on HIV disease than does pregnancy itself. There has been an increase in the incidence of STDs and medical complications among HIV-infected pregnant women but no discernible increase in obstetric complications or in poor birth outcomes (Williams, 1992). This situation contrasts with that in Africa, where maternal HIV infection has been associated with pregnancy complications, including prematurity, low birth weight, and fetal demise (Legg, 1993).

Early concern that pregnancy accelerated the course of HIV disease in infected women was based on knowledge that other infectious diseases carry a worse prognosis for women when they occur during pregnancy. Certain viral, bacterial, and fungal infections can be more common and more virulent during normal pregnancy (Ibid.). Pregnant women are considered to be vulnerable because of a natural deregulation of their immune system that allows maternal tolerance for the fetus. This response protects the fetus from being rejected by its mother.

Viral load has been associated with disease progression in nonpregnant individuals. However, it is not known whether viral load and replication are influenced by pregnancy. Nor is it known whether pregnancy shortens the life expectancy of infected women.

The extent to which pregnancy increases the immune burden and compromises the clinical course of HIV disease in infected women has not been established. Pregnancy does not appear to accelerate the progression to AIDS in asymptomatic women. Evidence for this lack of disease progression has been found in both early and later studies (Berrebi et al., 1990; Brettle et al., 1995; Hankins & Handley, 1992; Mandelbrot & Henrion, 1993; Mitchell, 1992). However, HIV-infected women who are pregnant may be more vulnerable to HIV-related complications as well as to non–AIDS-defining morbidity (Mandelbrot & Henrion, 1993). Overall, the care of pregnant women with HIV disease does not differ a great deal from the care of nonpregnant infected women except for the use of antiretroviral therapy (Hirschhorn, 1995).

Societal interest in perinatal transmission has focused almost exclusively on the suffering of infants and children (Pies, 1995). Yet the promising results from new drug therapies in preventing perinatal transmission sometimes obscure the plight of these children. Although the children may be free of disease, they will lose their mothers and, in many cases, their fathers too.

REPRODUCTIVE CHOICES

For an HIV-positive woman who does not want to have children, selecting a contraceptive method involves consideration of its effectiveness in preventing both pregnancy and transmission of disease. Thus she must take account of two concerns when making her decision.

Many women have found addressing both contraceptive and safer-sex concerns in just one method to be problematic. Some methods are more effective in preventing pregnancy than disease and vice versa. Barrier methods such as the male condom pose a problem for many women because they require the cooperation of male partners, and women are not always able to negotiate safer sex.

The male condom is the *only* barrier method proven to be effective against HIV (Stein, 1995). Some evidence of the effectiveness of condoms in vivo is provided by studies of discordant couples. A survey of studies found that condom use provided up to ninefold protection of the uninfected partner (Cates & Stone, 1992). In a European longitudinal study of discordant couples, no new infections occurred among consistent condom users (de Vincenzi, 1994). However, only 48% of the couples actually achieved the difficult goal of consistency.

Ironically, the age group of women most affected by HIV/AIDS is the very one that has never had to negotiate male-controlled contraception (Schneider, 1989). For adolescents, the challenge of introducing safer sex into a relationship is magnified compared to adults, who may have experience in negotiating sexual relationships. Adolescents, in contrast, may lack the insights or the skills that are necessary to enact safe-sex behavior. Also adolescents may be strongly influenced by their peers, an important source of their information about sexual behavior (Rotheram-Borus, Jemmott, & Jemmott, 1995).

Because of issues of gender power, much recent emphasis has been placed on the development of new female-controlled methods of contraception. (For more on gender power issues, see Chapters 4 and 5.) Spermicides, cervical caps, and diaphragms are examples of currently used methods that do not require male cooperation. Some concern has been expressed about the level of protection against HIV that these methods provide, however, compared to the male condom (Cates, Stewart, & Trussell, 1992). But when the male condom is not an option, female-controlled methods can provide fallback protection.

Currently, research on vaginal microbicides that have virucidal but not spermicidal properties is continuing (Elias & Heise, 1994). This research is considered to be important for women and men who want to have a child but still prevent disease transmission. Whether HIV is carried by sperm or only by semen and accompanying cells is open to debate (Stein, 1993). If the virus is carried by sperm, then prevention of sexual transmission necessarily involves contraception. If the virus is carried only by somatic cells in the semen, then contraception is not necessary for prevention. In the latter case, a virucide that inactivates the virus but does not kill the sperm could prove to be a much needed advance, particularly in societies with religions and cultures that place a high value on reproduction. A virucide with a chemical barrier that prevents disease transmission but permits conception would thus make an important contribution to prevention.

Few of the chemical and physical contraceptive methods developed recently have been tested adequately either for social acceptability or for effectiveness against STDs, particularly HIV (Stein, 1995). There is a real need for behavioral research on the social contexts in which these methods can best be used. At present more is known about the viricidal properties of these methods than about their sociological aspects.

Furthermore, as Worth (1989) points out, HIV/AIDS prevention efforts have been hampered by the separation between research on contraceptive behavior and research on sexual behavior. This separation has resulted in a lack of knowledge about the relationship between gender and cultural roles, sexual norms, and actual sexual behavior.

Women did not gain control over contraceptive decisions until the birth control pill and the intrauterine device (IUD) were introduced in the 1960s and 1970s. These methods of contraception clearly had important consequences for women's sexual decision making, but they also had important consequences for men. With the introduction of these new female-controlled methods, men were no longer required to use condoms or to practice withdrawal. Essentially men were absolved from contraceptive decision making. But the AIDS epidemic has now restored to men power over the consequences of sexual behavior (Stein, 1990). Women's reliance on the cooperation of their male partners to use condoms is a return to a female dependence on men similar to that of the 1950s. A woman must grapple with this aspect of sexual decision-making every time she asks a male partner to use a condom (Worth, 1989). The impact of the epidemic on both women's and men's sexual decision making cannot be overlooked.

Because a majority of women with HIV disease are in their child-bearing years, this is the context within which issues of reproduction and sexuality are examined. Reproduction is a complex personal choice for all women. A woman's decision to become pregnant or to continue with a pregnancy often involves concerns that HIV disease can only intensify. Superimposed on pregnancy, HIV affects the quality and length not only of women's lives but also of the lives of their children. All this takes place in an era of increasing attention to reproductive freedom.

It might seem that adolescents would be protected by their relative youth from negative social stereotypes about reproductive decisions. However, adolescents experienced the same punitive response to their reproductive decisions as HIV-infected adult women (King, 1996). Youth who are sexually active or who use drugs do not generate the same level of compassion that infants and young children evoke. Instead, their youth and relative immaturity are considered justifications for controlling adolescents' sexuality, pregnancy, and childbirth (Ibid.) even though adolescent women are less likely than adult women to have children out of wedlock (Males, 1996).

Reinforcing negative stereotypes is society's ambivalence toward and even denial of adolescent sexuality (Cohn & Futterman, 1995). There is a profound societal silence, particularly on female adolescent sexual desire (Bentley & Herr, 1996). The result of this silence is that adolescent girls lack knowledge of themselves as subjects of their own sexuality, which may impair their ability to make sexual decisions. AIDS education and prevention efforts have been seriously impeded by this societal reticence on adolescent sexual behavior.

More is known about adolescent sexual behavior than about adult behavior only because of society's concern about teenage pregnancy (King, 1996). Yet adolescent women are less likely than adult women to have children out of wedlock (Males, 1996). Most of the information is on intercourse, not on sexual behavior. And, as will be discussed in the last chapter, the compelling interest seems to be in controlling adolescent sexuality.

Reproductive Choices and HIV Disease

An immediate concern of infected women who are pregnant or who are considering pregnancy is whether they will transmit HIV to their unborn child. There is great uncertainty surrounding this question. Although there are indicators of higher risk or lower risk of transmission, there is no way to predict whether or not an infant will be infected because no safe antenatal screening test for HIV is available. As stated earlier, an invasive test could cause HIV to be transmitted from the mother to the fetus. Even if there were a safe test and the test of the fetus were negative, there is no assurance that the fetus would remain uninfected throughout the pregnancy and birth. The antibody test is not a reliable indicator of infection in newborns because the newborn infant carries passively acquired antibodies from its mother. Testing of newborns therefore is a reliable indicator of infection in mothers (though highly controversial when it is mandatory). Furthermore, the antibody test is reliable on infants after they have developed their own antibodies at 15 to 18 months. The lack of reliability of the antibody test as an indicator of HIV infection in infants was a particular problem in the early years of the epidemic when the antibody test was the only measure available. The lack of certainty surrounding transmission and testing creates difficult issues and decisions for women.

Diagnosis continues to be a major challenge for women with HIV disease. At most, 50% of infected childbearing women know they are infected when they give birth (Garcia, 1995). Many infected women learn of their own infection only after giving birth to an infected child. Had they known they were infected, knowledge of their own serostatus may have influenced their decision to continue their pregnancy although many infected women with this knowledge still choose to become pregnant or to continue their pregnancies. Women whose health is not compromised generally have the same attitudes and emotions regarding having children as they had prior to their diagnosis (Denenberg, 1997). It is also important to recognize that many pregnancies are unplanned and happen more by default than by intent.

Although prenatal testing policy in the United States is based on the assumption that cognitive information about seropositivity will affect reproductive choices, that assumption may not be entirely accurate. Even when women know of their own seropositivity, it is not always a major deciding factor in their reproductive decisions (Selwyn et al., 1989; Sunderland et al., 1992). This includes decisions to use contraception as well as decisions to terminate pregnancies. Several studies of diverse groups of women have found that knowledge of HIV seropositivity has little or no effect on contraceptive use (Fischl et al., 1987; Brown & Rundell, 1990). Seropositive women are no more likely to use contraception than seronegative women.

Decisions about pregnancy termination follow a pattern similar to decisions about contraception. Studies have found no difference in rates of pregnancy termination between seropositive drug-using women and seronegative controls (Selwyn et al., 1989; Sunderland et al., 1992). Pregnancy-related factors were more predictive of termination. In a review of research on reproductive decisions among HIV-infected women, Sunderland (1990) found that in most cohorts, 50% or more of the women continued their pregnancies to term. Overall, HIV-positive women make reproductive decisions that are similar to those of HIV-negative women.

Factors in reproductive decision making are many; serostatus is only one. The way these factors influence decision making is complex, and risks are not always weighed in a rational process. Moral concerns often translate into different outcomes. For example, some women may choose to have a therapeutic abortion to prevent potential suffering of a child whereas other women may take a pregnancy to term because of the belief that even a life shortened by HIV disease is of value (Kurth, 1993). Factors in influencing pregnancy continuation as well as termination are based on a complex of religious, moral, and psychological reasons. Those factors influencing women to continue a pregnancy include a desire to have a child, a chance to start anew, strong feelings against abortion, barriers to abortion service, inability to follow through with an abortion, denial of infection, unwillingness to reveal HIV status to a partner, and good maternal health (Kurth & Minkoff, 1995). Additional factors include a gender self-image that requires childbearing, a risk evaluation with acceptable odds, personal optimism, increasing age, religious faith, and prior experience with an antibody-positive child who seroreverted (Kurth & Hutchinson, 1990). A desire to please a partner and an unconscious desire to bear children in reaction to grief and loss have also been identified in decisions to continue a pregnancy (Selwyn & Antoniello, 1993). Finally, the familial and social support availabile to women are often critical in influencing continuation.

There are many complex factors that influence an infected woman's decision to terminate a pregnancy. She may fear her own HIV disease progression and fear infecting her child. Additional factors include perception of risk, poor maternal health, concerns about long-term care or child care, and the influence of the partner or family (Kurth & Minkoff, 1995). If she had prior experience with HIV and infant death she may feel stress from waiting for a child to serorevert. The decision to end a pregnancy may also involve a lack of placement options for the child, the desire to avoid physical illness in the child, a fear or inability to care for the child, and the desire to avoid HIV stigma for the child (Hankins, 1993).

Specific situations may affect women's reproductive decisions. For example, many women choose to carry a pregnancy to term because motherhood is a cultural expectation that they value. In having and caring for children, women often find a source of strength and a reason to live. For some infected women who are IDUs the goal of childbearing may impel them to get off drugs and to try to have a normal life (Mitchell, 1988). Even infected women who do decide to terminate, being more likely to have had a previous termination, may still have a subsequent pregnancy (Sunderland, 1990). And one study found co-residence to be an important factor in decision making (Pivnick et al., 1991). Infected mothers who had a child living at home were more likely to terminate a pregnancy than mothers who had lost children to child welfare systems.

It should also be noted that infected women do not live in a vacuum. They receive information about HIV disease from various sources. For example, a study by Johnstone and colleagues (1990) found that many women were influenced by media reports that risks of perinatal transmission were lower than previously estimated.

Risk assessment in reproductive decision making is a difficult task for women of all socioeconomic statuses. In trying to explain risk assessment, it has been suggested that women who live with risk in their daily lives may be more inclined to accept the risk of perinatal transmission. For example, the study by Selwyn and colleagues (1989) found this to be true of women who were IDUs. These women, who represent most of the women with AIDS, tend to be mostly from the lower class. But risk assessment by women from other social classes tends to be similar. These women are generally well-educated, employed, and live without risks other than sex with their infected male partner. Such women include women in the military (Brown & Rundell, 1990) as well as partners of hemophiliac men (Jason, Evatt, & Hemophilia AIDS Collaborative Study Group, 1990). Thus acceptance of risk seems to hold true also for women who do not ordinarily encounter great risk in their daily lives. In addition, the reasons for planned pregnancies and pregnancy continuations given by well-educated middle-class women are similar to those given by their lower-class counterparts (Hutchinson & Shannon, 1993). There may be a danger, therefore, in emphasizing socioeconomic aspects of reproductive decision making, with the implication that poor women have special reasons for having children whereas women of higher socioeconomic statuses make rational decisions.

So far this discussion has focused on women's reproductive choices. Little research has been conducted on men's role in making reproductive decisions, even though men are critical to the process. It could be that the reproductive choices of both men and women involve similar factors. However, a study of German HIV-discordant couples involving seropositive males that inquired into the motivations of each partner found that the wish that "a part of myself should live on" was a stronger factor for the men than for the women (Sonnenberg-Schwan et al., 1993). This study also found that the wish for a child was the commonly cited reason for abandoning the practice of protective sex (against advice to do so). It appears that pregnancy in the presence of HIV disease is common in both concordant and discordant couples.

In the public debate over HIV/AIDS and reproductive responsibility, attention to the role of men is notably lacking. This absence suggests that men have nothing to do either with the problem or with its solution (Pies, 1995). The single focus on women forces us to wonder where men fit within women's reproductive decisions. HIV disease places important demands on men in their role as fathers. Fathers need to be responsible in reproductive decisions because of the family-based nature of HIV disease (Sherr, 1996).

The emphasis on women's ability to transmit HIV perinatally to their children is rather curious when women's ability to infect is compared to that of men's (Pies, 1995). During a nine-month pregnancy, women can infect only one child. Owing to the greater efficiency of male-to-female transmission, however, men are able to infect any number of partners during the same time period. Many family planning and prenatal clinics acknowledge this irony when they promote HIV prevention by encouraging women to be responsible for getting their male partners to use condoms. This issue is raised again and covered in greater depth in Chapters 4 and 5.

Reproductive Counseling. The way in which information on risk is presented to women by reproductive health counselors may also influence women's decisions. Specifically, how a counselor frames the information may directly affect a woman's willingness to consider termination (Marteau, 1989). For example, women are more likely to consider ending a pregnancy if, rather than being told that they have a 75% chance of having a normal child, they are told that there is a 25% chance of giving birth to a child with an abnormality. Such negative framing, with its emphasis on the abnormal, is more likely to result in a decision to terminate (Sherr, 1991).

The desire of many women to continue a pregnancy, even when the risk is high, is often very strong. Examples here come from the field of genetic disorder screening. Faden and colleagues (1987) found that among middle-class non-drug-using women, the desire to continue a pregnancy is strong even when they have been told that there is only a 10% chance of a normal outcome. Their study asked a group of pregnant women about their attitudes toward abortion of fetuses with neural tube defects. More women responded that they would continue a pregnancy if there was only a 5% chance of having a normal child than if there was no chance at all (32% vs. 4%; Faden et al., 1987). This finding has important implications for approaches that can be used in reproductive counseling for women with HIV disease.

The ethics of different approaches used in reproductive counseling for women with HIV disease have been the subject of considerable debate. Central to this debate is the critically important issue of who should be the one to make reproductive choices. The genetic nondirective counseling approach has been offered as a model for reproductive counseling for HIV. This model is based on the idea of ethical neutrality and support for personal choice. The nondirective model was developed against a background of the eugenics controversy and therefore is sensitive to many of the issues of culture and racism that surround reproduction.

In the nondirective approach, the genetic counselor simply provides the client with information about risk. The client then makes a decision based on that information. The role of the genetic counselor is to translate scientific risk possibilities into personal risk calculations. Precise risk calculations are difficult to make for HIV disease because perinatal transmission depends on the course that the disease takes in the mother. In this way, because the health of the mother is necessarily affected, HIV is different from most other genetic diseases.

The maternal antibody test, as already mentioned, is not a good predictor of future infant health compared to other fetal tests. It may become possible to determine the actual risk of transmission with greater precision in the future. This risk determination would most likely be made through the identification of predictive maternal factors, but it may also involve intrauterine diagnostic techniques (Selwyn & Antoninello, 1993). This precision would be a major and welcome addition to prenatal counseling of HIV-infected women. However, as

Selwyn and Antoninello caution (Ibid.), a greater certainty of prediction should not change the general nondirective approach so that counseling becomes more coercive.

Reproductive counseling must go beyond helping a client merely to choose to have a child or not. It must also cover pediatric disease and assessment as well as care of the child with HIV disease. Many studies that have examined pediatric HIV disease have been child centered and, as such, have overlooked maternal and, especially, paternal issues (Sherr, 1993c). For example, much attention has been paid to variables in pregnancy and how they relate to outcome. Yet, outcome measures are usually limited to physiological characteristics of the newborn such as weight, body length, and head circumference. Psychosocial variables such as postpartum trauma, psychological adjustment, parenting perceptions, and maternal infant interaction are neglected (Ibid.).

It is vital that reproductive counseling facilitate the client in making her own decision. Thus the role of the nondirective counselor is to provide accurate information, encourage a full exploration of alternatives, and refer to appropriate resources. It is also important that counseling take into account the social and behavioral contexts in which clients will be making decisions (Selwyn et al., 1989). A counselor's insensitivity may cause women to feel alienated and distanced from the medical system with the result that the very population this system is intended to serve perceives it as increasingly irrelevant.

The aim of nondirective counseling is to empower women to make decisions about their reproductive health. The ultimate risk-reducing strategy is based on women's ability to take greater control over their reproductive lives. This means that women's risk must be understood in the context of gender power relations with men.

3

WOMEN AT RISK: DRUG USE AND PROSTITUTION

I got myself into a program in prison which taught me why I was an addict and how I could stop using and drinking. I learned all I could about my HIV status and became willing to change the way I was. From prison I was paroled into a program because I wanted to learn more about how to live drug free.

– Loretta

When I came back everything was sold. It was the drugs. There was nothing. This is the fourth time that he got rid of things. I was thinking of divorce.

One thing I give credit to him for is quitting drugs after dealing with drugs for so many years because he started so young. He started when he was about 12 years old. Because of his drug use he was found HIV positive.

– Leticia

I took a trick's wallet and then he came back on me. He bust me in the face with a beer bottle. I got raped by six men. They hit me in the mouth. That's why I ain't got no teeth.

I was 14 when I first shot heroin. I just tried to keep that fix every day. One time when my habit was $150, I'd go to bed with them for a spoon because I was sick. I let a guy pimp me just so I could hang around him. I thought he was cool. He told me that he liked me but all he wanted was me to keep his habit up.

When I was out there, I didn't give a damn. It was all about me. I had a couple of tricks – They would bring their sons to me and their sons would be about 14 years old. I know I have spread my disease but at the time I didn't care. It was all about the money. I didn't use a rubber and I knew I was infected. I was workin' the street for about 22 years.

I was so strung out I couldn't catch a trick. I tried to commit suicide when I was working the streets 'cause I was so tired sometime. I tried to cut my throat. I tried to OD. I took a bunch of valium. I've been on the mental ward three times for suicide. I was in a drug program. And again I went up to 35 days and relapsed.

– Eunice

It's been 8 years since I found out I am positive. And how do I deal with it today? It's like an everyday process. Even in recovery, I tell people I don't have one illness, I have two, you know. I have HIV and an addiction. And my HIV is the one that always takes me back out.

– Naomi

DRUG USERS AND THEIR SEX PARTNERS

The relationship between injection drug use and sexual behavior has been the driving force behind the heterosexual AIDS epidemic in the United States for the last decade. As discussed in Chapter 1, injection drug use is a critical risk behavior for women: Most women with AIDS are either injection drug users themselves or the sex partners of IDUs. The ratio of male to female IDUs is estimated to be 3 to 1 (Brown & Weissman, 1993). This ratio has also been found in statistics on needle-exchange programs (University of California, 1993). Because more drug users are men, most behavioral research on drug use has been conducted on the male drug subculture (Brown & Weissman, 1993; Rosenbaum, 1981; Weissman & Brown, 1995). As a result, little information on the relationship between drug use and sexual decision making is available, despite its importance to AIDS prevention (Worth, 1990).

Risk. Women are at particular risk from their male sex partners who are IDUs. Whereas a majority of the women who are the sex partners of male IDUs do not use drugs themselves, the men who are the sex partners of female IDUs also usually use drugs (Des Jarlais, 1984). The drug behavior of male IDUs is often clandestine; it is a behavior that they engage in with other men and keep secret from their female partners. Thus the female sex partners (FSPs) of these men are often not aware of their partner's past or present drug use. Many men take drugs for years without their female partners ever knowing. Furthermore, the role of men who are injection drug users is important in determining the HIV risk of women who inject drugs as well as of women who do not.

For both men and women, drug use is a difficult behavior to change permanently. As can be seen from the testimonies of Eunice and Leticia that open this chapter, many users have an early initiation into drug use and remain drug dependent for years. In addition, most drug users have high rates of relapse, and for many, their drug treatment is frequently intermixed with periods of drug use.

Crack use has been described as initiating a new form of prostitution (Chaisson et al., 1991; Inciardi, 1989). Often women addicted to crack exchange sex for crack. They have sex with multiple partners in crack houses – the places in which crack is sold and used. Thus numerous anonymous exchanges of sex for crack take place, and crack houses have been identified as important settings for heterosexual transmission. An additional concern about these sexual encounters is the age of the women. Quite often they are preteen-agers (Springer, 1992). The spread of STDs among adolescents because of crack use was noted in Chapter 1.

In contrast to heroin, which usually does not increase the sex drive, crack often results in prolonged sex. Under the influence of crack men have difficulty ejaculating; consequently, the women's vaginas will sometimes become dry. Vaginal and penile bleeding may occur, facilitating HIV transmission. In addition, open sores on the lips and tongues of crack users, which are the result of burns from hot crack pipes, are common (Inciardi, Lockwood, & Pottieger, 1993). This is a particular concern because much of the sex that occurs in crack houses involves women performing oral sex on men (Ibid.). One study of street prostitutes who used crack but not injection drugs also found a relationship between HIV infection and unprotected fellatio (Wallace et al., 1997).

Despite the high rate of awareness of and concern about AIDS in the crack houses, the use of condoms is rare (Inciardi, Lockwood, & Pottieger, 1993). A study of crack users in three urban neighborhoods found that although 71% of women who were regular users had exchanged sex for money or for drugs within the past 30 days, only 38% of them had used condoms (Edlin et al., 1992).

Gender Roles and Gender Differences

In general, female drug users hold traditional beliefs about gender-role behavior (Simpson & Williams, 1993). Women commonly rely on men – usually dealers – to supply them with drugs in exchange for companionship and sexual favors (Inciardi, Lockwood, & Pottieger, 1993). Women who inject drugs often report that they were introduced to drug injection by a man who was a sex partner or a family friend (Miller, Turner, & Moses, 1990). For men, the introduction to and progression in drug use and related criminal activity occur primarily through a male friend. Drug users typically have "running partners" – persons with whom they shoot drugs and spend time. Men prefer to run with men and to have sexual relationships with non–drug-using women (Connors, 1996). Women, however, prefer male running partners because of the protection they provide (Ibid.).

Women's efforts to secure a male running partner often involve increased needle sharing and sex for protection and access to drugs. For women, then, addiction is often closely tied to love and to their sexual relationships with men. This emotional involvement complicates the process of disengaging from drug use. Some IDU women who become sober remain sexually involved with a partner who uses drugs, and thus the women continue to be at risk for HIV.

Women also sometimes seek assistance with injections from the men who introduce them to drug use (Ibid.). Women share injection equipment primarily with their sexual partners or with close-knit groups that include their sexual partner (Kane, 1991). In contrast, male drug users are more likely to shoot drugs in gallery-type settings or in groups of casual acquaintances. Overall, female IDUs are more likely than male IDUs to have a drug-using partner and to share injection equipment with that partner (Brown & Weissman, 1993). They are also more likely to use equipment after their partner (as cited in Quina et al., 1997). Female users often perceive needle sharing as a networking strategy to increase access to low- or no-cost drugs (McCaul, Lillie-Blanton, & Svikis, 1996). When sharing needles during group injections, female users often go last because of their lower status in the drug subculture, thus heightening their risk.

Women make up a minority of prison inmates in the United States, as 90% of inmates are male (Dubler & Sidel, 1992). Criminal activity tends to be somewhat less common among female than among male addicts and tends to differ according to gender in type as well. Rosenbaum (1981) found that the two crimes most frequently committed by women addicted to drugs are forgery and prostitution. Women will generally avoid high-risk crimes such as armed robbery and larceny (McCaul, Lillie-Blanton, & Svikis, 1996). Women may perceive these crimes as carrying a greater chance of getting caught and longer prison sentences as well as a greater likelihood of injury to themselves or to others involved. Prostitution is seen by women as carrying less risk than the other kinds of criminal behavior. However, prostitution does put women at risk for HIV.

Sometimes women in a relationship will have primary responsibility for getting the money that both partners need to purchase drugs. These women turn to prostitution or to shoplifting, which are seen as "easier" crimes than burglary or the more violent crimes that male addicts may commit to get money (Williams & O'Connor, 1995). Yet, their role as primary provider of drug money does not bring women more power in their relationships with their male partners.

The career of addicted women is different from that of addicted men. These women face a greater narrowing of life options. These women are more likely to have young children and to be the sole support of those children (Shaw & Paleo, 1986). Indeed, twice as many women as men who use injection drugs have children living with them (as cited in Guinan & Leviton, 1995). Also, these women have fewer friends, and their educational and employment opportunities are limited (Rosenbaum, 1981). Female IDUs are less likely than male IDUs to be employed and more likely to rely on other means of support (Brown & Weissman, 1993). In addition, addicted women have lower self-esteem and higher levels of anxiety or depression than addicted men (Williams & O'Connor, 1995), they have fewer social networks and receive less support from their partners (Ibid.), and they have fewer psychological resources and skills for coping. These factors make the initiation and maintenance of behavioral change more difficult for women.

Women who use drugs suffer more stigma and discrimination than men who use drugs (Ibid.). The patterns, experiences, and implications of drug use are different for women than for men because of different societal expectations based on genders. Moreover, gender plays an important part in personality formation and role relationships, both of which are central to understanding the dynamics of drug use in women (Ibid.). To a large extent, the individual identity of and the resources and opportunities available to the drug user depend upon whether that person is a man or a woman.

There is often a strict separation of gender roles among poor people that leads them to have different expectations about the behavior appropriate for men and for women. Although society views drug use by anyone in a negative light, it judges a woman who uses drugs more harshly than it does a man (Ibid.). In particular, injection drug use is seen as unwomanly. In contrast, a man's drug use, although not acceptable behavior, is not seen as unmanly.

Gender also has consequences for the health of drug users. Female users have more medical problems than do male users (McCaul, Lillie-Blanton, & Svikis, 1996; Weissman & Brown, 1995). Women who use drugs often have gynecological complications, STDs, urinary tract and bladder infections, and menstrual irregularities. Many of these medical problems have serious implications for HIV risk and treatment.

Barriers to Risk Reduction and Service Delivery

The HIV risk behaviors of drug users are complex. They usually are based in interpersonal relationships and thus to reduce them requires changing not only the behavior of the drug user but also the behavior of that individual's drug-using and sexual partners (McCaul, Lillie-Blanton, & Svikis, 1996). A major difficulty encountered in targeted HIV outreach efforts is reaching women about the risk of disease they face from the drug-using men who are their sex partners. Although the FSPs of male IDUs are at risk, they may not perceive themselves as vulnerable to HIV infection, and, therefore, it is difficult to communicate with them about AIDS. Attempts to find non–drug-using FSPs through drug treatment and other programs designed for drug users have not been successful (Sterk et al., 1989).

Some FSPs are aware of their partners' drug use but are unwilling to confront them for various reasons including fear of losing their economic support and fear of physical violence. For example, women most at risk often depend on their male partners for economic security (Kane, 1991), and extremely high rates of domestic violence were found in a study of relationships between female sex partners and male IDU partners (Weissman, 1991a). The experience of violence is more common among women who use drugs and women who are the partners of male IDUs than among women who are not affected by drugs (Amaro, 1995). In addition, a large proportion of alcohol- and drug-dependent women report that they have been victims of childhood or adult sexual abuse, including rape and incest (Ibid.).

To avoid becoming infected, injection drug users are more likely to change their drug behavior than their sexual behavior. Specifically, they are more likely to alter their needle-sharing practices than they are to use condoms (Becker & Joseph, 1988; Des Jarlais & Friedman, 1988). It has been suggested that an IDU's sexual behavior may be more difficult to change because it usually involves other people and important social and emotional concerns (Worth, 1989). Both male and female IDUs resist using condoms in an established relationship (CDC, 1992). Because they do not have multiple partners, these drug users do not believe that it is necessary for them to use condoms. Men who use drugs often associate condoms with prostitution and promiscuity (Solomon & DeJong, 1989), and for this reason it is especially difficult for the female partner to introduce condom use into an ongoing sexual relationship with a male IDU. Some women fear that they will lose a desired partner if they insist that the man use condoms. Their male partner might interpret such a demand as an admission that the woman has been unfaithful to him or as an accusation that the man has been unfaithful to her.

The situation is further complicated when the male partner is also the woman's drug supplier (McCaul, Lillie-Blanton, Svikis, 1996). Here the dynamics involve a customer–supplier relationship as well as a social relationship. Women must be doubly skilled in negotiating reproductive decisions in this interpersonal context.

In another effort to reduce HIV transmission, needle-exchange programs allow users to exchange their used injection equipment for sterile equipment. These programs also provide AIDS information, condoms, bleach, HIV-antibody testing, and drug treatment referrals. Although these programs have proven to be effective in reducing the spread of HIV, they have shown limited effectiveness in reaching women. Women make up only 14–25% of the participants in needle-exchange programs in the United States (Weissman & Brown, 1995).

Women who have children are sometimes reluctant to utilize needle-exchange services, as they are other services, out of fear of being identified as drug users and, consequently, losing custody of or access to their children (Khoshnood & Stephens, 1997). For this reason, some women turn to secondary needle exchange when it is available. In secondary exchange, someone else exchanges needles for the user. It is an important service for programs to offer, particularly to women (Ibid.).

Women also make up just 25% of users entering drug treatment programs (Institute of Medicine, 1986). Although recent efforts to increase the number of women in treatment have had some success, women enrolled in treatment still represent only about 30% of the 1.5 million women in need (McCaul, Lillie-Blanton, & Svikis, 1996).

Men who are drug users are frequently pressured into treatment by their female partners. A man is less likely to press his female partner to seek treatment (Corea, 1992); rather, he will try to persuade her to stay home so that he does not lose her domestic services. Because women are more likely to have a partner who uses drugs, this pressure may add to the burden of seeking treatment and increase the rate of relapse (Denenberg, 1995). Another possible explanation for the underutilization of drug treatment by women may be related to the finding that female addicts have a higher rate of concurrent psychiatric illness than male addicts (Ibid.). Some drug treatment centers will not even accept a client with a psychiatric diagnosis.

Street outreach is the most common approach used to get information about drug treatment and HIV/AIDS to drug users. Outreach workers tend to go where men who use drugs gather. Generally, these are areas in which drugs are obtained and used, areas considered to be too dangerous for women or simply "off-limits" to female users (Weissman & Brown, 1995). This means that although outreach workers who go into the community to recruit users into programs can find many men who use drugs and get them into treatment, they frequently miss the women who are users.

Most treatment programs have developed from men's drug use patterns and needs and therefore have a male profile (Wagner & Cohen, 1993). Most programs are for heroin users, and much less treatment is available for polydrug or crack users, who are also more likely to be women (Ibid.). Both in absolute numbers and in proportion to need, fewer drug treatment centers serve female users than male users (Shaw & Paleo, 1986). Because of drug treatment's male profile, women who enter treatment are placed in settings in which men dominate both as clients and as staff. Men who are ex-addicts are presented as the role models in these programs (Williams & O'Connor, 1995). The result is that the special concerns of women are often overlooked (Weissman & Brown, 1995). Such women's concerns can include resolving issues of physical and sexual abuse, learning about the effects of drug use on an unborn child, learning how to manage a pregnancy and how to parent effectively, and developing skills that will help them provide for themselves and their children.

As might be expected, the retention rate for female addicts in drug treatment is lower than that for male addicts (Williams & O'Connor, 1995). Drug treatment often takes a "therapeutic community" approach, and such an approach can reflect negative societal views toward female addicts. Treatment staff might describe women in drug treatment as emotional, manipulative, and more ill and difficult to treat than men (Ibid.). For women, successful rehabilitation is defined more by their gender-role behaviors, relationships, and mothering skills than by their completing their education or obtaining employment (Ibid.).

There is a lack of research on whether women do better in drug treatment programs that offer them specialized services or in those with mixed-gender settings. One study of alcohol treatment that compared the two types of settings found that women receiving specialized services stayed in treatment longer and had higher rates of program completion than women in the mixed-gender setting (McCaul, Lillie-Blanton, & Svikis, 1996). In addition, the children of women in specialized treatment settings were less likely to be placed in foster care than were the children of women in alternate programs.

Although children are often central in the lives of women who use drugs, some residential treatment centers will not house women who are pregnant or who have children with them. A class action suit in 1992 gave pregnant women access to treatment (Connors, 1996), and as a result, in recent years, the accommodation of women and children in treatment programs has improved somewhat. However, liability associated with the care of pregnant women still prevents some residential treatment centers from accepting them (McCaul, Lillie-Blanton, & Svikis, 1996). Furthermore, although some drug treatment programs take in both women and children, these programs are typically more concerned about the recovery of the mother than the needs of the children (Barth, 1993).

Many women who use drugs fear that they will lose their children if they seek treatment. Few programs help women accepted for treatment arrange child care. Quite often going into treatment means a woman must give up her children to foster care. This is why many women go into treatment only after they have already lost their children or have been arrested on drug charges (Corea, 1992). Few drug treatment programs are women focused, but those that are and that do not separate women from their families tend to have the best results in terms of both retention in treatment and low rates of relapse (Wagner & Cohen, 1993). In other words, the most successful programs address the specific needs of women in a women-centered environment.

Women who go through drug treatment with the help of support groups also have fewer relapses (Alemán et al., 1995). However, the struggle to remain drug free is constant, especially in the inner city. Many women are unable to maintain their resolve to be drug free, despite their best intentions.

Not all residential treatment centers that allow women and children are well informed about HIV and sensitive to clients with the infection. There is a lack of treatment centers that accommodate HIV-infected women. One exception is the Tarzana Treatment Center in Southern California. Unfortunately, the future of this program is uncertain because of budget constraints and the high costs of residential treatment. The cost of residential drug treatment for a single woman and child is $23,000 a year (Roberts, 1993).

Traditional treatment programs such as Alcoholics Anonymous and Narcotics Anonymous also do not always meet the needs of women who are HIV infected besides being alcohol- or drug-addicted. These programs too are not invariably well informed about and responsive to HIV disease. As a result, infected women sometimes feel isolated in these programs. This type of isolation led to the creation of the special support group for HIV-infected, drug-and-alcohol-addicted women that provides some of the vignettes in this book.

The vast majority (85–90%) of drug users do not enter any type of drug treatment (Polych, 1992). Therefore, attempts to reach IDUs in drug treatment with information about AIDS have only limited effectiveness. Nor is HIV-prevention information routinely available at most prisons. Thus it has been necessary to find other forums for the delivery of HIV risk-reduction materials. Street outreach using peer education has become the primary approach used.

The National Institute on Drug Abuse (NIDA) has funded projects to recruit women using injection drugs who are not in treatment in order to provide them with HIV counseling and education and drug treatment programs (NIDA, 1990). These projects received funds under National AIDS Demonstration Research (NADR) and AIDS Targeted Outreach Model (ATOM) contracts. Most of these projects used a street- and community-based outreach approach as their principal means of recruiting women in the target population. Underlying this strategy was the assumption that women who are IDUs cannot be reached through existing institutions such as health clinics, welfare offices, shelters, prisons, and jails.

An analysis of these projects found that a large portion of the female participants actually had had some type of exposure to an institution or agency that could have been a gateway to appropriate drug treatment, HIV prevention, and other services (Gross & Brown, 1993). However, the service delivery system that they had encountered was fragmented, uncoordinated, alienating, and irrelevant to many of these women. Thus, outreach was important in linking drug-involved women to treatment and other services.

This analysis also found that IDU women had not been motivated to seek treatment for three main reasons: (1) competing basic life needs and priorities; (2) denial that drug use is a problem; and (3) frustration in reaction to barriers imposed by traditional drug treatment programs (Ibid). Thus, a more effective approach to getting women to enter treatment is to facilitate their identification of their most urgent concerns and address those first before dealing with other issues such as drug treatment and HIV prevention.

In an analysis of projects in the NADR program, Weissman (1991b) found that participants did not fit neatly into programs such as substance abuse, prenatal care, or AIDS because most of the women had multiple problems, among them drug abuse, homelessness, legal problems, poor health, lack of financial support, lack of social support systems, and dysfunctional or destructive interpersonal relationships. Thus, it was recommended that those who are designing programs take into account the complex and different contexts that shape the lives of these women.

The strategy of "targeted outreach" has been employed by NADR to reach women directly. Projects have had considerable success in contacting women through outreach in a variety of settings: laundromats, beauty shops, factories, and bars; health fairs and community events; public health and family planning clinics, OB-GYN clinics, well-baby clinics and hospital emergency rooms; social service agencies (including AFDC and WIC); jails and prisons; battered women's and homeless shelters; housing projects and door-to-door (Weissman & Brown, 1995).

A survey of 1989 NIDA demonstration projects that examined barriers to help seeking by female IDUs found that traditional male referral networks such as employers and the criminal justice system failed to account for the majority of treatment referrals for women. For these women, medical providers and child-protective services were the primary referral agencies (McCaul, Lillie-Blanton, & Svikis, 1996). The most frequently cited positive influence on help-seeking behavior of female IDUs was the encouragement they received from family members other than a partner or spouse (e.g., children, parents, siblings). The most frequently cited factor that discouraged help seeking was the women's concern about their children, including child-custody issues and the availability of child-care services.

HIV Prevention Strategies for IDUs

The numbers of IDUs reached through drug treatment is limited. But for those users who do participate, exposure to drug treatment programs that provide AIDS information has been associated with reduced risk of HIV infection due to a reduction in needle-sharing practices (Lewis & Watters, 1991). Sexual risk reduction among users in treatment, however, is affected less by education than by personal experience, by either knowing someone who is living with AIDS or by having one or more friends who has died from AIDS (Ibid.).

Peer education programs have had some success in getting IDUs to use safe injection practices (Miller, Turner, & Moses, 1990; Turner, Miller & Moses, 1989). These programs have been less influential in changing sexual behavior, however, particularly in getting IDUs to use condoms. IDUs are known to be inconsistent or ineffective users of contraception (Miller, Turner, & Moses, 1990).

Many IDUs who have changed to safe injection practices are still unlikely to use condoms (Miller, Turner, & Moses, 1990; Turner, Miller, & Moses, 1989). This was true in San Francisco, where safe injection practices increased with only a small increase in condom use by IDUs (Lewis & Watters, 1991). Among IDUs in the city, men were more likely than women to report never having used a condom. Intensive street outreach did convince some of San Francisco's male IDUs to use condoms more frequently. The percentage of male IDUs that used condoms increased from 15% in 1987 to 22% in 1989 (Ibid.).

One study of street IDUs found that peer support and a sense of self-efficacy or personal empowerment were related to changes in their sexual behavior (Ibid.). In another study, situational factors, such as availability, were predictive of condom use, whereas self-efficacy was not (Ibid.). These findings suggest the need for more research on variables predictive of condom use. It may be that factors that lead to changes in sexual behavior are different for street users than for users in treatment or in prison.

It should be noted that IDUs have reported changing their sexual behavior in the absence of formal intervention programs. Most frequently they reported reducing the number of their sexual partners and increasing their use of condoms (Friedman et al., 1993). One study of non–injection-drug-using women who were the current or potential partners of IDUs and who reported having had more than one sex partner in the previous 12 months, found that 62% of the women said they had changed their sexual behavior because of AIDS (Sogolow, Des Jarlais, & Strug, 1991). As might be expected, these women accomplished this change by reducing the number of their partners and increasing their use of condoms. However, a methodological limitation of the studies just mentioned as well as of most other studies of HIV-risk reduction is that they are based on self-reporting. Self-reported behavioral change may be different from actual behavioral change.

PROSTITUTES AND THEIR SEX PARTNERS

Prostitution and injection drug use have always had a close affinity in the AIDS epidemic in the United States and Europe. These behaviors have provided an important interplay between sex and drug use. Eunice's vignette illustrates this close connection. As discussed earlier in this chapter, the more recent introduction of crack cocaine also has an intricate tie to prostitution. James, who examined the process of becoming an addict-prostitute, found that prostitution can lead to drug addiction and that addiction frequently leads to prostitution (1976a). Rosenbaum (1981) similarly determined the relationship between prostitution and addiction to be inextricable. Moreover, both behaviors are illegal in the United States – drug use everywhere and prostitution everywhere except in brothels in rural Nevada. Cities with large numbers of IDUs also have large numbers of prostitutes.

Because a commercial sex worker can engage in sexual occupations besides prostitution, "prostitute" is a more specific term. However, "commercial sex worker" is used in much of the literature. For this discussion, "prostitution" is defined as an exchange of sex for money or drugs. Street prostitution is its most visible form (James, 1976b), although it represents only about 20% of all forms of prostitution in the United States (Cohen, Alexander, & Wofsy, 1988). Prostitutes can also work in massage parlors, outcall and escort services, bars and cafes, and brothels. Street prostitution, which is primarily an urban phenomenon, is the form of prostitution most often associated with injection drug use (Ibid.). Because of its visibility, street prostitution is also the type of prostitution most likely to result in the prostitute's arrest (James, 1976b).

Risk. Prostitutes are considered to be at risk for AIDS and for other STDs because they have sex with multiple partners who they are usually not able to screen. Also, they may be asked by their customers to engage in sex without proper prophylaxis. Thus prostitutes and their paying partners are considered to be primary groups at risk for HIV infection. Secondary groups at risk are the nonpaying partners of prostitutes and the male or female partners of clients.

The role of prostitutes in the spread of HIV/AIDS has been given considerable attention, just as it has in the spread of other sexually transmitted diseases (Brandt, 1987). Immediately after the several early cases of AIDS were identified among heterosexual women in 1982 (CDC, 1983), epidemiologists began to study the role of prostitutes in the spread of HIV/AIDS (Kreiss et al., 1986; Van de Perre et al., 1985). Prostitutes were targeted because they were considered a conduit for infection to the heterosexual population (Clumeck et al., 1985; Piot, Quinn, & Taleman, 1984; Redfield et al., 1985).

Several early studies on heterosexual transmission involved prostitutes (Clumeck et al., 1985; Piot, Quinn, & Taleman, 1984), and female prostitutes, as a group of sex partners, received most of the attention in them. Initial epidemiologic studies of prostitutes demonstrated that they were infected with HIV. However, the risk factors for transmission of HIV were a subject of debate. Some of the first studies involved African prostitutes who had high rates of other STDs, particularly syphilis and chancroid, which are risk factors for heterosexual transmission (Kreiss et al., 1986; Rosenberg & Weiner, 1988).

Much of the early concern about the role of prostitutes in the heterosexual spread of HIV/AIDS in the United States was based on surveillance data from men who reported contact with prostitutes. The reliability of these data was questioned. It was thought these data might be inflated because of the unwillingness of infected persons to admit to homosexual behavior or to injection drug use (Potterat, Muth, & Markewich, 1986). In particular, there were doubts about the reliability of surveillance data on the military because homosexuality and drug use are grounds for dismissal (Polk, 1985; Potterat, Phillips, & Muth, 1987). Because epidemiologic data on persons who had had heterosexual contact with prostitutes were lacking, female-to-male transmission of HIV remained a topic of considerable discussion at this time (Schultz et al., 1986; Wykoff, 1986).

An additional confounding factor in assessing the prevalence of HIV infection in prostitutes in the United States was their possible involvement in injection drug use. Infected prostitutes who shared injection equipment during injection drug use could have become infected parenterally rather than sexually.

In one effort to determine the role of parenteral transmission of HIV in these prostitutes, the CDC conducted a multicenter study from 1985 to 1987. In this study, 12% of 1,396 women enrolled were found to be infected with HIV. Rates of infection ranged from zero at a legalized Las Vegas brothel in which no injection drug use was reported to 48% in northern New Jersey where high levels of injection drug use were reported (Table 10). Of the 1,396 women, 693 reported that they were IDUs or sex partners of IDUs. Of these 693 women, 138, or 20%, tested positive for the HIV antibody.

Women at Risk: Drug Use and Prostitution

Table 10. *HIV seroprevalence among female prostitutes in the United States*

Site	IV-drug Use (%)	N	No IV-drug Use (%)	N	Total (%)	N	N
Las Vegas	0	0/10	0	0/27	0	0	37
Atlanta	1.5	1/65	0	0/58	0.8	1	123
Colorado Springs	3.8	2/52	0	0/46	2.0	2	98
Los Angeles	3.7	6/163	4.4	6/137	44.0	12	300
San Francisco	9.9	10/101	0	0/111	4.7	10	212
Miami	26.6	46/173	7.5	20/267	15.0	66	440
Southern New Jersey	42.9	6/14	0	0/14	21.4	6	28
Northern New Jersey	58.3	67/115	18.6	8/43	47.5	75	158
Total	19.9	138/693	4.8	34/703	12.3	172	1,396

Source: Centers for Disease Control (1987a); Darrow, Biggler, Deppe, French, et al., 1988.

In general, the variation in these rates reflected the extent of drug usage among prostitutes at different study sites as well as the extent of drug-related AIDS cases in corresponding cities. The changes in rates suggested that drug-use practices, particularly needle sharing, vary geographically. Furthermore, prostitutes who used injection drugs or who had sex partners who were IDUs were less likely to use condoms than those who had no connection to drugs, confounding the attempt to determine the role of injection drug use in transmission. Risk factors for antibody to HIV took in many variables associated with injection drug use, including visiting a shooting gallery and frequency and duration of drug use (CDC, 1987a). Those prostitutes at most risk reported having injected drugs 30 or more times in a month and having injected drugs for at least 12 months during the past 5 years (Ibid.).

HIV infection in prostitutes who were not involved in drug usage or in sex with drug users was associated with a seromarker for hepatitis B, recent syphilis infection, and sexual activities with large numbers (> 50) of nonpaying partners (Darrow et al., 1988). Of the 703 women in the CDC study who reported that they did not use injection drugs and were not sex partners of IDUs, 34 (5%) tested positive (Table 10). A majority of these prostitutes (20 out of 34) came from Miami, which differs from other AIDS epidemic areas in the United States because that city has a pattern of migration back and forth to the Caribbean where heterosexual transmission is more common (Pheterson, 1989). Young women who drift into Miami often resort to prostitution because they are not qualified for any other work. They usually do not speak English, and in addition to lacking job skills, they lack the social networks that would give them access to other types of work. These women do not have the basic characteristics of prostitutes in the area: they are younger, they are more desperate, and they generally have little awareness of STDs (Ibid.).

The CDC has estimated the infection rate for IDU prostitutes in the United States who use injection drugs to be four times higher than for non–injection-drug-using prostitutes (CDC, 1987b). In addition to the CDC multicenter study, numerous other studies of prostitutes in the United States and Europe have found that prostitutes' primary risks are injection drug use and sex with an IDU (CDC, 1987b; 1992; Luthy et al., 1987; Schultz et al., 1986; Smith & Smith, 1986; Sterk, 1989; Tirelli et al., 1986). That the sexual partners of prostitutes are most often IDUs is, therefore, significant (CDC, 1987a; 1987b; Sterk, 1989; Sterk et al., 1989).

Gender Roles

The role of female prostitutes has received far more attention than that of their sexual partners in studies of the heterosexual AIDS epidemic. This attention reflects deep-rooted sexism in society. When the first heterosexual cases appeared in the early 1980s, the risk that prostitutes faced from their customers was not considered of concern. Rather, the concern was that prostitutes could infect their customers who might in turn infect their wives and girlfriends. Media accounts of the HIV epidemic enhanced this view (Patton, 1994; Wofsy, 1987).

Women most often enter prostitution because of poverty. In recent years, much notice has been taken of the "feminization of poverty" – of how poverty has become an increasingly female problem (Pearce, 1978; 1982). By virtue of their profession, prostitutes must depend on men for economic support, and this is the dilemma that prostitution presents for feminism. On the one hand, prostitution may be viewed as an alternative to other lower-paying traditional female jobs. On the other hand, prostitution seems to be the ultimate example of sexual exploitation wherein women's age-old economic dependence on men is perpetuated. Thus there is no real consensus about prostitution in the women's movement (Wilson, 1993). Radical feminists oppose prostitution, as they do pornography, on grounds that it is a form of violence against women (Dworkin, 1981). Liberal feminists, in contrast, stress women's freedom to live and work as they choose (Delacoste & Alexander, 1988). The lack of consensus among feminists results in programs for prostitutes that are isolated and fragmented.

Barriers to Risk Reduction and Service Delivery

The social environment in which prostitutes work has a major effect on their lives (Carmen & Moody, 1985; Cohen, 1980). The greatest barrier to HIV-risk reduction for prostitutes is the illegality of what they do. That prostitutes generally live on the margins of society affects both their vulnerability to HIV disease and their responsiveness to HIV/AIDS-prevention efforts (Cohen & Alexander, 1995). The primary motivation for working as a prostitute is economic, and frequent incarceration can interrupt a prostitute's work patterns and income. Prostitutes remain in an extremely vulnerable situation with constant threats of arrest and incarceration.

A description of the legal system of prostitution in Nevada may, by comparison, also shed light on the work lives of street prostitutes who operate illegally. Prostitution is legal in 11 of the 17 counties in Nevada (Stein, 1987). Statewide, there are 37 legal brothels and about 350 licensed prostitutes (Ibid.).

The Nevada Board of Health requires prostitutes in county-licensed brothels to be tested weekly for gonorrhea and monthly for syphilis (Nevada Statewide AIDS Advisory Task Force, 1987). A prostitute found to be infected is not permitted to work until the appropriate time after treatment when follow-up tests indicate she is negative. A woman who tests positive for the HIV antibody is denied employment as a prostitute. Between 1988 and 1993, more than 20,000 HIV-antibody tests were conducted in Nevada; none of the women employed at any of the state's brothels tested positive (Quarterly HIV/AIDS Surveillance Summary, 1993). However, 19 brothel applicants tested positive on preemployment tests during this time (Ibid.).

In 1987, Nevada's brothels voluntarily adopted a mandatory condom policy (Nevada Statewide AIDS Advisory Task Force, 1987). This policy was ratified by the state as a mandatory condom law in March 1988 (Albert et al., 1995). This law requires that condoms be used for all sex acts, including oral sex.

Prostitutes at the brothels are protected by their legal status. They are registered and identified in the legal system and possess a county work card. Brothel policy places prostitutes in a strong position to reject customers and to enforce condom use. Thus prostitutes have some control over the types of sex acts in which they agree to participate.

The main work benefit from legalization is that prostitutes are free to work without fear of arrest. This is in contrast to the situation of most prostitutes who work illegally, particularly those who work on the streets. Street prostitutes are more physically vulnerable than licensed prostitutes. They have an adversarial relationship with law enforcement and are usually unable to seek help if they find themselves in physical jeopardy. Some street prostitutes are reluctant even to carry condoms, especially large quantities of them, for fear that the condoms will be confiscated as evidence by the police.

Prostitutes who work illegally also have a different relationship with the health care system than do licensed prostitutes. They often enter the health care system because of their contact with the legal system, that is, as a result of an arrest or conviction for prostitution. For example, several states now enforce mandatory HIV-antibody testing for women who are arrested for and convicted of prostitution (Bayer, 1989; Fumento, 1990). By 1989, mandatory testing of these women was in place in 13 states (Alexander, 1995). In some states, California for example, both prostitutes and their customers must be tested, but there is a double standard because the customers are arrested less often than are the prostitutes. In California, as a condition of probation for the first offense, a prostitute or her customer must attend an AIDS education course in addition to being tested for the disease. A second conviction for an infected prostitute or customer can result in a felony charge.

Although prostitution is a misdemeanor in most states (James, 1976b), in the majority of states with mandatory testing of convicted prostitutes, an HIV-infected prostitute may be charged with a felony upon a subsequent conviction for prostitution. Thus an infected prostitute can acquire a serious criminal record upon a subsequent conviction for prostitution. Mandatory testing of prostitutes is intended to control HIV by getting infected women out of prostitution. Ironically, it may actually impede an infected prostitute from leaving prostitution because of her more serious criminal record acquired because of her seropositive status (Campbell, 1990). Moreover, support services for occupational change by prostitutes, such as vocational training, are woefully lacking.

Mandatory testing of unlicensed prostitutes can also make them more dependent on pimps (Leigh, 1988). Street prostitutes have pimps primarily because prostitution is illegal (James, 1976b), and a pimp will post bail and provide a lawyer when one of his prostitutes is arrested. In addition, a pimp gives financial and moral support to a prostitute who must serve a sentence. With the increased criminal penalties based on seropositive status, an infected prostitute may need a pimp even more, thus diminishing her chances of getting out of prostitution (Campbell, 1990). Mandatory testing thus has important implications for the social mobility of prostitutes.

In August 1987, the U.S. Public Health Service (PHS) recommended that men and women who work as prostitutes be counseled about and tested for HIV infection and that seropositive prostitutes be instructed to stop practicing prostitution (CDC, 1987c). However, the recommendation that prostitutes get out of prostitution to reduce their risk of HIV infection has only limited effectiveness. The CDC study (1987a; 1987b) found that the most likely source of infection for prostitutes was their nonpaying partners because prostitutes are less likely to use condoms with them. Seventy-eight percent of the prostitutes in the CDC multicenter study reported using condoms with paying partners compared to only 16% with nonpaying partners (CDC, 1987a). Other studies have also found that prostitutes are more likely to use condoms in professional rather than in personal relationships (CDC 1987b; Philpot et al., 1988; Sterk, 1989). Nonpaying partners pose a further risk to prostitutes because they often have histories of injection drug use.

Because of prostitutes' risk of infection from nonpaying partners, their pursuit of career alternatives other than prostitution may not reduce their risk of HIV disease (Darrow, 1990). Nonpaying partners frequently do not consider themselves at risk because their female partners use condoms with clients. Cultural values, including the trust and love inherent in intimate relationships, apparently do not promote condom use. The strict separation between a prostitute's personal and professional life poses a major obstacle for AIDS prevention (Day, 1988).

Attempts by prostitutes to persuade their paying partners to use condoms are often met with resistance. Prostitutes worldwide report that the main reason they do not use condoms with paying partners is the partners' resistance or refusal (Population Reports, 1989). Frequently, customers will simply offer a prostitute more money to engage in higher-risk sex.

In the United States, women's use of crack cocaine also has undermined the amount of money prostitutes can make from prostitution. Some women are willing to engage in high-risk sex in exchange for small amounts of crack that are worth much less than the sum of money ordinarily requested by a prostitute (Sterk, 1989). If a crack-addicted prostitute does ask for money it is usually a very small amount, as little as $3 for vaginal sex (Worth et al., 1989). According to non–crack-using prostitutes, this new crack-related sex trade has deflated the prices that they are able to command for sex, and, as a result, is more difficult for these prostitutes to get out of prostitution.

HIV Prevention Strategies for Prostitutes

Most efforts to target prostitutes with prevention information have been street based. Many prostitutes are wary of institutional programs, and street outreach tends to be more relevant to their lives. But street outreach has limitations because street prostitutes are a minority of all prostitutes. Efforts to reach prostitutes in other settings have had limited success.

Condoms are a principal component of AIDS prevention. However, as stated earlier, prostitutes' condom use varies with the context of the sexual encounter. Nonetheless, most AIDS prevention programs for prostitutes have focused on increasing their use of condoms. In fact, prostitutes often equate safe sex with condom use (Sterk, 1989). Yet because customers are such an important part of the sexual equation, HIV/AIDS-prevention programs that promote condom use and target just the prostitutes can be only partially successful.

One program in Massachusetts recognized the importance of targeting men. In response to their clients' refusal to use condoms, prostitutes erected a billboard with the message: "WE CHARGE FOR *SEX, AIDS* IS FREE." These prostitutes also designed a shopping list of strategies to protect themselves (as cited in Connors, 1996).

Not only do prostitutes and customers need to be encouraged to use condoms; they also need to be instructed in how to use them correctly. Evidence that regular condom use may lead to mastery comes from a study that found the lowest rates of condom breakage and slippage to be in Nevada's legalized brothels (Albert et al., 1995).

On the whole, prostitutes are a good group to target with AIDS education campaigns. Many have been responsive to AIDS education and research projects (Chickwem & Gashau, 1988; Darrow, 1990). They have been interested in learning more about AIDS, have been willing to participate in prevention projects, and have taken condoms when offered (Darrow, 1990). The personalities of some prostitutes, specifically, their assertiveness about condom use, can also be effective in promoting safer sex. Their knowledge of safe alternative nonpenetrative sexual practices and their expertise in eroticizing these practices also can be valuable skills in AIDS-prevention efforts.

As a natural result of their profession, prostitutes come in contact with many persons who engage in high-risk behaviors. Their clients tend to be drawn from broad segments of the population. They are usually not a well-defined group and have little in common besides their utilization of commercial sex services. As a result, they are often difficult to target and reach with AIDS information.

The cooperation of pimps is also important in AIDS education efforts. Pimps have considerable influence over the behavior of prostitutes. Other persons in prostitutes' social networks – bar employees and security personnel, hotel staff, brothel owners, taxi cab drivers – can also convey AIDS-prevention information.

One study that surveyed prostitutes on their views regarding effective AIDS education found that those programs designed to reflect their specific needs and perceptions were the most effective (Cohen, 1987). Outreach efforts based on respectful, caring, and honest relationships were important in reaching the target population. Prostitutes reported that they disliked being treated in a manner that was impersonal, intellectual, or judgmental. For this reason, peer education is valuable in encouraging HIV prevention among prostitutes.

Peer education programs for prostitutes have existed in the United

States since 1989 (Alexander, 1995). Programs that involve prostitutes in project design and implementation tend to be the most successful (Cohen & Alexander, 1995). Programs that exemplify this approach can be called "community organizing" because such programs have an ongoing involvement in the community to bring about social change.

Many HIV/AIDS prevention programs for prostitutes in the United States have come from organizations of and activism by prostitutes. In California, COYOTE, an acronym for Call Off Your Old Tired Ethics, was formed in 1973 to focus on prostitutes' rights (Delacoste & Alexander, 1987). The National Task Force on Prostitution, founded in 1979, grew out of COYOTE (Ibid.). The goal of the Task Force was to educate the public on prostitution through lectures, workshops, and consultations.

In 1985 the California Prostitutes Education Project (CAL-PEP) was formed to educate prostitutes about AIDS. CAL-PEP's AIDS Prevention Project was designed and implemented by prostitutes, former prostitutes, and advocates for prostitutes' rights to help prostitutes protect themselves and their partners from AIDS. Utilizing peer education, CAL-PEP has trained prostitutes as AIDS educators to conduct outreach to other prostitutes and to customers in stroll areas (areas where prostitutes walk). CAL-PEP provides prostitutes with condoms, HIV testing, information about AIDS, and drug treatment referrals through street outreach and workshops, and its staff consults with similar AIDS-agencies on developing and implementing AIDS-prevention programs for prostitutes. The staff also provides on-site training at CAL-PEP or at the location of the inviting agency. In addition, CAL-PEP publishes a training manual, *Prostitutes Prevent AIDS: A Manual for Health Educators.*

Another peer education response to the personal safety issues of prostitutes relied on informal mutual support networks among street prostitutes. Through these networks, prostitutes conveyed broadly defined safer-sex messages to each other, including information about violent clients (Barnard & McKeganey, 1996). Descriptions of troublesome or violent clients from prostitutes' own experiences and knowledge were distributed in places where prostitutes congregate.

HIV/AIDS-prevention programs have had to recognize that prostitutes often have competing needs and that the disease is not always uppermost in their lives. Most prostitutes have basic needs for food, housing, and child care. Also, because many street prostitutes use injection drugs, they may need assistance in coping with their drug habit. It is therefore important that HIV/AIDS-prevention programs have good working relationships with drug treatment programs. Prostitutes' various needs must be addressed before HIV/AIDS prevention can be effective.

One program in Southern California offered free methadone maintenance to heroin-addicted street prostitutes. Most women who were invited to participate enrolled in the program. After one year, the participants' personal income from prostitution and other crime decreased by 58%, and their income from legal sources increased by 86% (Bellis, 1993). This study demonstrates the importance of available and accessible drug treatment in reducing risk for HIV/AIDS.

Housing is a primary need for women who want to get out of prostitution. Two residence programs for homeless prostitutes have responded to this need: Off the Streets in New York City and the Threshold Project in Seattle, Washington (University of California, San Francisco, 1996). Most of the residents at Off the Streets are drug users, and one-third are estimated to be HIV infected. Male and female prostitutes in this program are helped with finding a permanent residence, vocational training, and drug treatment referrals (Ibid.). The Threshold Project – a two-year program offering clients a series of progressively more independent living experiences – assists homeless youth acquire the skills necessary for them to live on their own without having to engage in prostitution. Most of the young women at Threshold have been emotionally, physically, or sexually abused. Results from follow-up show that roughly half (42%) of the participants had remained in stable living situations without engaging in prostitution (Ibid.). These results are encouraging, particularly because the program's target population is so vulnerable.

Although it is true that once their basic needs are met, prostitutes may be more ready to practice HIV/AIDS prevention, such change will not occur rapidly. Prostitutes report that it sometimes takes them as long as a year to fully implement safer-sex practices (Cohen & Alexander, 1995), and prevention programs must keep this time frame in mind.

4

GENDER, CULTURE, RACE, AND CLASS

My husband has threatened my life a couple of times. When he beat the hell out of me, he was picked up for spousal abuse. I brought charges.

He intentionally infected me because I left him. Fortunately my two children aren't infected. I'm trying to get them back but they judge my HIV status as my ability to take care of my kids.

— Denise

He would have a bad temper and be angry. And we would argue. There was a lot of pressure with bills, the rent, stuff for the children or the doctor. Since he doesn't have papers, he doesn't have Medi-Cal, and it would cost money to get his medicine or for a doctor's appointment. That was putting pressure on him. I felt as if we, the children and myself, were a burden to him.

I became desperate and I looked for job after job. And since I didn't have papers and the children started coming, it was no, without papers we can't give you a job. I didn't even know English. These are great barriers that one has here. You can't get ahead with them.

I was not making enough. Our economic problems returned. He made little money because of his not having papers. He had to handle too much, the rent, the bills, and all that. Later I started to clean houses even though it was little. I was trying to help him.

— Rosemary

I went to downtown L.A. where I'm from. Same people, doing the same thing, looking the same tore-up way. I just feel real grateful today that I was able to unglue myself from downtown. It's a miracle that I'm outta there. Same old cardboard boxes, same old thing.

— Loretta

I got a job with some Koreans and there we made blouses, skirts, and pants. I started work at 7:00 A.M. to 7:00 P.M. Monday through Friday and Saturdays it was 7:00 A.M. to 3:00 P.M. I had to hurry because I had to pick up my daughter from this lady that did us the favor of taking care of her.

He would scream at me or he would reprimand me in front of our daughter. He would threaten me at times with killing me and my daughter. He would come home very angry and he would say that since the three of us had no hope, that he was going to take our lives, first my daughter, then me and later him.

– Juana

I was transporting dope. I didn't even know there was dope in the suitcase. I opened it up and there was $50,000. I was 14. We got busted. So I went to juvenile hall.

I was wearing the same clothes over and over. The only time I'd bathe was when I'd go – when a trick would take me to a motel, or I'd go to McDonald's, go into the bathroom and wash myself.

I was gettin' down behind the garbage can. The police pulled up I finished hitting myself. Then they took me to jail. I have a lot of "under-the-influence" and a lot of "prostitution" cases. I never been in the penitentiary.

I got used and used people. I ripped them off – purses, watches and rings, and stuff. One woman tried to give me a job keeping her house clean, and I set it up to get burglarized.

When I was on drugs, I did not have anywhere to go. I was on drugs so bad. I did not have any money. I was homeless when I went into treatment.

– Eunice

I went back to my country [Guatemala]. It was supposed to be 2 weeks, but it ended up being 6 because I wanted to get my green card. He was – I was getting it through him because he was a citizen.

When I came back, everything was sold. He said, "I got rid of a few things." It was the drugs. There was no TV, there was no car, there was nothing. This was the fourth time it happened that he got rid of things. So I was getting ready to – I was thinking of divorce then because I am thinking the children are growing up, and I didn't want to have that. If I'm not going to have a husband that is going to keep the values, then I think I can do it on my own.

– Leticia

GENDER-BASED POWER RELATIONS

Power relations based on gender have been ignored in most HIV/ AIDS-prevention approaches (Amaro, 1995; Campbell, 1995; Wingood & DiClemente, 1995). As indicated earlier, a majority of risk-reduction interventions target prenatal women and prostitutes. In some instances, however, interventions are gender neutral, meaning that they do not differ between the sexes. Such an approach assumes gender roles are static and fails to take into account the socialization process that influences women's risk for HIV infection. In particular, it ignores the importance of sexual relationships between men and women and the adverse effect these relationships can have on women's ability to adopt and maintain HIV-preventive behaviors (Wingood & DiClemente, 1995). Therefore, gender power relations are central to an understanding of women's HIV-risk behavior.

Drawing on Jean Baker Miller's 1986 book, *Toward a New Psychology of Women*, Amaro (1995) identified four essential components of any theory about women's HIV-risk behavior: (1) women's social status is a central feature in women's risk; (2) connection and the relational self in women's development and the fear of disconnection because of conflict are critical features in women's risk; (3) male partners are key role players in women's risk; and (4) experience and fear of physical and sexual abuse are important barriers to risk reduction among some women. Accordingly, a gender-specific approach to prevention recognizes that the risk of HIV infection among all women, particularly among poor and addicted women, must be viewed in a larger social context of what Miller refers to as women's "permanent inequality" in status and power. For most women, sexual risk for HIV occurs within their relationships with men. Indeed, for some women, their major (and only) risk factors are associated not with their own behavior, but with that of their male partners (Sherr, 1993).

In her book, Miller (1986) proposes a "Self in Relation Theory" according to which the "relational self" is at the core of women's self-structure and the basis for their growth and development. Miller argues that women are essentially oriented toward others. As a result, the building and the maintaining of relationships are highly charged with meaning. Yet these relationships, particularly with men, must still be viewed in the larger context of women's "permanent inequality," which stems from women's ascribed unequal status based on gender, race, and class.

If the Self in Relation Theory is applied to HIV prevention, it then suggests that the risk involved in initiating HIV-risk-reduction changes in intimate relationships is greater for women than for men. This disparity may undermine women's intentions and their attempts to adopt safer sex practices (Auerbach, Wypijewska, & Brodie, 1994). According to the Self in Relation Theory, giving to others is a central aspect of women's identity within the unequal role ascribed to them. In this way, sex becomes something that a woman gives to a man, and this definition prevents her from realizing her own sexuality (Miller, 1986). But the safer-sex negotiations needed for HIV/AIDS prevention require women to step out of their assigned role and, potentially, to engage in direct conflict with men.

Miller (1986) also identified qualities characteristic of women's ascribed status, such as submissiveness, passivity, docility, and dependency. But HIV prevention requires that women display assertiveness in negotiating safer sex, which is not among the traditional female characteristics identified by Miller (Amaro, 1995). In safer-sex negotiations, therefore, women must act contrary to their socialization as the subordinates of men. As a result of the unequal social statuses of men and women, negotiations between them for safer sex are more complex than if they were between equals. For those women who must depend on men for their social and economic support, the ways in which they can reduce their risk of HIV infection may therefore be limited.

Women are victims of domestic violence and domestic sexual abuse more often than men (Denenberg, 1997). Gender inequality actually promotes spousal abuse by limiting the social and economic options of women. Women who are confined to the home or to low-paying jobs are especially vulnerable to domestic violence (Currie & Skolnick, 1997).

Their gender places girls at greater risk than boys for childhood sexual abuse (Denenberg, 1997). Many HIV-infected women report a history of childhood sexual abuse (Cook, 1997; Denenberg, 1995; Wyatt, 1997), and unresolved abuse often leaves women vulnerable in later sexual situations. As a result, women who were abused as children are more likely to experience adolescent pregnancy, substance abuse, domestic violence, and HIV infection (Denenberg, 1995). These women may feel powerless in all sexual situations. Not only do they have histories of childhood sexual abuse, these women are also often abused as adults, especially women who use drugs (Connors, 1996). Their long histories of drug and physical abuse may cause women to believe that they cannot control their lives or what happens to their bodies, particularly in transactions with men involving drugs and sex (Ibid.). Thus, advising women with histories as victims of sexual violence to negotiate safer sex may not be effective.

Gorna (1996) maintains that mutual monogamy also is not a viable HIV-prevention option for many women precisely because of gender power differentials, that is, because their male partners may not be monogamous. Gorna is critical therefore of the promotion of mutual monogamy as an HIV-prevention strategy for women. She maintains that it is overpromoted and is actually quite dangerous. Many women subscribe to the standards of monogamy, but with tragic results if their partners do not. According to Gorna, 80% of HIV-infected women worldwide became infected from their one and only partner.

Sherr (1995) offers another view on gender power relations. She points to the numerous studies reporting women's lack of power in sexual decision making. According to Sherr, such assumptions are demeaning and may actually endorse and perpetuate the imbalance they describe. An understanding of gender power relations may highlight positive aspects of female expression rather than negative (Sherr, 1995). For example, it is known that women will often tend to the needs of others in their family before their own. Sherr argues that this may not simply reflect a lack of power but rather an alternative lifestyle and a philosophy that should be praised rather than criticized.

Sobo (1995) also differs with the view that impoverished women engage in unprotected sex because they are not empowered. This view holds that economic dependency is paramount in women's relationships with men. But Sobo argues that women may choose to engage in unprotected sex with men for status and for emotional fulfillment rather than for economic benefit. Economics do not play a central role in these relationships because the financial assistance that men give inner-city women is often not steady. In addition, many women are unwilling to accept financial resources from their male sex partners because to do so might increase gender-related status inequities that these women reject.

Adolescence. Adolescence is a critical time for the development of power relations based on gender. A power imbalance appears to exist in adolescent relationships: Female adolescents are perceived as having and asserting less power in interpersonal relationships with male partners (Wells, 1980). Girls attempt to solve problems in relationships by silencing themselves and avoiding disagreement (Bentley & Herr, 1996).

It is particularly relevant that for adolescent girls a sexual relationship may be among the first ways they can separate themselves from their parents and develop an adult identity (Cohn & Futterman, 1995). Because these early sexual relationships represent independence, they may assume an exaggerated importance for these young women. Moreover, these girls may feel that they are not in a position to make demands on their partner – to suggest he use a condom or be faithful – for fear of jeopardizing the relationship.

Also, young women tend to have sexual partners who are older than they are. Girls perceive these men as having power because of their maturity, life experience, and financial resources. This age differential is reflected in that a majority (two-thirds) of the fathers of babies born to teen mothers are adults (Males, 1996; Roan, 1995). The age differential also makes young women more vulnerable to HIV/AIDS because these men are more sexually experienced and more likely to be infected (Rotheram-Borus, Jemmott, & Jemmott, 1995). Yet not using a condom may be seen by these girls as a small price to pay for the attention that they get from these men and the concomitant opportunity to break away from their parents. In addition, adolescent girls may consider parenthood to be a desired outcome of sexual intercourse (Ibid.).

Young women sometimes enter into abusive relationships with men but lack the experience necessary to get out of these relationships and take control of their lives. It is especially disturbing that for many of the youngest teens, sex is not a voluntary choice. One study found that a majority (74%) of young women who had sex before the age of 14 reported they did so involuntarily, as did 60% of those who had sex before the age of 15 (as cited in King, 1996).

Adolescent socialization has a powerful influence on sexual behavior. Traditional socialization teaches adolescents to believe that the prescribed sexual behavior for women is passivity, lack of interest, and feigned naiveté (Frieze et al., 1986). The prescribed behavior for men, in contrast, is to be sexually aggressive (Gross, 1978). In this male role, conquests are more significant than relationships (Carroll, Volk, & Hyde, 1985). Communication for both partners is kept at a minimum.

Thus adolescent socialization is in direct conflict with those guidelines that instruct women to be assertive and informed about safer sex. Safer-sex guidelines emphasize communication and negotiation, both of which are lacking as values in adolescent socialization.

Gender differences in sexual scripts are also evident in adolescent relationships. Stereotypical gender roles have been found in focus group discussions on sexual relationships. Adolescent girls report that their role is to "say no" to sex, and adolescent boys report that their role is to "get as much as you can" (Rotheram-Borus, Koopman, & Bradley, 1989). Differences in meaning in communication between young people are also evident. Trust means something different to young women than it does to young men. Young women expect young men to disclose previous risky sexual activities. Young men, on the other hand, expect young women not to have had previous sexual experiences (Maticka-Tyndale, 1992). A study of young African American men found that on sexual topics, they will often say what they think their partner wants to hear (Gilmore, DeLamater, & Wagstaff, 1996). Communication thus becomes critically important in these relationships.

Adolescents' perceptions of monogamy are also relevant. Often both adolescent boys and girls see themselves as practicing monogamy when, in fact, it is serial monogamy. As perceived and practiced by adolescents, monogamy typically has a duration of 3 to 6 months (Rotheram-Borus, 1997). This finding suggests a need to stress the importance of long-term monogamy as part of safer-sex practices for this population.

HIV-Discordant Couple Relationships. Much can be learned about gender power relations from examining the relationships of HIV-discordant couples. In an HIV-discordant couple, one partner is HIV positive, and the other, HIV negative. As noted in Chapter 2, in discordant relationships women are much less likely to abandon an infected partner than the converse (Sherr, 1993). A similar tendency has been found among women who are the partners of alcoholic or mentally ill men. However, economic dependency in these relationships often limits women's options. Also as stated in Chapter 2, women in discordant relationships are less likely to withhold information about their own serostatus from their partner, and they are less likely to be informed about their partner's serostatus (Ibid.).

The dynamics of gender power relations in the context of HIV disease in the United States have not been much studied. One test of discordant couples' counseling interventions, which was conducted by Padian and colleagues (1993), did not analyze gender power differentials, although these differentials could have been relevant in explaining gender differences in behavior (Amaro, 1995). The limited research that is available concerning gender power relations comes mainly from counseling intervention studies made in developing countries. One study of discordant couples in Zaire found that pregnancy was more common if the HIV-positive partner was the man rather than the woman (Kamenga et al., 1991). Another study of discordant couples, in Rwanda, found that condom use was more consistent when the man was the HIV-negative partner (Allen et al., 1992). In all instances in which the HIV-negative partner seroconverted during the course of the study, the male partner was reported to drink alcohol regularly. Male sex partners in discordant couple relationships are discussed in detail in the next chapter.

Gender power relations are determinants not only of women's HIV risk, but also of women's participation in clinical research. Whether or not women enroll in clinical trials depends upon social and economic factors that are specific to their status as women and reflective of gender power relationships (McGuire, 1997). Women's decisions to participate in clinical trials may be influenced by male partners. Men put women at risk but may also interfere with their access to clinical trials. Efforts to improve women's access to clinical trials have not yet adequately addressed the ways in which gender differentials shape women's relationship to care.

Cultural Influences

The previous section showed how traditional female socialization conflicts with guidelines that advise women to be assertive in negotiating safer sex. But cultural influences are also important in explaining sexual risk behavior. Thus this section focuses on cultural factors in the sexual behavior of Hispanic/Latino women and African American women, the two groups of women at highest risk for HIV/AIDS. The overrepresentation of Hispanic/Latino and African American women among AIDS cases is even more pronounced for women than it is for men (Cochran, 1989).

Hispanic/Latino Women. In Latin culture, women are expected to defer to men (Worth & Rodriquez, 1987). This deference stems from the cultural concept of "machismo," the belief that men, by their gender alone, should exercise authority over women. Culturally prescribed behaviors associated with machismo include extramarital sexual activity, heavy drinking, and physical abuse (Stevens, 1973).

Within the culture of machismo, men are expected to be sexually experienced; an active sex life, including sex with prostitutes, is promoted as a way to demonstrate virility and to achieve sexual satisfaction (Carrier, 1989). The use of prostitutes is common among unattached immigrant men in large cities such as Los Angeles (Marin, 1989). These men, who come into the United States alone, sometimes leave girlfriends or families behind in their native countries (Magaña, de la Rocha, & Amsel, 1996).

The female counterpart of the cultural concept of machismo is "marianismo." Marianismo promotes the idea that Hispanic/Latino women should emulate the Virgin Mary by being morally and spiritually superior to men and by enduring any suffering caused them by men (Stevens, 1973). Hispanic/Latino women are expected to be virgins at the time of marriage and to remain faithful to their husbands throughout marriage. Machismo and marianismo are helpful for understanding the double standard found in Latin culture (Carrier, 1989).

In a Hispanic/Latino culture such as Mexico's, women are not expected to be knowledgeable about, or to show any interest in, sex (Worth & Rodriquez, 1987). For a woman to be knowledgeable about sex is considered a violation of her proper cultural role (Ibid.). Women in Mexican culture are protected, which includes protection from information about sex. In contrast, Mexican men have access to information about sex from their male friends and relatives. The cultural attitude that women need to be protected is in direct conflict with HIV-prevention approaches, which encourage open discussion and advise women to be knowledgeable and assertive about safer sex. Furthermore, disease-prevention approaches that promote condom use are

Gender, Culture, Race, and Class

also in opposition to this cultural reticence as well as to the teachings of the Catholic Church.

The power balance in male–female relationships in Hispanic/Latino culture also influences sexual behavior. For women, *respeto*, or respect for authority, including one's husband or boyfriend, together with sexual modesty, means giving priority to the needs of men (Cochran, 1989). Besides being obedient to male authority, women are expected to be sexually inexperienced, and if a woman requests that her partner use a condom, she may be stigmatized as "loose" (Ibid.). In addition, in traditional Hispanic/Latino cultures, husbands sometimes have the right to make decisions about contraceptives (Ibid.). Approaches to preventing AIDS that encourage open discussions of condom use clearly conflict with cultural values such as obedience and deference to male authority.

Women's deference to men has been demonstrated in a study of 2,527 Hispanic men and women in the northeastern United States. Focus groups were formed to discuss barriers to HIV risk reduction. In a majority of the women-only groups, unequal power and gender roles emerged as critical barriers to risk reduction (Amaro & Gornemann, 1992). In contrast, in the mixed-gender groups, these issues were not discussed as often. This reticence in the mixed groups suggests that women may find it difficult to discuss freely with men the gender roles and power differentials that operate in relationships.

Another example of women's deference to men comes in a study involving focus group interviews of low-income Hispanic women from Los Angeles (Flaskerud et al., 1996). The program aimed to teach these women about HIV/AIDS in the hope that they would in turn educate their male partners about the disease. However, the perception that these women had of their own social status prevented them from assuming the role of credible educator with their partners.

Finally, an emphasis in Hispanic/Latino culture on the value of motherhood can be another connection for women to their male partners and another barrier to HIV-risk reduction through condom use (Amaro, 1995). Among Hispanic women the strong cultural value placed on motherhood and childbearing can be an especially formidable barrier to risk reduction (Ibid.).

African American Women. Culture also influences the sexual behavior of African American women. In many African American communities, there is a serious shortage of eligible male partners owing to social factors such as homicide, incarceration, heart disease, and AIDS. High rates of drug use and unemployment compound this shortage of "marriageable" African American men. The effect of this sex-ratio imbalance is greater family instability and higher rates of sexual activity outside marriage (Cochran, 1989). Because of their limited options, women may be willing to tolerate objectionable behavior by their male partners. For example, there is evidence that African American women may be willing to tolerate their partner's having other women (Worth, 1989), a practice that is referred to as "man sharing." Although not an ideal situation, particularly because it heightens their risk for HIV, these women may not feel that they have many other options. For them, man sharing means a choice between having a man in their life or having no man at all.

Because of the sex-ratio imbalance, African American men may see their sexual options as unlimited and may feel less pressure to develop commitments. They may perceive themselves as having greater power in their relationships with women and fewer behavioral constraints. Thus the monogamy encouraged by HIV/AIDS-prevention programs may not be relevant to these men and women and may not be an achievable goal. For this reason, consistent use of condoms may be more practical and effective as an AIDS preventive.

Sobo (1995) maintains that to gain status and build self-esteem African American women may appear to believe in the ideal of good partner choice and monogamy. These women represent themselves as having used wisdom in making their partner choices and as having excellent monogamous relationships. Therefore, using a condom would undermine their confidence in their ability to choose partners who are honorable and free of disease. To others, they can claim that they have perfect intact unions with loyal, honorable partners although they are actually engaging in unsafe sex. Thus the ideal of monogamy interferes with their ability to practice safe sex.

Cultural Sensitivity. Research has shown that ignorance about HIV/AIDS is not the reason that many women fail to protect themselves from contracting the disease (Weissman, 1991). Rather, women fail to reduce their risk because the necessary behavioral changes may involve real or perceived threats to their economic survival, their relationships, and their culturally sanctioned roles (Mays & Cochran, 1988; Worth, 1989, 1990; Worth & Rodriquez, 1987).

Structuring preventive messages so that they are gender specific and culturally appropriate is therefore critical. These messages must take account of the realities of gender-based power relations in women's lives. Not only may advice to be monogamous and to be assertive about condom use be irrelevant to women, it can place them at risk of verbal abuse or physical violence (Peterson & Marin, 1988). For example, Hispanic/Latino women may fear a partner's anger if they ask him to use a condom, so they do not ask (Gomez & Marin, 1993). AIDS prevention approaches must account for female subordination and take care not to make women vulnerable to physical harm from partners.

AIDS-prevention programs must also be sensitive to the history of family planning in the United States. In many states, forced sterilization of women on welfare continued into the 1970s (Dalton, 1989). Many of these women were either African American, Hispanic/Latino, or American Indian (Auerbach, Wypijewska, & Brodie, 1994). In one example, in the 1970s, two African American sisters, 14 and 12 years old, were sterilized as part of a federal effort to reduce poverty (Banks, 1996). These particular sterilizations were exposed, and federal regulations governing involuntary sterilizations were implemented in response. Yet, even today there is evidence that poor women of color are sterilized involuntarily with the support of government funds (Ibid.). Health care providers may judge some patients incapable of using some birth control methods effectively. In these cases, they may promote methods that are either long-term or permanent. For example, most states provide Medicaid funds for voluntary surgical implants of the contraceptive Norplant, which is a temporary long-term form of sterilization (Ibid.). But although government-financed sterilization is available, government-financed abortion is not (Ibid.).

Given this history, it is understandable why poor women may not trust health care institutions; and why African Americans in the United States distrust European-American culture (Levine et al., 1993). African American women are skeptical of family planning efforts, which some have interpreted as having genocidal implications. Their suspicion and feelings of mistrust often impede the African American involvement in HIV-prevention efforts (Dalton, 1989). Messages that promote condom use are sometimes seen as feeding into racist agendas by suggesting that African Americans stop having children altogether. Thus concerns about selective genocide were expressed by one group of African American women participating in an HIV/AIDS intervention based on culturally sensitive skill building (Levine, et al., 1993). Clearly, to reach all segments of American society, HIV/AIDS-prevention programs must become more culturally sensitive.

INSTITUTIONAL BARRIERS
Health Care

Besides gender and culture, institutions can be barriers to reducing the risk of HIV for women in sexual relationships. One such institution is the health care system itself which can raise barriers for women at risk with respect to their diagnosis and access to care.

Diagnosis and Seroprevalence of Female Cases. In the past, physicians were slow to recognize the symptoms of HIV disease in women, and as a result, the disease was often in an advanced stage before it was accurately diagnosed. For many women, primary contact with the health care system was through their obstetrician-gynecologists, specialists who may not have been alert to the possibility of HIV disease in their female patients (Kurth, 1993). Many infected women were presenting with gynecological symptoms such as abnormal pap smears, pelvic inflammatory disease, or recurrent, intractable candida vaginitis, and obstetrician-gynecologists did not necessarily see initial symptoms as being related to HIV disease. The potential for misdiagnosis existed. In many instances, AIDS was simply the diagnosis that was left at the end of a long process of exclusion. Many women had to endure recurrent symptoms and repeat visits to the doctor before an AIDS diagnosis was finally made.

That women were experiencing symptoms that were not included in the CDC's surveillance definition of AIDS also masked the true number of female cases of the disease. Severe undercounting occurred because many women died without having been given an AIDS diagnosis. Consequently, the original definition of AIDS was based on clinical presentations of a white gay male population.

Although the surveillance definition of AIDS was expanded in 1987, it still did not include female-specific conditions. The expanded definition cited 23 indicator illnesses that, when they occurred in the presence of HIV seropositivity, constituted AIDS (Kurth, 1993). These indicator illnesses were based on the "Spectrum of Disease Study," a natural history conducted by the CDC. Nevertheless, by 1990, still only 7% of the study participants were women (Burkett, 1995). However, the expanded definition did give more attention to conditions that affected the health of children, such as multiple or recurrent bacterial infections. Thus pediatric AIDS became an indicator of AIDS in women, but conditions appearing exclusively in women remained excluded from the definition (Corea, 1992). As a result, infected women continued to die without being given an AIDS diagnosis.

Female AIDS activists continued to exert pressure on the CDC to include female-specific conditions in the definition of AIDS (Ibid.). Finally, in January 1993, the case definition was again expanded. Pulmonary tuberculosis, invasive cervical cancer, and recurrent pneumonia were the indicator illnesses added to the previous list of 23. Included in the female-specific conditions were vulvovaginal candidiasis, cervical dysplasia, cervical carcinoma in situ, and pelvic inflammatory disease (PID) (CDC, 1992). Cervical cancer rather than cervical dysplasia or cervical carcinoma in situ was chosen as the appropriate AIDS-indicator illness because the latter two diseases frequently do not progress to invasive disease (Ibid.). Also cervical dysplasia and carcinoma in situ among women with severe cervicovaginal infections (which are common in HIV-infected women) can be difficult to diagnose (Ibid.). The diagnosis of cervical cancer is generally unequivocal.

The three indicator illnesses added in 1993 tended to affect or were specific to women (Kurth, 1993). Pulmonary tuberculosis is preventable. Cervical cancer is preventable with proper recognition and treatment of cervical dysplasia (CDC, 1992). Because these illnesses are preventable, the expanded cases definition highlighted the importance of access to care for infected women. The addition of cervical cancer as an indicator illness also underscored the need for integrating gynecologic care into medical services available for HIV-infected women.

The expanded 1993 definition resulted in an increase in cases of AIDS identified among women, racial and ethnic minorities, adolescents, IDUs, and persons infected through heterosexual contact (CDC, 1994). Both the 1987 and 1993 definitions helped give a more accurate picture of the impact of HIV disease on women. The problem though was that the first AIDS cases among women appeared in 1981, and it was not until 12 years later that female-specific conditions were added to the case definition.

Without an AIDS diagnosis, many infected women were ineligible for Social Security Disability Income (SSDI). The reason is that the Social Security Administration relied on the CDC's definition of AIDS to determine eligibility, and it was not until 1993 that the definition was changed to include female-specific indicator illnesses (McGovern, 1997). The change in SSDI eligibility was the result of a class-action suit brought by HIV-positive disabled individuals in addition to careful scrutiny by Congress (Ibid.). The issue then has been not only one of undercounting female AIDS cases but also of ensuring access to care and services.

In addition to its case definition of AIDS, the CDC used other classifications that masked the number of female cases. As stated earlier, the transmission categories in the CDC's surveillance reports through 1983 did not list heterosexual transmission as a separate category. And even when heterosexual transmission was made a separate category, it still obscured risks. As noted in Chapter 1, just as there is one for men who have sex with men, a separate category is needed for heterosexuals who also engage in drug use.

CDC classification systems have also obscured the risk of infection faced by lesbians. Although female-to-female transmission has been documented, the CDC's surveillance reports do not include a category for female-to-female transmission. This lack creates an inaccurate picture of lesbians' actual risk (Cole & Cooper, 1991). Cases involving female-to-female transmission are simply put into the "other/risk not reported or identified" category. As noted earlier, the percentage of female cases that fall into that category is nearly double that of male cases (13% compared to 7%). It is also true that most instances of HIV/AIDS among lesbians have involved the additional risk of injection drug use. In the late 1980s, the CDC established a category separate from the injection drug category for men who have sex with men and also engage in injection drug use (Patton, 1994). However, the category homosexual/female was usually simply marked "not applicable," and no separate category was established to identify lesbians' additional risks (Ibid.). As a result of CDC surveillance definitions and methods, lesbian women with HIV disease remain officially uncounted (Morrow, 1995; Ibid.), and the idea that transmission between women is non-existent and that lesbians are sexually risk free from HIV disease is perpetuated.

The categorization of female sexual identity also presents problems for women in recognizing their own risk particularly because sexual identity and sexual behavior are not always consistent. Some women who self-identify as lesbian may still have sex with men. Some women who self-identify as heterosexual may have sex with women. The relationship between sexual identity and behavior is complex. Some women may choose not to describe themselves in terms of either their sexual identity or sexual practices. For example, women who have sex with women may not identify themselves as a lesbian but as a "mother," "caregiver," "drug user," "woman in recovery," "African American" or "Hispanic/Latino."

The underdocumentation of AIDS cases among lesbians as a result of how the sexual identity of women is categorized also has implications for services for women. Lesbians are underserved in the health care system and, furthermore, are at risk of discrimination from health care providers (Stevens, 1993). Almost no services have been developed specifically to respond to the needs of HIV-infected lesbians (Richardson, 1994). Yet, the needs of lesbians with AIDS may be different from those of other HIV-infected populations. For example, some lesbians may not feel comfortable in support groups with infected heterosexual women. Most AIDS service organizations have not responded to women's concerns based on sexual identity. Few have addressed issues of risk and services for lesbian, bisexual, and transgendered women (Weiser, 1997).

During the early years of the epidemic, there was little analysis by gender in the CDC's publications on AIDS appearing in the *MMWR*. From 1981 to 1987, there were only five articles on seroprevalence in women (CDC, 1981; 1982a; 1982b; 1983; 1987): one on infected infants and, by implication, on pregnant women; one on prostitutes; and three – none of which included an analysis by gender – on modes of transmission and opportunistic infections.

Only in 1985 did researchers begin to study women-specific manifestations of HIV disease. Until that time, medical journal articles would often simply omit analysis by gender. Thus a majority of natural

Women, Families, and HIV/AIDS

history studies were on cohorts of gay men (Rodriguez-Trias & Marte, 1996). Concentrated research on disease progression in women did not start until 1990 (Patton, 1994). Women were underrepresented even in natural history studies of special groups such as IDUs, which did not include gynecologic manifestations of HIV. In an example of this research bias, none of the studies for the panel on "Gender-Related Variations in Natural History," held at the Eighth International Conference on AIDS in 1992, included gynecological manifestations of HIV (Rodriguez-Trias & Marte, 1996).

Health Status, Access to Care, and Quality of Care. Women have not shared the same access to care and quality of care as men. By virtue of their being poor and often members of minorities, infected women have been at a disadvantage, tending to seek care only during a health crisis (Mitchell et al., 1992). For poor people basic survival – the need for food and shelter – take precedence over health concerns. In addition, the poor often lack health insurance. As a result, people who are poor and ill frequently have their first contact with the health care system in the emergency room of a hospital. Their disease can be in a fairly advanced state by that time.

The social circumstances of infected women tend to differ from those of men, in part reflecting the higher proportion of women from traditionally underserved and disadvantaged populations (Hirschorn, 1995). Many infected women have competing medical, economic, and social needs that create barriers to their access to care, especially to care equal to that received by infected men. Women are more likely than men to be poor, minority, and less connected to community organizations (Mays & Cochran, 1988). Women are also more likely than men to be either uninsured or underinsured (Connors, 1996). In seeking health care, infected women are more likely than men to turn to public facilities, to be suspicious of institutions or agencies, and to be crisis oriented in their health-seeking behavior (Mitchell et al., 1992). Compared to infected men, infected women who are already in the medical system receive fewer services, are less likely to have a primary provider of care, and are more likely to use emergency services (as cited in Goldstein, 1997).

Evidence on gender differences in health status suggest that culturally prescribed gender roles, with their associated traits and behaviors,

98

have a negative impact on women's health status (Verbrugge, 1989). In relation to HIV/AIDS in particular, women are socially vulnerable because of their low social status, which places them at risk for the disease (Travers & Bennett, 1996).

Race is another important variable in a person's access to health care. In general, African Americans and Hispanics/Latinos have not shared the same access as non-Hispanic whites to clinical trials (Murrain, 1995). For example, white men have the highest rates of receiving AZT therapy and PCP prophylaxis, and African American women, the lowest, even when their immune status is the same (Kurth, 1993). Race, class, and gender, which together affect perceptions of illness and kinds and availability of care, are the three factors most determinant of a person's health status and degree of well-being (Schneider, 1991).

Because early in the epidemic there was little recognized therapy for HIV disease, experimental drugs and clinical trials were often the only treatment. Women comprised only 3% of those who received AZT during its initial availability for compassionate use (Legg, 1993). Although clinical trials were often the only way in which women could get treatment, women were largely excluded from these trials. Women were less likely than men even to be told about clinical trials by their doctors (Connors, 1996). By 1990, only about 8% of trial participants were women even though at that time women accounted for nearly 10% of AIDS cases (Legg, 1993). These were major issues for female AIDS activists.

The AIDS Clinical Trials Groups (ACTGs) that began in 1987 required that participants have a primary care physician (Corea, 1992). This requirement excluded a majority of women with HIV/AIDS because they could not afford a primary care physician and used public health care facilities instead. The location of drug trials also affected the participation of women. Although New York and New Jersey both had high caseloads of infected women, the trials took place in other states. No child care or transportation was provided participants, and scheduling did not accommodate school hours of participants' children.

The exclusion of women in AIDS clinical trials is not in any way unique (Cotton, 1990a, 1990b). The norm in clinical trials for a wide variety of diseases has been to exclude women. The Food and Drug Administration and the National Institute of Allergies and Infectious Diseases guidelines for clinical trials excluded women of childbearing age from participation in AIDS trials unless they could provide proof of adequate and detectable contraception, which meant an intrauterine device (IUD) or birth control pills (Burkett, 1995; Corea, 1992). However, the IUD had a potential role in causing intrauterine infections in women, and there was little information on the relationship between the pill and HIV disease. Although condoms and diaphragms posed no health risks, they were not acceptable to the FDA. This response from the FDA was seen by women as irrational and paternalistic (Ibid.).

The FDA barred women of childbearing age from most drug studies to protect women's reproductive systems and their potential fetuses. The FDA's requirement for birth control was based on regulations written in 1977 in response to birth defects caused by the drug thalidomide (Burkett, 1995). Before a woman was allowed to try a new drug in clinical trials, its effect on the reproductive system and on offspring had to be tested on female animals. Its effect on the male reproductive system and on sperm production was never mentioned as a concern (Ibid.). The impact of the FDA regulation was that most drugs licensed for the market were never tested on any women. Women were being protected from experimental medications. Yet, drugs tested on men were being sold to women as well as to men, despite evidence that each group reacted differently to many drugs.

Like AIDS diagnosis, then, AIDS treatment had a male profile. In this AIDS was not unique, because drug therapy for many diseases has often been based on extrapolations from studies of men (Cotton, 1990a, 1990b). Yet, as was just mentioned, there are known gender differences in drug metabolism, toxicity, and efficacy (Legg, 1993). But gender differences affecting drug therapy for HIV disease, like those for many other diseases, were not addressed.

Barriers such as those just described prevented women from participating equally with men in clinical trials. Thus virtually no data emerged on the impact of AIDS drugs on women. Even AZT was never examined specifically for its safety and efficacy in women (Burkett, 1995). Yet animal reproduction studies indicated that AZT might cause cervical dysplasia in women (Burkett, 1995; Corea, 1992).

The AIDS Clinical Trial Group 076 study that examined the efficacy of AZT in preventing perinatal HIV transmission raised immediate concerns for female activists. A majority of infants born to infected women were HIV negative *without* AZT, meaning that these fetuses would have a drug with known toxicity administered to them in an attempt to prevent transmission that would not have taken place anyway. Caesarean section also offered some potential in reducing the risk of perinatal transmission.

The contradiction in the 076 study was immediately evident to women. Earlier, when ACTG studies had offered a potential benefit to HIV-infected women for their own illness, pregnant women were excluded from those trials. Now, the 076 study offered a potential benefit not to women but to fetuses, and pregnant women were actively recruited for the trials (Ibid.). Rather than the strict procedures that had guarded against pregnant women being administered AZT, women given AZT in the 076 study were required to be pregnant. The sudden inclusion of pregnant women did a lot to reinforce the idea that women were important in the AIDS epidemic only in their role as vectors of disease to their unborn children or male partners.

Demands made by female activists to stop drug trials that excluded women created a conflict of interest for male activists. In particular, these demands threatened men's access to experimental drugs. Male activists had achieved considerable influence at the FDA. The FDA had given in to their demands on approving drugs, despite there being no proof of effectiveness and minimal proof of safety (Burkett, 1995). However, although men had gained considerable influence, they did not use this influence to advance the needs of women in any way.

Women's access to clinical trials did not change a great deal later in the epidemic, despite progress with new drug therapies. Women lacked access to later clinical trials with combination therapies just as they had lacked access to earlier trials with AZT (Wolfe, 1997). Historically women have experienced a double standard of treatment. Men with HIV/AIDS were allowed to take greater risks in the hope of obtaining effective treatments whereas women were excluded from doing so. This double standard has hindered the development of effective disease-management strategies for women.

The Media

Heterosexual Risk. By 1988, it was clear that women could be infected through heterosexual contact. Yet the media did little to alert women of their risk and, in fact, was the source of considerable inaccuracy and distortion. The media downplayed the risk of heterosexual contact, particularly its risk to women. The *New York Times* ran a series of editorials in 1987 that lulled readers' fears about the heterosexual spread of AIDS (Corea, 1992), which was described as happening more slowly than anticipated. Fear that AIDS would spread into the heterosexual population was thought to have no basis. In the editorials' pie charts and graphs illustrating risk factors for AIDS, women who were infected heterosexually were referred to as "others," a term that obscured the women's risk. At the time, 25% of female cases in New York City were from heterosexual transmission (Ibid.). In all of the discussion and debate over the heterosexual epidemic, gender differences were never mentioned, even though the epidemic among women already differed sharply from that among men.

In 1988 an article appeared in the January 1 issue of *Cosmopolitan* that minimized heterosexual risk even more. The article, "Reassessing News about AIDS: A Doctor Tells You Why *You* May Not Be at Risk," was written by a psychiatrist, Robert E. Gould. Its appearance in *Cosmopolitan* is especially relevant because the magazine had a readership of 11 million between the ages of 18 and 34 (Ibid.). Gould stated, "There is almost no danger of contracting AIDS through ordinary sexual intercourse" (Gould, 1988). He based this assertion on his own studies, on published reports on AIDS, on discussions with leading researchers in virology, and on visits to hospitals. Gould added that by "ordinary sexual intercourse" he meant penile penetration of a well-lubricated vagina – penetration that is not rough and does not cause laceration. According to Gould, repeated unprotected sex with an HIV-infected partner does not present a risk as long as the genitals of both partners are "healthy," meaning that they have no open lesions or infections.

Gould did not elaborate on his studies or on the other published reports that he mentioned in the article. He questioned whether infected women were really truthful about vaginal sex being their only risk and suggested that they may have actually engaged in anal sex but were unwilling to admit it. Gould asserted that the harm in advising women to be careful about vaginal sex was that to do so reminded women once again "that sex is wrong, dirty, bad ... even deadly." Gould argued for a return to the enlightenment of the sexual revolution of the 1970s, a time when people were much more carefree about sex.

When Gould made his assertions, the number of female heterosexual cases had been increasing annually since 1982, and it had been established that most heterosexual AIDS cases occurred through vaginal rather than anal sex (Guinan & Hardy, 1987; Wofsy, 1987). Gould's statements brought on a strong reaction from AIDS experts as well as from female activists in ACT-UP (AIDS Coalition to Unleash Power). Members of ACT-UP initiated a meeting with both Gould and Helen Gurley Brown, the editor of *Cosmopolitan*. Gould agreed to the meeting but Brown declined. When questioned by the activists, Gould admitted that many women do have small vaginal abrasions, but he stated that these abrasions were not involved in transmitting HIV. According to Gould, vaginal secretions produced during sexual arousal keep the virus from penetrating the vaginal walls. Gould held strongly to the statements in his article. Following the meeting, 300 activists staged a demonstration outside the offices of *Cosmopolitan* at which they chanted, "For every *Cosmo* lie, more women die!" Ironically, *Cosmopolitan* was nominated for a National Magazine Award for general excellence that same year (Norwood, 1990).

Images of Women. Not only did the media provide inaccurate information about AIDS, it obscured women's risk by focusing on prenatal women and on prostitutes. Wofsy (1987) notes how headlines such as "Nursing Mother Gives Baby AIDS" and "Infected Hooker Spread AIDS" contributed to the public perception of women as infectors. A widely distributed poster reinforced the stereotype of prenatal women as infectors. The poster shows a little girl, and the accompanying caption reads: "She has her father's eyes and her mother's AIDS," which suggests a greater contribution from the mother than the father to the child's medical condition (O'Leary et al., 1993). Children were overrepresented in the media and were often portrayed as "innocent victims" in contrast to their mothers who were depicted as guilty and selfish (Ibid.).

Other articles also depicted women in a negative light. One, reporting on a U.S. Army study of rampant promiscuity and venereal disease among men in the armed services, focused not on the danger that these men posed for women, but on how women, as transmitters of AIDS, were a danger to the men (King, 1990). An analysis of articles on prostitutes and AIDS appearing in the *New York Times* and the *Washington Post* between 1985 and 1988, found that they expressed little concern about the health of prostitutes, only about the prostitutes' role as disease vectors (Ibid.). The majority of press articles on women with AIDS referred to the prevalence of HIV among prostitutes and emphasized the prostitutes' role in spreading the disease (Sacks, 1996).

Media attention to pregnant women and prostitutes promoted an image of women as vectors of transmission. These women were portrayed as irresponsible reservoirs of infection. Many stories covered poor and minority women who were infected but had babies nonetheless (Norwood, 1990). The picture that accompanied a 1985 *Newsweek* article showed prostitutes against a dark, ominous background as they worked the streets (Treichler, 1988).

Media images of heterosexual men were quite different from those of prostitutes. Pictures of men who had AIDS often showed them as emaciated from the ravages of the disease (Sacks, 1996). These images tended to evoke pity rather than blame. Thus a *Newsweek* article in 1992 juxtaposed two pictures, one of a Thai bar girl massaging a client, a Western man and, next to it, a picture of a gaunt Thai man languishing in a hospital bed. The bar girl is shown as the infector, the men the infectees – the victims.

Women have been portrayed as infectors in popular culture especially in the lyrics to some popular rap songs. Early in the epidemic, rap delivered a lot of messages about the importance of safe sex for preventing AIDS. However, many of the songs' lyrics described women as infectors spreading the disease and warn men to stay away from these women (Hampton, 1996). The rapper Eazy E, who died from AIDS in 1995, attributed his infection to his having had multiple female partners over the years.

Even though cases of AIDS among women were mounting, in the early years of the epidemic women were rarely featured in articles on the disease except in their secondary and traditional roles as mates and caretakers (Treichler, 1988). Women were generally not consulted for the articles (Norwood, 1990). Although infected women and women who provided care could have served as sources, the media failed to draw upon their expertise. As a result, the articles presented the issues entirely from a male perspective. A good example here is the matter of partner notification. Although partner notification clearly has important implications as a prevention strategy for women, it was treated as solely a concern of gay men by the *Washington Post* and the *New York*

Times and by other New York dailies (Norwood, 1990). In surveys conducted both nationwide and in New York City women (the vast majority of whom were African American and Hispanic/Latino) expressed a desire for partner notification (Ibid.). Yet such notification was treated as a confidentiality and civil rights matter pertaining only to gay men (Burkett, 1995). That partner notification might present different issues for women than for men was never acknowledged. This, despite that partner notification was identified as the single prevention strategy with the greatest potential to save women's lives (Ibid.).

Stories that did feature women with HIV/AIDS speaking for themselves often did so as a journalistic device to draw readers rather than as a serious attempt to examine women's AIDS issues (Norwood, 1990). The media also tended to neglect organized events involving women with AIDS. From 1988 through 1989, no leading AIDS reporter from New York's four daily newspapers (except the medical editor of the *New York Post*) covered a single AIDS event organized by women (Ibid.). These events included major conferences, symposiums, state hearings, and the first women's AIDS protest. Thus the media did little to provide a forum for women's advocates to reach other women.

Although the media paid little attention to women's risk early in the epidemic, once it did, ironically, women became the focus of attention, to the exclusion of both gay and heterosexual men. The primary targets of condom advertisements became women even though condom use required the cooperation of male partners. In 1987, New York City sponsored a series of television advertisements created by a Madison Avenue firm to promote condom use among heterosexual women (Fumento, 1990). The advertisements understandably drew the wrath of homosexual activists because New York City had been slow to respond to the AIDS crisis, and when it finally did, there was no mention of homosexuals. In an analysis of print media, including the major newspaper and magazine articles on AIDS and heterosexuals written from 1988 through 1989, Norwood (1990) found no mention of the role of heterosexual men in AIDS prevention strategies.

Mass media campaigns targeted women. The second year (1988) of the five-phase national media campaign "America Responds to AIDS" was aimed at women and sexually active adults with multiple partners (CDC, 1991). The subject index of the campaign's catalog lists 22 references to women and only 15 references to men, excluding one reference to gay men (Ibid.). (The *HIV and AIDS Education and Prevention Catalog* published by the Centers for Disease Control and Prevention lists 26 references to women and 6 references to men, excluding one reference to gay men in its subject index [CDC, 1993]). The America Responds to AIDS campaign sought to reach a broad range of women, including women with multiple sex partners, women who were the sex partners of injection drug users, and women who were college students, single parents, and newly divorced (Miller, Turner, & Moses, 1990). Although this effort is laudable and the attention was clearly overdue, it threatened to reinforce the idea that only women are responsible for safer sex. This is especially true when a similar campaign specifically targeting men is not made.

Media campaigns are important. They affect public awareness about protection against HIV and, in particular, about condom use. Campaigns that advise women to use condoms or to get their partners to use condoms are inherently sexist, especially when men are not similarly advised (Wermuth, Ham, & Robbins, 1992).

It should be noted that there have been efforts to produce posters directed at both men and women, particularly in England. One such poster promoted condom use with the slogan "Women's self-defence and men's responsibility." There was also a campaign that promoted the idea "Take care of the one you love," with an equal focus on men and women (Bury, 1992).

Through the late 1980s and early 1990s in the United States, condom advertisements and safe-sex guidelines appeared in most magazines with female audiences but not in magazines aimed at men. Articles appeared in issues of *Ms.* magazine in May 1989 and January/February 1991 and in *Essence* in April 1990 (Kurth, 1993).

Films also promoted condom use. The film *Sex, Drugs, and AIDS* was made to target adolescents. In that film, a group of young women discuss how they approach their boyfriends about using condoms. However, the film does not show a similar scene with young men discussing condoms (Wofsy, 1987).

There is an inherent contradiction in presenting women as responsible for both causing infection and promoting safer sex but denying them the power to change behavior. Indeed, the focus on women's responsibility reinforces the idea that it is "women's work" to ensure that safer sex is implemented and to exert control in an area in which they have little power and few options (Strebel, 1995; 1996). Moreover, although women were made responsible for AIDS prevention in media campaigns, they were largely invisible in discussions of prevention policy (Norwood, 1990). In other words, women were designated risk managers but not allowed to engage in actual decision making.

The media also inaccurately depicted the role of race in the AIDS epidemic. When more concern was finally given to heterosexual AIDS in the mid- and late 1980s, magazines portrayed it as a white middle-class epidemic (Fumento, 1990). Eight of the ten women whose faces appeared on the cover for the issue of *People* magazine containing the article "AIDS and the Single Woman" were white (Ibid.), ignoring the fact that a majority of women with AIDS were African American and Hispanic/Latino. Of the six experts interviewed about heterosexual risk for the article, all were white and five were men (Norwood, 1990). None was directly involved in issues related to the epidemic among women.

Racial depictions on television, like those in the print media, also did not represent those people actually affected by HIV/AIDS. The 1988 series *Midnight Caller* featured a white woman who had been infected by a bisexual man in a one-night stand. By 1989 a new AIDS poster person had emerged: Alison Gertz, a 23-year-old middle-class white woman who had gone public with her disease (Fumento, 1990). Gertz, like the female character in *Midnight Caller*, became infected through a one-night stand with a bisexual man. Both the *New York Times* and ABC's *20/20* did stories on Gertz, and, later, ABC produced "The Alison Gertz Story." Thus television drama too neglected the fact that most women with AIDS were African American or Hispanic/Latino and IDUs or the sex partners of IDUs. These women did not become infected from a one-night stand with a bisexual man and they were not middle-class.

The message that AIDS was a threat to the white middle class was often reinforced by the media. The film *Sex, Drugs, and AIDS*, mentioned earlier, had been made for the New York City Board of Education and was later shown in high schools around the country. Although the girls talking about condom use in the film are white, the film was originally made for a school district that is 80% black, Hispanic/Latino, and Asian (Fumento, 1990). Public service ads also represented AIDS as a disease affecting the white middle class. The victims of AIDS depicted in these ads were generally white, and they appeared to be comfortably well off (Sacks, 1996).

The 1987 mass media campaign conducted by the CDC to bring AIDS to the attention of people in minority groups was also misleading. The campaign presented AIDS as an "equal opportunity disease," one that did not discriminate: No one was safe from AIDS, and everyone was at risk. Seeking to appeal to minorities, the campaign described AIDS as "color-blind." The ads also tried to convey the idea that AIDS was not exclusively a gay disease, that minorities were at equal risk. In reality, however, AIDS clearly did discriminate, and race was a factor in who it struck (Fumento, 1990). Minorities, particularly minority women, were at significantly greater risk. The media simply did not accurately depict those most affected by the epidemic.

In 1992 both the Republicans and Democrats featured a woman with HIV disease at their national conventions (Burkett, 1995). On the surface, this act seemed laudable and long overdue. However, the two women who spoke at the conventions did not represent most women with HIV disease. Both of them were white and middle class. Including them in the conventions may have been perceived by the parties as a safe way to talk about AIDS without visibly embracing a "gay cause."

Finally, the unrepresentative depictions of women with AIDS may be related to societal disapproval of drug use, that is, to an unwillingness to recognize that for a majority of women HIV risk and drugs are connected. Societal disapproval may also be influenced by a perceived relationship between drug use and poor mothering (Sacks, 1996).

In summary, a number of barriers prevented an early response to women's risk of AIDS from heterosexual relations. Initial focus was on two types of women, prostitutes and pregnant women, who were seen as vectors of transmission. The concern was not about the risk to the women themselves but rather about the risk to men and children. A white, gay male profile permeated the epidemic, and the seriousness of the heterosexual epidemic was downplayed. Men's and women's respective risks, needs, issues, and interests were treated as one and the same. When the heterosexual epidemic was finally accorded greater importance, a major and sudden change occurred. Women were made responsible for controlling the spread of the disease. What did not change, however, was the primary concern about risk to men and children.

Gender, Culture, Race, and Class

The Intersection of Gender, Culture, Race, and Class

We might ask then what the impact of the institutional response from the health care system and the media has been on women. The personality traits that Miller (1986) identified as feminine – submissiveness, passivity, docility, and dependency – were barriers to HIV risk reduction because of gender power dynamics. (It should be stressed that not all women are actually submissive, passive, docile, and dependent at heart.) Rather, it is society's pressure on women to demonstrate these traits – in effect, to prove their femininity – that actually increases the women's risk for HIV disease. These socially preferred traits are relevant to a discussion of the institutional barriers because infected women often find themselves dealing with agencies that respond to them in ways that reinforce the traditional role of women. Moreover, HIV disease must be understood in the context of urban poverty. The disease affects the inner-city poor predominantly, with a disproportionately high concentration among African American and Hispanic/Latino women. A majority (around 73%) of mothers with HIV-infected children receive public assistance (O'Leary & Jemmott, 1995).

Women are often involved in providing informal care to family members stricken with AIDS. A disproportionate number of the women providing informal AIDS care in families are minority women. Caregiving is demanding work that often occurs at the expense of the caregiver's own health and frequently goes unrecognized by our society. Chapters 6 and 7 will consider issues related to women's caregiving more fully.

Women seeking services on behalf of their children often must deal with the welfare system. Welfare has often been accused of treating women in a paternalistic way (Glassman, 1970; Iglitzen, 1977). Women on public assistance remain economically dependent, their dependency on men simply replaced by a dependency on welfare. The institution of welfare has been examined for its role in perpetuating women's dependency, passivity, and resignation (Campbell, 1979). When stereotypically feminine traits are promoted by institutional structures, the outcome for women is often to isolate them from support systems in society.

As with other reportable diseases in the United States, reports on AIDS do not include information about victims' socioeconomic status

(Rhatigan, Connors, & Rodriguez, 1996). Although there is a lack of government-collected data, it is nonetheless clear that poverty plays a critical role in HIV disease among women. Infected women are often disenfranchised and dispossessed. Indeed, the stresses and problems encountered by the poor may actually *contribute* to their HIV risk (O'Leary & Jemmott, 1995). For example, one study of women who were IDUs found that their residential instability was a predictor for sexual HIV transmission (Brown & Weissman, 1993). To poor people, HIV disease may seem a distant threat and may rank far below their immediate survival needs on a list of their concerns. Yet poverty is at the center of the intersection of gender, race, and class.

What will it take to empower women to overcome institutional barriers and gender power imbalance? Real empowerment will require long-term solutions such as changing paternalistic institutions and ending women's economic dependency on men. For women to become truly empowered, occupational segregation and the feminization of poverty must cease (Pearce, 1993). To bring this about is, of course, no easy task.

Women must also acquire greater control over their bodies as well as a concept of sexuality that is more women-centered (Strebel, 1996). Control of the heterosexual epidemic will require a close look at gender-role socialization – not only of women's roles but also of men's roles.

5

MEN, GENDER ROLES, AND SEXUALITY

If it wasn't for my daughter, I don't know what I would do. I take care of myself. I take care of my problems, take medicines. I'm very depressed. I lost everything in a few months. I used to have a lot of connections with my family.

I don't know what it is but I always find a way to take care of my daugher and she helps me, keeps me alive. We haven't heard from nobody in the family. That's okay. I'm just going to this group where I met some other people just like me. I got a lot to live for now, especially for my daughter.

– Ed

I'm a single father. I have one child. She's 3 years now. My wife passed away 2 years, 5 months ago. I don't have family here. My own family's living in Mexico City.

I need a break. I need time for me. Because all the time I have is for my daughter. I have friends here which give me help or sometimes they care for my daughter. My friends help me . . . For me it is very difficult to play mother to my daughter. For a man, raising a child is difficult but life sends many surprises and teaches you to live better. The same way it deals difficult blows, it also brings good news. I have learned to live a better life one day at a time and to try to be better and to give my daughter the best in life.

– Jose

He would go to work and call me later really drunk. He wouldn't take his medicine and I would have to beg with him then. I never argued about money with him. When I worked, it was different because the money I made I would save but on one occasion I told him that I wasn't going to save. And he got angry. We went out and we were arguing. Just because I was working I didn't discontinue my obligations to him and my daughter. I always had the clothes clean and ironed and in order.

He didn't like talking about the illness. I liked to listen to others. If I didn't listen to the doctors or the people that gave me advice on how I should care for myself, it would be too late for me, if I don't pay attention to how to take care of myself. To my husband, the world had ended after he knew the consequences that stem from this illness.

– Juana

And I would say to myself, "Is it my fault he is sick?" We would argue a lot. Sometimes I would complain. I wanted to bear the burden of the disease with him. I said to myself little by little I'll make him understand to change his temper. But it was like I was married to another man. He was very different, his way of being, his way of thinking.

He tried to take his life three times about our situation. One time we had a slight disagreement. I went to see what was going on and I saw him with a bottle of pills. I had to call 911. And I told them with what little English I knew that he had tried to take his life. He didn't want to tell them what had in reality happened. It's like, he can't accept it, his illness. It's been many years but he can't accept it.

– Rosemary

We separated for a whole year and he ended up going to jail. Financially I was just really down. I was going back and forth from place to place and this was really hard. When he got out of jail, he decided to stop doing drugs and he started working. It was the first time I saw him stable. I'm surprised because it's not an easy thing to deal with – emotions after the person quits with this dependency.

But he really was an inspiration to my life. He was a loving husband and a caring dad. When the children asked him for things, he kept his promises. He was a good man. The most I miss about him is his friendship. He became a really good friend of mine.

– Leticia

Although prevention efforts have sought to educate women about their risk for HIV infection, the success of many of these efforts depends on behavioral changes by their male sex partners. Women may know about the dangers of unprotected sex and the benefits of using condoms but still not be able to use condoms because their male partners object.

Thus despite their concerns about risk, women may be prevented from acting on the information provided them.

As has already been discussed, HIV/AIDS prevention strategies often treat women's risk behavior separately from the risk behavior of men, without acknowledging gender power differences (Richardson, 1990; Strebel, 1995; Ulin, 1992; Wingood & DiClemente, 1995). Prevention is focused on the behavior of the individual, and the sociocultural context in which individuals interact is neglected. As has been noted, prevention approaches may ignore the reality for women that they do not control the behavior of their male partners.

AIDS prevention strategies targeting women often emphasize the importance of communication and negotiation with male partners regarding safer sex practice. The goal is to get men to change their behavior by relying on the negotiating skills of women. There is even a book entitled *How to Persuade Your Lover to Use a Condom* (Breitman, Knutson, & Reed, 1987). This focus on women as negotiators has ignored the role of men in sexual decision making and has reinforced the belief that women are responsible for safer sex. Women have even been blamed for failing to persuade their male partners to use condoms (Gollub, 1995).

One reason that women have been the primary target of AIDS prevention efforts is that they are considered to be easier to reach and more approachable than men (Eighth International Conference on AIDS, 1992). A study of women-focused HIV/AIDS prevention programs found that those located in places where women already have reason to visit were effective (Center for Women Policy Studies, 1993). The diverse settings in which women may be reached include family planning clinics, women's health clinics, AFDC application sites, food stamp program offices, the kitchens of migrant worker camps, and their own homes.

In addition to women being more accessible than men, women may also be more likely to be interested in health information. An example is the 1991 announcement by the popular basketball player Earvin "Magic" Johnson that he is seropositive. Johnson's revelation had a greater impact on women in the African American and Hispanic/Latino communities than on men in these communities (Mills & Fischer-Ponce, 1992; Rapkin el al., 1992). The women showed up in greater numbers to be tested.

The attention to women's risk has perpetuated traditional beliefs about gender roles. Women are made responsible for men's health behavior. This focus on women makes it difficult to know if men will respond to AIDS prevention information when they are targeted. The field of preventive health behavior has given considerable attention to gender differences in health-seeking behavior and utilization of services. It may be useful to examine these differences to determine their application to AIDS.

MALE GENDER ROLES AND SEXUALITY

In general, differences in the health-seeking behaviors of men and women have been explained as a result of gender-role training (Graham, 1984, 1985). Women have a more sharply defined sense of the future and thus are more responsible about their health concerns (Blackwell, 1967; Freeborn et al., 1977; Graham, 1957). They are apt to use health services more often and receive more preventive care than men (Meininger, 1986). As a consequence of socialization, women perceive more symptoms and take them more seriously once they are aware of them (Anson, Carmel, & Levin, 1991). Women may find it easier than men to seek assistance in health-related matters because women are traditionally dependent, submissive, and compliant. Men may fear that responding to their own health concerns will make them seem weak rather than strong and in control.

Because of sociocultural gender roles, women are the family caregivers. They take responsibility for the health of their entire family, including their sexual partners. This caregiving role puts women in frequent contact with the health care system.

Male Reproductive Health

There is a particular lack of attention paid to male reproductive health as a societal health issue. This lack of attention is reflected in contraceptive decision making. As in HIV/AIDS prevention, in decisions about contraception most of the focus has been on women. Even in family planning studies testing the efficacy of condoms, women were taught how to use the condoms, but their male partners were not (Edwards, 1994). Men have been treated as the silent partners in contraceptive decision making.

The marginalization of men in health services is tied to the concept of the "absent father" (Blum, 1993). Yet empirical support for the notion of the absent father is not totally convincing. For example, one study of impoverished unmarried couples found that the vast majority of the men are willing to declare their paternity and sign the birth certificates of their children (as cited in Edwards, 1994). However, some men are not given the opportunity to do so by hospital staff. About half of teen fathers do stay in touch with their female partners, as do most men whose female partners undergo abortions (Blum, 1993). These data clearly negate the idea of the absent male. Their involvement in these health concerns suggests a need for family health settings that are more welcoming environments for men.

Although it advocates an expanded focus on reproductive health, the family planning movement does not provide for the inclusion of services for men. Men are largely absent from family planning clinics both as clients and as staff (Stein, 1996). In ironic contrast to family planning clinics, clinics that treat sexually transmitted diseases serve men predominantly (Ibid.).

Public health's separation of family planning services and STD-prevention services is not in the interest of either men or women. Just as men should not be excluded from family planning services, women should not be excluded from STD-prevention services. After all, men, either passively or actively, are involved in contraceptive decision making, and at least as many women as men are affected by STDs and with more serious morbidity (Ibid.). Family planning services and STD-prevention services, however, function independently of one another, and there is even tension between the two (Gollub, 1995). Advocates for family planning have expressed concern that HIV/STD prevention will involve a return to condoms and women's barrier methods, which are less effective methods of contraception than the pill. Likewise, advocates for AIDS education and STD prevention have been concerned about the neglect of HIV/STD counseling in family planning settings. Certainly, any tension between these kinds of services is not in anyone's best interest as they both play such important roles in helping to maintain positive health behavior.

Another reason to involve men in family planning emerges from research on discordant couples (Kamenga et al., 1991) (see Chapter 4). That study found that pregnancy was more common when the couple's male partner was HIV positive than when the female partner was. Yet, as Sherr (1995) points out, this finding is rarely highlighted. In particular, it has not been translated into policy in prenatal and family planning clinics that serve women rather than men.

Men also need to be involved in family planning programs because their approval is a critical factor in women's decisions to use contraception (Berer & Ray, 1993). In England, various strategies to get men to attend family planning clinics have been explored, and targeting men separately has been found to be effective (Ibid.). Clinics offer men-only sessions because men feel intimidated when they must be in waiting areas that are dominated by women. England's Family Planning Association sponsored a "Men Too" campaign that distributed leaflets directed at men. In Colombia, the Family Planning Association has used its satisfied male clients to reach other men in vasectomy-promotion campaigns.

Whether involving men in contraceptive decisions actually improves the use of contraception and reduces unwanted pregnancy is hotly debated (Edwards, 1994). There is not a great deal of solid research in this area. Some experts, however, believe that it is important to involve men in the process of contraceptive decision making, regardless of the outcome, because it will encourage them to forge a stronger bond with their children and will promote more responsible sexual behavior and more familial responsibility (Ibid.). Emphasizing men's involvement will potentially enhance their personal growth and development. This can have important benefits for their female partners and children.

Most research on men and contraceptive decision making has been done in developing countries (Ibid.). Although some United States studies of sexual activity and contraceptive use have included men, few have examined their psychosocial aspects such as men's attitudes about contraception and pregnancy (Ibid.). Only with the advent of AIDS and other STDs, along with high rates of unintended teenage pregnancies, has the male role in contraceptive decisions been examined. As a result, most U.S. data on men's involvement in contraceptive decisions is for adolescents (Ibid.).

However, research on contraceptive decision making in developing countries has found that men favor family planning (Population Reports, 1986). It is a lack of communication between the partners, rather than the man's opposition, that usually accounts for failure to use condoms (Kasprzyk, Montano, & Wilson, 1992). But even though most men believe that decision making about family planning is a joint responsibility, many prefer that their female partners take responsibility for contraception (Population Reports, 1986). And family planning programs have found that contraceptive methods used by women that do not involve partner consent are most effective for preventing pregnancy (Guinan, 1992; Stein, 1990).

Research has found that although men are interested in family planning, they do not want to learn about it from their wives (Panos Dossier, 1990; Population Reports, 1986, 1989). Even so, most men report that they learned about family planning from either their wives or their friends rather than from health care professionals (Population Reports, 1986). It appears that a lack of information and services designed for them, not a lack of interest, has prevented men from taking an active role in family planning. The few programs in the U.S. that have involved men have been well received (Edwards, 1994).

Heterosexual men have been treated as marginal in both family planning and HIV/AIDS-prevention efforts. HIV/AIDS-prevention approaches did not draw on lessons learned earlier in family planning. An examination of the information about HIV disease reveals that it ignores men and reinforces traditional gender roles. Even when it targets men, the information tends to be general rather than gender specific. A good example is the brochure *Men, Sex, and AIDS* produced by the American Red Cross (1988). Despite its title, this brochure does not address specific male concerns about AIDS; its contents do not differ very much from a more general brochure, *HIV Infection and AIDS* (1989). Another brochure, however, *Women, Sex, and AIDS* (1988), does contain information specific to women's concerns, including information about pregnancy. Yet, because of its relevance to their role as fathers, this information would seem appropriate to brochures for men.

Much informational literature advises women who think they might be at risk for HIV infection and are considering having children to be tested. The same advice is not given to men who are considering becoming fathers (Richardson, 1990). And whereas the impact of a positive antibody test on women's decisions about childbearing has been explored in depth (e.g. Fadin, Geller, & Powers, 1991; Shepherd,

1994), the impact of a positive test result on men's decisions about having children has not. No comparable work on HIV/AIDS and male reproductive health has been done.

Research indicates that an emphasis on fatherhood could be an effective approach in reaching men with HIV/AIDS prevention messages. A study conducted by the National Institute on Drug Abuse (NIDA) found that drug-using men were motivated to use condoms out of concern about fathering an "AIDS baby" (Rabin, 1994). Condom campaigns that target men with the aim of helping them protect their families may thus be effective.

The neglect of the role of men in family planning and AIDS prevention suggests a need to redefine these efforts to encompass male health issues. More attention must be paid to reproductive counseling for men as potential fathers. Men's decisions do not affect only them, and lowering the rate of HIV infection among men has consequences for the women who are their sex partners and for their future offspring.

Masculinity

As already discussed, there has been a lack of attention to male reproductive health. Men may find it difficult to assume responsibility for their health by adopting safer-sex practices because their traditional socialization teaches them that "real" men initiate sex and are in charge from beginning to end. As a result many men believe that to remain in control they must appear to know everything about sex. Thus men may have a difficult time accepting information about sex or about HIV/AIDS from women.

Gender-typed socialization places a lot of responsibility on men. In reality, men do not always know as much about sex as they think they do or as much as society thinks they ought to. A good example comes from a study of heterosexuals at an urban STD clinic. Men who attended a "condom skills" course as their intervention had the lowest rates of new STD infections (as cited in Kurth, 1993).

Traditional training also socializes men into thinking that "real" sex must involve penetration. They see penetration as a goal in all sexual encounters. However, this goal conflicts with safer-sex goals that emphasize activities that do not involve penetration. According to traditional socialization, such nonpenetrative types of sex not requiring condoms are a poor substitute for the real thing. In some instances, couples may practice nonpenetrative sex but only as foreplay leading up to penetration. The traditional idea that sex is tied to male performance and must involve penetration remains unchanged.

Traditional gender-role socialization also results in men and women responding differently to using condoms. For men, sex is tied to male performance, and they see condoms as interfering with that performance. Women, however, are not supposed to be knowledgeable about sex or to let their sexual needs and preferences be known to their partners. Consequently, women may be reluctant to take the initiative in practicing sex that does not involve penetration. Women's sexuality continues to be tied to reproduction (Santos & Arthur, 1992).

Traditionally, men are trained to appear as though they are always ready and willing to have sex. In response, women are trained to control men's sexual appetite by saying no. Women are seen as needing to be seduced and coerced into having sex. Safer-sex options focus on a male, heterosexual construction of sexuality. This construction reflects the traditional view of a sex drive as an impulse for which men are not responsible but that women are expected to curb (Holland, Ramazanoglu, & Scott, 1990; Juhasz, 1990).

Traditional gender-role socialization promotes different views and values about sex for men and for women. Men are encouraged to be the aggressors – the active partners in all sexual encounters – and women, the passive recipients (Gross, 1978). Boys learn that sex is something that they are expected to do to girls, whereas girls learn that sex is something that is supposed to happen to them (Richardson, 1990). Because it must be responsive to male initiative, women's sexuality is reactive rather than proactive (Wilton & Aggleton, 1991). Furthermore, for many women, sex is associated with dangers such as unintended pregnancy, health risks, and violence. For this reason, talk of safer sex is a contradiction for these women (Strebel, 1996).

Traditional gender-role socialization is also reflected in men's sexual behavior. Men are trained to see the sex act as a conquest; the number of women with whom they have sex – their conquests – becomes the indicator of their manliness (Carroll, Volk, & Hyde, 1985; Fasteau, 1975). This attitude runs counter to safer-sex guidelines that promote monogamy. According to traditional socialization, monogamy is not to be valued as a way to demonstrate masculinity.

There are limited data on gender differences in beliefs about sexual behavior related to HIV/AIDS. One small study that examined the gender differences in beliefs about safer sex in focus groups found that the men were less likely than the women to mention monogamy as an AIDS-preventing option (Kasprzyk, Montano, & Wilson, 1992). This belief is also reflected in a study of HIV-infected heterosexuals that found that before diagnosis, the men had fewer monogamous relationships than did the women (4% compared to 55%). After diagnosis, 14% of the men but none of the women reported having multiple partners (De Bertolini et al., 1996). Another study found that men reported more negative than positive aspects of safer sex practices (as cited in Quina et al., 1997).

An example, perhaps an exaggerated one, of society's acceptance and of the value it places on male promiscuity is provided by well-known male professional athletes. When basketball's Magic Johnson announced that he was HIV infected in 1991 at age 32, he explained that he had engaged in sex with many different women during his time with the National Basketball Association (NBA). (As noted in Chapter 4, the rapper Eazy E gave a similar explanation.) A star player and a womanizer, Magic had had unprotected sex (many times, one-night stands) with women all over the country (Stine, 1993). Similarly the former NBA star Wilt Chamberlain, though not infected, stated in his autobiography that he had had sex with over 20,000 different women during his 14-year career (Ibid.). Their promiscuity is accepted because our society tends to idolize well-known athletes such as Magic Johnson and Wilt Chamberlain. Promiscuous heterosexual behavior appears to be regarded with widespread tolerance and even condoned. Male promiscuity is actually encouraged, but it makes the women who are the sex partners of promiscuous men very vulnerable, particularly to HIV infection. For their part, women are often attracted to the status and power of professional athletes and derive their own sense of identity out of the sexual relationships that they have with them.

Cultural influences are also relevant to a discussion of the sexual behavior of men. For example, a survey of Latino heterosexual men in the United States found that their traditional gender-role beliefs, such as the belief that women should be subordinate to men, interfere with condom use (Marin et al., 1996). Another study of Latino men in California identified cultural factors that affect sexuality. These include a sense of fatalism and an avoidance of open discussion about sex (Forrest et al., 1993). Most of the heterosexual men in the study, even those who engaged in sex with prostitutes or with women they met at bars, did not perceive themselves to be at risk for HIV. Most of these men did not use condoms at all or used them inconsistently. Cultural influences related to masculinity can thus be barriers to safer-sex practices.

Also related to manliness, traditional socialization teaches that "a real man" is heterosexual (Richardson, 1990; Schneider, 1988; Wilton & Aggleton, 1991). To be manly is, above all, not to be homosexual. Having many female partners also serves as a way for men to demonstrate that they are not gay. Young single men often feel they need to be sexually active to maintain their reputation as heterosexual. The contraceptive behavior of young men is also influenced by homophobia. For some men, impregnating a woman is the strongest way for them to prove that they are not gay (Edwards, 1994). Clearly, a goal of proving one's heterosexuality can be in direct conflict with both preventing pregnancy and HIV/AIDS prevention.

It is significant that men show higher rates of homophobia than women and that gay bashing is especially prevalent among young men in their teens and twenties (Schneider, 1988). In families with HIV-infected gay members, homophobia is more common among male members (fathers and brothers) than among female members (mothers and sisters) (Brown, 1988). Moreover, by ignoring safer-sex guidelines heterosexual men could be trying to disassociate themselves from AIDS because of its association with homosexual men. As long as these homophobic fears exist, men will continue to deny that HIV has any relevance to their lives. They will continue to deny their own risk of infection and the risk of infection that they pose for their female partners.

It is clear that masculine identity plays an important role in heterosexual relations. A negative portrayal of how men behave in heterosexual relations also contributes to problems in achieving safer sex. For example, in their books on women and AIDS, Kaplan (1987) and Norwood (1987) assert that men are not to be trusted in sexual matters. In fact, these authors base their arguments on this belief (Schneider, 1989). HIV/AIDS mass-media campaigns may also portray both male and female heterosexuality as negative. One such campaign, aimed at women, shows a sexy young man labeled "Lady Killer," and in a campaign aimed at men, the caption of a poster showing a sexy woman asks, "Does She, or Doesn't She?" In contrast, materials targeting gay men are positive, depicting sexuality in a healthy way (Edwards, 1994).

Men in Couples

Part of the problem one encounters in understanding men's role in couple relationships is that no clear profile of male AIDS cases is available. It would be helpful, then, to construct such a profile based on what is known about the gender roles and sexuality that are reflected in male AIDS cases. The three main groups of men who have HIV/AIDS and are members of male-female couples are injection drug users (IDUs), men who have sex with men and women (MSMW), and hemophiliacs. For both adults and adolescents, injection drug use is the primary link to the heterosexual population.

Injection Drug Users. Injection drug use accounts for the largest transmission category for heterosexual men. This category comprises 22% of male HIV/AIDS cases (CDC, 1997). Because there is a separate category for men who have sex with men who also inject drugs, this transmission category includes only heterosexual men.

Men are also at risk for HIV from drugs such as methamphetamine (which is sometimes injected), and crack cocaine (which is discussed in Chapters 1 and 3), and alcohol. Alcohol presents a risk because it lowers inhibitions. Men are more likely than women to use alcohol and other drugs (McCaul, Lillie-Blanton, & Svikis, 1996). A study of heterosexuals in an alcohol treatment program in San Francisco found the infection rates among the men to be 3% – higher than the rates (0.5%) found in a survey of heterosexuals outside of treatment (Avins et al., 1994).

Risk behavior of IDUs is closely tied to the criminalization of drug use. IDUs may engage in risk behavior for HIV because that behavior ranks fairly low in their risk hierarchy. For example, needle sharing is seen as carrying a lower risk than stealing to obtain money, dealing drugs, carrying a needle, and obtaining drugs (McCaul, Lillie-Blanton, & Svikis, 1996). Reducing risk by reducing needle sharing is therefore perceived to directly increase risk of carrying a needle and risking arrest.

As mentioned in Chapter 3, the introduction to drugs for men and their progression in drug use and related criminal activity occur primarily through a male friend. Because what is known about injection drug users is tied mainly to their contact with either drug treatment and/or prison, most information about them concerns their socioeconomic status and their criminal behavior. Much less is known about their gender identity and sexuality.

Most imprisoned men with AIDS have been infected through sharing drug-injection equipment (Dubler & Sidel, 1992). Inmate populations tend to be drawn heavily from the IDU population outside prison. Incarceration is often associated with drug use in some way: Up to 50% of criminal offenses leading to incarceration are drug related (Brewer & Derrickson, 1992); almost all poor drug users will at some time rely on criminal behavior to support their habit (Dubler & Sidel, 1992); and many drug users were using drugs at the time they committed the crime for which they were incarcerated (Institute of Medicine, 1986). Up to one-half of inmates report injection drug use, and up to one-third report homosexual activity during the time they are incarcerated (Brewer & Derrickson, 1992).

Both consensual and coerced sex between inmates occurs in prison. Many men who engage in consensual sex with men in prison return to a heterosexual life upon release. These men will usually self-identify as heterosexuals. They regard sex with men as a temporary, situational behavior. For this reason, they may not be aware of the risk for HIV infection that their behavior poses to themselves, and to their female partners upon their release.

A health crisis such as AIDS takes a heavy toll on African American men who comprise about one-third of state prison inmates (Fears, 1998). Because of the high number of incarcerated African American men, there is concern about the risk of AIDS to their female partners. The widespread practices of homosexual sex and drug use are contributing to the high number of HIV-infected inmates and, in turn, to the growing infection rates among African American women (Ibid.).

More injection drug users are in prison than in any other setting, including drug treatment centers and hospitals (Brewer & Derrickson, 1992). Public health authorities believe that correctional facilities are the best means of access to a group that otherwise eludes educational efforts. The recommendations of public health officials, however, are often at odds with those of correctional officials. This is unfortunate because prisons have the highest concentration of HIV-infected persons in the world. AIDS infection in prison is six times higher than it is out on the streets (Fears, 1998).

Drug treatment has been shown to be effective in reducing the needle sharing behavior that is a risk factor for HIV. Reductions in needle use have been found to be greatest among patients enrolled in drug treatment (McCaul, Lillie-Blanton, & Svikis, 1996). However, most drug treatment programs address high-risk behaviors related to drug use, not sexual-risk behaviors for HIV.

As reported in Chapter 3, drug users are more likely to change their drug behavior than their sexual behavior to avoid becoming infected with HIV. They are also more able to talk about their drug use and its corresponding risk for HIV than about their sexual practices. Apparently, there is a shame barrier when talking about sex. Both male and female drug users resist using condoms in established relationships. Like prostitutes, drug users are more willing to use condoms with casual partners than with their regular partners.

HIV/AIDS prevention programs have been far more successful in getting IDUs to use safe injection practices than in getting them to use safe sex practices. As was noted earlier, IDUs are known to be inconsistent or ineffective users of contraception (Miller, Turner, & Moses, 1990).

Men Who Have Sex with Men and Women (MSMW). The categorization of homosexual and bisexual men into one transmission category in surveillance reports – "men who have sex with men" – is highly problematic because of inconsistencies between sexual identity and sexual behavior. The category identified as bisexual can include men who self-identify as gay but report a female partner at some time in the past; men who are bisexual and who self-identify as such; and men who self-identify as heterosexual but occasionally have sex with men (Lifson, 1992). All these categories, as well as the exclusively homosexual category, can include men who have sex with men for pay.

An international research project on MSMW found that very few self-identify as bisexual (Soesbeck & Tielman, 1992). Bisexual identity appears to vary among cultures. Most native men in Mexico who practice the active, insertive role in male-to-male sex, and who also have sex with women, do not view themselves as homosexual or bisexual (Chu et al., 1992). The behavior patterns of immigrant Mexican men usually resemble patterns established in their native country, unless they have undergone intensive acculturation (Ibid.). The reported higher prevalence of bisexual behavior among Hispanic/Latino and African American men than among white men has been associated with ethnic or racial community norms and values that promote rigid gender roles and reject homosexuality as unmanly (Doll & Beeker, 1996). Because homosexuality is so unacceptable, some men engage in bisexuality in order to maintain their heterosexual identity.

In an analysis of surveillance reports from men with AIDS who reported having had sex with men, African American men reported bisexual practices more frequently than did white or Hispanic/Latino men (Chu et al., 1992). From data on HIV-infected male blood donors, bisexual behavior was reported more often by African American donors than by white or Hispanic/Latino donors (Ibid.). It has been suggested that African American men, in particular, may adopt the bisexual self-identity because of the stigma surrounding homosexuality in the African American community (Chu et al., 1992; Doll et al., 1992). It may be more culturally acceptable for African American men to have many partners, including male partners, if these men are the insertive partner, have one or more female partners, and are financially compensated (Doll & Beeker, 1996).

The setting in which sex occurs is also important, and some men will have sex with men only under specific circumstances. For example, in prison some men may have same-sex relations because they prefer these, but others have same-sex relations because that is their only available option. This also may be true in the military. Sex between men may occur in other settings that involve prolonged isolation from women such as the work environments of migrant labor. Because their behavior is situational, these MSMW may self-identify as heterosexual. In some contexts, men may lead "heterosexual front lives" by living in communities with their wives and children but engaging in sex with other men in hidden, informal settings (Ibid.).

The risk posed by MSMW is further increased because they are often injection drug users (Chu, Peterman, Doll, Buehler, et al., 1992). In a study of injection drug use, bisexual-identified men were twice as likely as gay-identified men to report drug use (Ibid.). However, bisexuality among drug users has been given little attention, despite its potential significance for HIV risk among several intersecting populations (Doll & Beeker, 1996).

Male prostitutes are also often IDUs and usually have sex with men (Elifson, Boles, & Sweat, 1993). For many injecting drug users, bisexual behavior is an artifact of their trading sex with other men for money or drugs. Both the male prostitutes and their male sex partners do not necessarily self-identify as bisexual or homosexual. If fact, a substantial number view themselves as heterosexual and report having female sex partners (Ibid.). And although male prostitutes have paid sex with men, more of their unpaid sexual encounters are with women (Boles, Elifson, & Sweat, 1989).

Because of the clandestine sexual and drug behavior of MSMW, their female sex partners are often unaware of their risk for HIV. Less than half of MSMW disclose their sexual behavior with men to the women they have sex with (Doll & Beeker, 1996). In one study of MSMW, over half (54%) of their female partners did not know about the same-sex behavior of these men. A majority (65%) of the men had engaged in unprotected sex with the women (Stokes, McKirnan, Doll, & Burzette, 1996). It appears that the same-sex behavior of MSMW is even more closeted than their drug use. One study compared male IDUs and MSMW and found that 94% of the IDUs revealed their drug use to their female partners whereas only 21% of MSMW revealed their same-sex behavior to their female partners (Wolitski, Rietmeijer, & Goldbaum, 1996). It is especially significant that in an analysis of surveillance cases of AIDS from 1981 to 1990, one-fourth of the men who self-identified as bisexual were married when they died (Chu et al., 1992).

Bisexual men who live in different social contexts manage their bisexuality differently and, as a result, have different practices with regard to safer sex. One study that compared three groups of MSMW – bisexual identified, gay identified, and heterosexual identified – found that bisexual-identified men practiced safer sex with both men and women (Boulton et al., 1991). However, gay-identified and heterosexual-identified men practiced safer sex with men, but not with women (Ibid.). Because of the range of social contexts in which MSMW interact, there is a need for health education campaigns to target these men as members of these particular contexts.

The only behavior that some MSMW have in common is their anonymous use of public sex sites (Japenga, 1992). AIDS educators have used these sites as settings for the distribution of risk-reduction materials (Ibid.). MSMW are often very closeted and usually do not respond to gay-identified educational programs (Tielman, Hendriks, & Soesbeck, 1992). Because of the lack of accurate self-identification among MSMW, educators may need to target these men in hetero-sexual settings such as the workplace (Doll et al., 1992). MSMW who do self-identify as bisexual appear to be the group that is most respon-sive to safer-sex education. Therefore, it is important that they be tar-geted as a separate group. There is also a need for therapy and support for bisexual men and for greater visibility of bisexual organizations (Lever et al., 1992; Wolf, 1987).

Adolescence is a critical time for gay and bisexual youth. Young men who have sex with men often lack the emotional and social support available to heterosexual youth. They do not share the same opportuni-ties for dating and initial sexual exploration in settings that carry a low risk for HIV transmission (Doll & Beeker, 1996). These youth are often isolated and confused and are sometimes able to express their sexuality only through clandestine sexual encounters. These encounters some-times take place with older men who present a risk for HIV because they have had more partners over the years. Encounters between homo-sexual adolescents and their partners may also involve drugs and vio-lence. This is why expanded services for gay and bisexual youth are especially needed so that they may have access to communities and institutions that support their sexual identity (Ibid.).

Compared to the other groups of male AIDS cases, far less is known about behavioral change among MSMW. This is due to the problems in identifying and targeting this group of men. The risk that MSMW present to women has to do in part with their clandestine sexual and drug activity. This group of men serves as a good example of how be-havioral strategies need to focus on men rather than on women because the female partners of these men are often unaware of their partner's sexual and drug activity and thus are unaware of their own risk.

Hemophiliacs. Hemophiliacs are different from IDUs and MSMW in that their infection is not the result of either sexual or drug-using behavior. Rather, it is the result of their having received contaminated factor concentrate, the blood product that they need to treat their medical condition. Hemophiliacs suffer from a blood-clotting disorder and must receive factor VIII concentrate to control bleeding. Hemophiliacs accounts for 1% of male HIV/AIDS cases (CDC, 1996).

Heterosexual transmission has most often been studied among couples, and many of the studies, particularly studies of discordant couples, have been confined to hemophiliac couples (Sherr, 1993). The risk that hemophiliacs present to their female partners is through unprotected sex.

The risk for HIV that hemophiliacs pose for women is related to the number of men who are infected. From the onset of the epidemic, the level of infection in this group has been very high. As a group, the hemophiliac population has the greatest proportion of cases in the United States relative to their representation in the population (Wride, 1992). The National Hemophilia Foundation estimates that the level of infection among this country's 12,000 severe hemophiliacs could be as high as 90% (Ibid.). Despite this, behavioral change to reduce the risk to the female partners of hemophiliacs has been slow to develop. This group illustrates the difficulty of getting people to change their behavior, especially because as a group, and compared to other groups of male AIDS cases, hemophiliacs are generally more enlightened about health, a result of the demands of their own illness.

Despite their close contact with the health care system, hemophiliacs do not use condoms consistently (Kolata, 1988; Markova et al., 1990; Miller, Turner, & Moses, 1990). The level of unprotected sex practiced by discordant couples, even after being apprized of the dangers, varies. These couples often had to make decisions about having children because of concerns about transmitting a genetic disease prior to the advent of AIDS. They face the risk of having not only an affected son but also a carrier daughter. However, hemophiliac couples may desire to become parents so much that they will have unprotected sex deliberately in order to conceive (Sherr, 1993).

When they could not personally control their bleeds, hemophiliacs would often hide the nature of their illness out of fear of discrimination (Wilkie, 1990). Today, hemophiliacs have less contact with the medical system than they once had because they are now able to self-administer their infusions. Factor concentrate has liberated hemophiliacs and allowed them to achieve normalcy in their lives. Now, however, they are again reluctant to disclose their hemophilia to friends and employers because of its association with AIDS. Their lack of openness is not in the interests of their own health because when bleeds, which can be life threatening, do occur, immediate action must be taken to control them. A great deal of passing and denial exists among the hemophiliac population because of this medical stigma (Scheerhorn, 1990). The National Hemophilia Foundation was itself initially reluctant to take action about contaminated factor concentrate because this concentrate had done so much to improve the lives of hemophiliacs (Shilts, 1987).

The reluctance of hemophiliacs to disclose their hemophilia and their HIV seropositivity may also be an attempt to avoid associating themselves with homosexuality or injection drug use. The National Hemophilia Foundation contributed to homophobia by its initial recommendation that gay men be prevented from donating blood as a way to control contaminated factor concentrate (Ibid.). Hospital staff have reported that hemophiliac patients with AIDS tend to go out of their way to make their sexual identity and the origin of their illness known (Bosk & Frader, 1992). Also in an effort to differentiate themselves from homosexual patients, the infected hemophiliac patients will "display" their wives and children.

Perhaps in part because of homophobia, hemophiliacs have not sought out AIDS education or counseling in great numbers. There are early reports of a few isolated hemophiliacs who sought information about AIDS from gay service agencies because these agencies were the only sources available to them. For the most part, however, this group of men appears reluctant to deal with HIV disease (Kolata, 1988). Initially, upon learning that some factor concentrate was contaminated, some men chose not to be tested for HIV even though they suspected that they had been infected (Ibid.). Others chose to cut down on their factor concentrate treatments (Shilts, 1987; Wilkie, 1990). Generally, hemophiliacs have not been in the political forefront in the AIDS epidemic as gay men have, even though a majority are infected. The National Hemophilia Foundation reports that few seek out therapy for HIV or attend support groups; instead, it is much more common for their wives to do so (Norwood, 1987). One study of hemophiliac couples found differences in the kinds of support needed by men and by women (Sherr, 1993). Women expressed a specific desire for dialogue about safer sex.

The previous sections discussed three main groups of male AIDS cases: IDUs, MSMWs, and hemophiliacs. In reviewing the various types of male sex partners, it is apparent that the task of providing men with information on how to reduce their risk of contracting HIV can be difficult. In some instances, and for various reasons, men will not self-identify as sex partners. In other instances, because of the various roles that men take on as sex partners, they may not constitute a well-defined target group. In either event, they are not reached with information about AIDS. Even after a profile of male AIDS cases has been constructed, information about the gender roles and sexuality of men with AIDS is limited. For this reason, it may be useful to examine the behavior of men in other roles such as those of partners in discordant couples and sex partners of prostitutes.

Discordant Couples

Hemophiliacs have been given attention particularly as infected partners in discordant relationships. Discordant relationships can reveal a great deal about male gender roles and sexual behavior. These relationships can inform an understanding of patterns of behavioral change and of the sustainability of these patterns over time.

Whether discordant couples actually constitute a group is not clear (Sherr, 1993). Discordant couples do not gather together, self-identify, or have a common purpose. The only defining characteristic of discordant couples is that one partner is infected and the other is not.

Most studies of discordant couples involve situations where the man is HIV positive and the woman, negative (Ibid.). In examining discordant-couple relationships, it should be kept in mind that all HIV-positive concordant couples were at some point discordant. There is a great interest in understanding what is unique about those couples who remain discordant compared to those who become concordant.

In their study of discordant couples, Kamenga et al. (1991) found that at-risk men were more likely to protect themselves than at-risk women and that infected men were more likely to place an uninfected woman at risk than an infected woman was to place an uninfected man at risk. When the husbands were at risk of infection, their rate of sustained condom use was higher than when they were the positive partner and risked infecting their wife. A husband who was HIV negative was more likely to abstain from marital sex than if he were HIV positive. Infected husbands who were abstinent from sex within marriage reported that they had unprotected extramarital sex, whereas no infected women reported extramarital sex. The study found that infected women were younger and married for a shorter time than infected men. More psychological problems occurred in relationships in which the wife was the infected partner, and more HIV-negative husbands divorced their seropositive wives than vice versa.

Most research on discordant couples has involved couples counseling (Allen, Serufilira et al., 1992; Allen, Tice et al., 1992; De Vincenzi, 1994). One study found that counseling men and women together increased their consistent use of condoms. Of the couples who used condoms consistently for vaginal and anal intercourse, none of the HIV-negative partners became infected (De Vincenzi, 1994). Discordant couples comprise a diverse population, and approaches in counseling need to address this diversity. In particular, such approaches need to consider the gender power relations in discordant couples.

Paying and Nonpaying Partners of Prostitutes

As noted in Chapter 3, prostitutes have received a great deal of attention for their role in the heterosexual HIV/AIDS epidemic – far more attention than their clients have received. Prostitutes and their paying partners, who are often IDUs, are considered to be primary groups at risk for HIV infection. Secondary groups at risk include the prostitutes' nonpaying partners and the partners of clients.

The nonpaying partners of prostitutes are less likely to use condoms than their paying partners. Moreover, nonpaying partners often do not consider themselves to be at risk because their female partners do use condoms with clients. Even with clients, however, condom use is inconsistent. The primary reason that prostitutes do not use condoms with clients is the client's resistance or outright refusal. Furthermore, prostitutes report that they nearly always must be the partner who initiates the use of condoms (Mak & Plum, 1991). Clients rarely propose using them. Although clients may agree to protect themselves from risks in commercial sex, they do not show the same concern about infecting their partners, whether paid or unpaid (Leonard, 1990). A large number of clients also have women who are not prostitutes as their regular sex partners, and a significant number of clients are married (Ibid.).

AIDS-prevention programs for prostitutes recognize that the control of HIV infection will ultimately require behavioral change by the clients of prostitutes. Condom-promotion efforts that target only prostitutes will have only limited success because clients can either offer the prostitute more money for sex without a condom or boycott any prostitute who insists on using a condom (Alexander, 1995).

Although many programs have been successful in reaching prostitutes, reaching clients has proven to be more difficult (Population Reports, 1989). Clients are not a well-defined group. Like MSMW, they share only one feature. MSMW have in common their use of anonymous sex sites. In the same way, prostitutes' clients have in common their use of commercial sex services.

Prostitutes, particularly street prostitutes, are a much more clearly defined group than are their clients. One defining factor is that prostitutes who go to STD clinics are part of the public health care system (Rosenberg & Weiner, 1988). Clients, in contrast, are usually not part of this system. If they do seek services from the health department, it is simply as male sex partners.

In the United States, peer education programs for prostitutes have been in place since 1989 (Alexander, 1995). However, only a small number of projects have focused on clients. Even when clients were included in prevention efforts, often the advice given to them was simply to not have sex with prostitutes.

Some HIV/AIDS prevention programs employing prostitutes as peer educators have been successful in reaching clients (Panos Dossier, 1990). A few programs have included all persons in the prostitutes' social network. These programs also have used the men working in bars, brothels, and hotels to educate clients (Panos Dossier, 1990; Sepulveda, Fineberg, & Mann, 1992; Wilson et al., 1990). In the Netherlands, clients of prostitutes organized Men in Prostitution, which distributed condoms and safer-sex information to other clients in Holland's legal red light districts (Alexander, 1995; Population Reports, 1989).

Many of the efforts made to educate clients have been in developing countries (Alexander, 1995). Programs in Africa targeting potential clients of prostitutes include interventions aimed at truck drivers and at men in the military (Sepulveda, Fineberg, & Mann, 1992). The social network of truckers, which includes people who provide various services at truck stops, was also targeted. Programs have also conducted outreach and workshops in bars and in places that employ large numbers of men, such as factories (Alexander, 1995).

In Ethiopia, the Department of AIDS Control developed a client project in response to prostitutes' complaints about clients' refusals to use condoms (Ibid.). Men were trained to be peer educators and motivators in the workplace. They sold condoms at subsidized low prices and held condom-promotion events at sports stadiums and other public sites. This particular project targeted the clients first and then the prostitutes in contrast to most programs, which expand from prostitute to client.

A project in Bulawayo, Zimbabwe, which began as a study of prostitutes and clients, eventually became a peer-education project (Wilson et al., 1990) in which prostitutes and clients received training as peer educators. As in the Ethiopian project, clients were included in response to prostitutes' frequent complaints about the clients' refusal to use condoms. This project became the model for programs in other countries in the region.

In Thailand, a government-implemented program enforcing 100% condom use in brothels reduced HIV-infection rates considerably among young Thai men. Rates among those men who were in the army and who frequented prostitutes declined from 13% in 1993 to 7% in 1995. Similarly, condom use during sex with prostitutes increased from 61% to 93% (Nelson et al., 1996). Compliance was enforced by the police and public health workers. It is important to note that the pressure to see that condoms were used was placed on the brothel rather than on the prostitutes.

Because clients of prostitutes are an ill-defined group, a project in India used socioeconomic mapping to locate the areas from which a majority of clients came (Bhattacharya, Chowdhury, & Chakraborty, 1996). This project then developed a client profile. It found that most of the clients frequented 15 geographic areas, 35 liquor stores, and 12 gambling dens. These areas were targeted with outreach approaches involving the social marketing of condoms and peer education. These approaches were well accepted.

A project in Bali, Indonesia, offered HIV-education sessions to prostitutes, clients, and pimps (Ford & Wirawan, 1996). This project found that the most important predictor of condom use was the STD knowledge of the three groups and that STD knowledge of clients had the most effect. This project demonstrated the importance of including clients in educational interventions.

Data about HIV/AIDS interventions with clients are limited. It is sometimes necessary to rely on anecdotal accounts, and quite often, these accounts are from prostitutes, not clients. In the Ethiopian project the prostitutes felt encouraged and reported that their clients asked for condoms and sometimes even brought their own (Alexander, 1995). Stronger data on client involvement in HIV/AIDS prevention programs are clearly needed.

Need for a New Focus on Men

The focus of AIDS prevention on women has been shown to be misguided in that it has made women primarily responsible for safer-sex practices, without attention to important gender power differentials. Controlling HIV disease will require acknowledging the fundamental differences in power relations between men and women. In particular, the growing number of AIDS cases among adolescents highlights the need to recognize and change gender power relations that promote the continued spread of the epidemic. This process requires that sexism and homophobia are confronted early in the socialization of heterosexual males.

One problem in understanding the behavior of heterosexual men is the lack of research on heterosexual adults generally. In addition, researchers have not studied the social context in which men interact with one another, and with women, as it relates to AIDS prevention.

What is known about men is fragmented and unclear. Often a focus on men quickly shifts to women. A good example here is provided by the topics included at the International Conference on AIDS held in Amsterdam in 1992. There were 22 formal sessions on issues specific to women (Eighth International Conference on AIDS, summary report, 1992a; Eighth International Conference on AIDS, 1992b: Sessions 110, 185, 235, 252). However, there was only one session devoted to changes in the attitudes and behavior of heterosexual men, and that session actually discussed women, not men (Eighth International Conference on AIDS, Session 16). (Even one of the presentations at that session referred to women rather than men in its title [Rapkin et al., 1992].) According to conference organizers, only a few abstracts on the session topic were submitted to the conference, and as a result, no conclusions were reached on how to change male attitudes and behavior (Eighth International Conference on AIDS, summary report, 1992). Nevertheless, the need for rapid development and implementation of programs to change the behavior of heterosexual men was emphasized in the summary of conference proceedings (Ibid.).

One of the major themes of this conference was women's empowerment (Long, 1996). Women were given more attention at this conference than at any previous conferences (Ibid.). With so little attention paid to men at the conference, its theme seems somewhat ironic. For women's empowerment to be realized, changes in the behavior of men must occur. In this regard, it is encouraging that "Male Sexuality" was included in the Twelfth World AIDS Conference held in Geneva, Switzerland, in 1998.

The National Conference on Women and HIV, held in Pasadena, California, in 1997, did include several sessions on gender power relations and female-controlled microbicides. But male behavior, particularly gender role socialization, must be studied further so that effective prevention strategies for women can be developed.

The lack of research on the behavior of male sex partners is critical. Data are extremely limited and usually confined to developing countries. More attention has been given to men in developing countries than in the United States because the epidemic in those countries is primarily heterosexual. Men's involvement in contraceptive decision making has received some scrutiny in developing countries. The main focus of research in developing countries, however, has been on men in discordant relationships and men as sex partners of prostitutes. These data, therefore, involve highly specialized groups of men. Both groups include men only as they are members of couples, and the data are on male and female behaviors together, not separate. More information on the range of behaviors exhibited by other male sex partners is especially needed.

Men must be the focus and priority of AIDS research and education. Researchers need to study how men differ from women in their perceptions of risk, interpretations of AIDS prevention information, and determinants of risk behavior. Of course, AIDS prevention for women remains important. What is learned about behavioral change among men can inform and affect AIDS prevention for women. For example, a change in drug and sexual behavior by men will have health consequences for the women who are sex partners.

The new interest in men is not intended to end the targeting of women. However, women should no longer be made to feel personally responsible for the behavior of men. Rather, they should be offered alternative gender roles designed to empower them in their relations with male partners.

Often the term "heterosexual" is used to describe women or men as members of a couple but not men separate from women. AIDS-prevention strategies must be sensitive to the multiple and often clandestine sexual practices of heterosexual-identified men. These strategies require the development of a clearer profile of men. Then these strategies must target men directly, not as members of couples, and not through women. Women may have male sex partners who display a wide range of risk behaviors. Until there is an accurate profile of these men, their female sex partners will continue to be vulnerable.

The problems that affect AIDS prevention for men are part of a larger problem with educational messages. Because targeting has been selective, it has fostered divisiveness and a sense of otherness (Ehrhardt, 1992). Information about AIDS is conveyed to men as members of different groups of male AIDS cases, such as IDUs or hemophiliacs (Panos Dossier, 1990; Wilton & Aggleton, 1991). Men have not been targeted as a composite group of heterosexual male sex partners.

Men also need to be contacted in more diverse settings. For example, men can be reached at gyms, barber shops, or sporting events (Population Reports, 1986). Men can be targeted in many of the same ways that women have been. Just as AIDS prevention has targeted women in their role as mothers, it can target men as fathers. In the same way in which women have acted as peer educators in educating other women, men can be peer educators to other men. Finally, in addition to couples counseling, HIV-prevention programs should provide counseling for men and by men themselves.

HIV interventions for men should stress consistent and correct use of condoms as well as monogamy. Safer-sex practices should be presented as a collaboration of men and women, one requiring communication and disclosure. Programs that help men improve their communication and disclosure skills are critically needed. Effective HIV interventions may require men to rethink notions of intimacy. Approaches aimed at skills building may be useful tools to help men control their impulses to be violent, coercive, or promiscuous.

Social marketing of condoms may be an effective approach in targeting men. In African American communities, a culturally sensitive program has marketed the condom Umoja Sasa, or Unity Now, with the slogan "Protect the Blood." In Zaire, a careful consumer study produced a culturally sensitive and affordable condom known as "Prudence." In one year (1988–1989), sales of Prudence increased 443% (Ferreros et al., 1990). In fact, in many regions of Zaire, "Prudence" became a generic substitute for the term "condom."

Men's issues related to AIDS are long overdue for consideration and must become part of men's health agendas. HIV/AIDS needs to be redefined as a health issue affecting men. The recent men's movement would appear to be an appropriate forum for these changes because this movement deals directly with men's health issues and with the ways in which traditional roles oppress men.

AIDS-prevention strategies must not contribute to gender role stereotypes that hinder the effort to control HIV disease. These strategies will have to be sensitive to the way in which reinforcement of traditional masculine identity encourages the continued spread of the epidemic. Control of the epidemic will require that men be given clear and concise gender-specific information about AIDS. But men must not merely be given the information; they will be expected to act on it. Unless men become a major focus of research and prevention efforts, women will continue to be at risk for HIV disease.

6

WOMEN, MOTHERHOOD, AND THE FAMILY

My partner [James] is infected with HIV too. Yesterday we went to pick up the wedding band. A lot of times I think I want to marry him because I don't want to be alone. I know I don't want to give my disease to anybody else.

It feels good to have somebody in your corner that has some kind of time to be there. The only thing I'm confused about, you know, I'm gonna give this man my whole life, to be with him the rest of my life and I think that I can do this.

When I went into the program, I met James. He was usin' rocks but right now he just drinks his beer. I'm still drinking but I'm on methadone. If it wasn't for James, I'd probably be back on the street 'cause I didn't have nowhere to go. And so me and James – we ended up fallin' in love, got our own place and stuff. Just ain't no reason to go to the streets now. I'm lookin' at life different now.

– Eunice

I had a real problem. I thought I had to tell my family about my HIV. I had been holding that from them 'cause I was afraid of losing them again. You see, I just got back with my sister this past year after 10 years of not talking.

And with that, I didn't know what her perception of me as a person was, being she never used drugs and she has been a great support for me. Yet, I knew if I told her, she would tell the rest of my family and I didn't want to take that chance cause I didn't want to be alone. But I went ahead and told her cause I'm in the process of getting my 3-year-old son in my custody and I thought someone should know in case I got sick or something. I was surprised she showed no pain in her facial expression and real understanding. I feel like a weight has been lifted.

– Louann

We had plans of the three of us returning to Hildalgo but unfortunately it didn't happen that way. When I lived with him, the saddest thing was when I saw him in a coma from which he never got out of and my God took him so that he wouldn't suffer any longer. I give thanks to God for being so lucky to still be alive with my daughter and continue ahead.

I had to face reality that this is going to happen, not to try to change things but to face things like the illness and that this is my life now. And I start cooking. I love to cook, to help my sister. I take care of her daughter. I bathe her. I play with her and the truth is my life is very different. There is a lot behind me and I have another life here.

My sister doesn't like me to cry. She doesn't want me to be sad and mope around here alone. She always calls me from work and asks me how I am. She takes very good care of me. I am very happy with her, so much support. She supports me so much.

– Juana

And then he told me he was sick and that he had gotten infected. Thank God the children aren't sick. Well, now you see the life I lead because of his illness. I decided to see if I can live with him like this, with the illness. And we were together but it was like I was in denial.

– Rosemary

One good thing that happened, the family got closer. Bobby got really attached to Marvin. He was feeling a little guilt or a lot of guilt because the child came out positive and he would blame it on himself.

We tried to give Marvin the best we could although we were going through financial problems. On the other hand, we neglected Bobby and Tabatha because we were so focused on Robert and Marvin. He was so sick. So we kept leaving Bobby and Tabatha with friends, with my sister, with Church people. It was a blessing because they would help us a lot but then the children would feel that mom and dad were not there for them.

I went to pick up my daughter at my sister Sara's. Then I went to buy some things for my children's birthday party. And at 5 P.M., the celebration began. It was a fun day for the family.

Bobby was here last year. I remember we celebrated the children's birthdays. I have pictures from last year. He had so much fun and so did I together with the children. It's not easy sometimes. When the memories come back, it's difficult when all of a sudden I realize my partner of life is gone. I miss him when I watch *MASH* late at night by myself and he is not here to laugh with.

– Leticia

My family is very supportive. All my family knows. My close friends, they all know and they're really supportive.

We have two support groups that meet twice a month. We have families. We have foster parents. We have single moms, single dads. It's just a real mixed group. We have people who have known of their diagnosis for a long time. We have people who just recently found out.

– Mariana

THE IMPACT OF HIV DISEASE ON FAMILY LIFE

Research on the psychosocial impact of HIV disease has focused on the individual (Bor, 1995). Gay men have been studied most frequently; women have received less attention (Sherr, 1995). By now, the literature on the psychosocial impact of HIV disease on gay men is comprehensive. However, the psychosocial consequences of HIV disease for women are different than they are for gay men. Because of the epidemic's white gay male profile, services were designed around the needs of this clientele. This same model was used for women despite their different roles.

Although it has been evident for some time that HIV affects more than just individuals, little work has been done on the psychosocial impact of HIV on the entire family (Bor, 1995). Not until the Eighth International Conference on AIDS in Amsterdam in 1992 were the special needs and problems of families affected by HIV/AIDS finally addressed in a comprehensive way (King, 1993). The first conference devoted entirely to families with HIV disease was not held until 1998.

Families and Illness. Many different types of family situations exist in the context of HIV disease. Some families have only one member who is infected; other families have multiple members. Some families are married couples; others are single parents. Some single-parent families are headed by women; others are headed by men.

This diversity is illustrated by the experiences of the individuals who are profiled in Appendix B and whose quotations open each chapter. Among them is Leticia, an infected woman whose husband and child died from HIV/AIDS. She is now raising two children who are not infected. Mariana is not infected herself but has a child who was infected from a blood transfusion. Rosemary is not infected but has a partner who is and three uninfected children. Juana was infected by her husband, who died, and now raises a child who was infected from breast-feeding. Ed is an infected single father who has a child who is not infected. And Jose is also an infected single father, but his child is infected.

Not only are these family situations different, but they also came about through different routes of transmission: Leticia was infected heterosexually by her husband who was infected from injection drug use; Mariana's son was infected through a blood transfusion; Juana and Jose were infected from heterosexual partners; and Loretta is a lesbian-identified woman who became infected through injection drug use. These differences demonstrate just how complex family relationships in the context of HIV can be.

These individuals also have varying levels of social support. Ed receives no support from his family; he relies heavily on a support group for HIV families. Leticia and Mariana have a great deal of support from family and friends, and both are active in public speaking about their experiences with HIV/AIDS. Juana also derives a lot of support from family members. Louann, after a long history of drug use, is now hoping to gain acceptance from her family. Denise relies heavily on her HIV support group and is trying to get her children back from foster care.

Some of the families interviewed are dealing with special issues such as language barriers and immigration problems. Both Juana and Rosemary are immigrants who speak only Spanish. Juana is originally from Mexico and Rosemary from Honduras. Both women describe the problems they encountered because of their immigration status in attempting to find work in the United States. Immigrants like Juana and Rosemary maintain contact with extended family members in their native countries. Thus Leticia's mother came from Guatemala to help her and the children, and Jose's parents came from Mexico to help him and his daughter.

To understand the effects of HIV disease on families such as these, it is helpful to look at the impact on families of other chronic illnesses. Tay-Sachs disease can cause fatal illness in infancy, and both cystic fibrosis and sickle cell disease can produce serious disability (Wissow, Hutton, & McGraw, 1996). In addition, children are born to mothers with serious and even fatal diseases such as cancer, lupus, and multiple sclerosis. In all of these illness situations, families must deal with the possibility that a child will be affected or that a parent will not live to see his or her child grow up.

Considerable research has been done on the stress experienced by families with critically ill children, including children with cancer and juvenile-onset diabetes (Baker, 1992). However, the existing literature on chronic childhood illness has profiled middle-class families (Boland, Czarniecki, & Haiken, 1992). This research therefore may not apply to families with HIV/AIDS, who are often poor, minority, single-parent families. In addition, much of the research on chronic childhood illness has involved families with only one ill member (Ibid.). In families that have children with perinatal HIV infection, there are at least two members who are infected. The parents of a child with cystic fibrosis or sickle cell disease may be carriers of the disease or may have other affected children, but they are unlikely to have the disease themselves (Wissow, Hutton, & McGraw, 1996). No model of a fatal illness comparable to AIDS, striking both parents and children, exists (Boland, Czarniecki, & Haiken, 1992). Thus the dynamics in families with multiple HIV infections can be expected to be different. HIV disease presents families with a unique constellation of challenges.

Research on pediatric HIV disease has focused on medical and clinical issues rather than on family issues (Nehring, Malm, & Harris, 1993). As a result, little is known about the impact of pediatric HIV disease on the family. However, it is readily apparent that varying degrees of chaos already exist in many families affected by pediatric AIDS. Families with maternal-child HIV infection are frequently beset by a multitude of problems – poverty, homelessness, illegal drug use, incarceration, physical and emotional abuse, absentee parents, and school truancy (Andiman, 1995) – that often make it difficult for the families to cope with the additional burden of HIV disease.

It has been shown that children with chronic diseases are more likely to experience emotional, behavioral, and educational problems (Barlow & Mok, 1993). These children have well-documented problems in psychosocial development (Wissow, Hutton, & McGraw, 1996). But the burdens of having HIV disease, particularly the secrecy and stigma associated with it, may be worse than those of other illnesses.

Behavioral and emotional disturbance can also occur in the well children in families with HIV/AIDS (King, 1993). These children are referred to as "affected" rather than "infected." The needs of affected siblings are sometimes neglected because of the family's focus on the infected child. Affected siblings of chronically ill children are likely to receive the least emotional support of any family member (Wissow, Hutton, & McGraw, 1996). Moreover, they are sometimes required to take on additional responsibilities within the family (Ibid.). This may take place with greater frequency in families with HIV disease than in families dealing with other chronic illnesses because in a family with HIV/AIDS, the parents themselves are often ill and/or single parents (Ibid.). Feelings of anger, abandonment, guilt, and loneliness are common in affected siblings (Nehring, Malm, & Harris, 1993). Affected siblings fare particularly poorly if parents withhold information about the infected sibling's condition (Wissow, Hutton, & McGraw, 1996). This problem may be more common among families with HIV disease because of the secrecy surrounding disclosure.

Similar issues and problems have been found in families with children who suffer from chronic diseases other than HIV/AIDS (King, 1993). Studies of parents of children with chronic illness have found that anxiety, depression, guilt, and grief about the fate of their children are common (Wisson, Hutton, & McGraw, 1996). The parents may blame themselves for the child's illness and worry about the child's future. There is often a wide range of emotions as the child's condition improves and then deteriorates.

Families of children with chronic diseases describe altered self-images, decreased social interactions, isolation, altered daily routines, financial problems, and the "sick role" (Nehring, Malm, & Harris, 1993). In families of children with terminal cancer, social, emotional, and financial issues are major concerns (Ibid.). Families of children with developmental disabilities describe marital problems, chronic sorrow, lessened expectations, and a sense of the child's being "different" (Ibid.). Pediatric HIV disease is an unhappy combination of all of these concerns. In addition, pediatric HIV disease largely affects an already disenfranchised population. The multiple strains placed upon these fragile families are evident, as are illustrated in Juana's and Leticia's vignettes. Moreover, it is clear from the research on families with chronic diseases, as well as from the limited research on HIV/AIDS, that caregiving is critically important to the functioning of these families.

Caregiving

A majority (approximately 75%) of women with HIV disease have children (Forsyth, 1995). Infected women have an average of 2.6 children, roughly the same number as other women (Smith, 1996). Infected women are generally young, poorly educated, and have few job skills (Simpson & Williams, 1993). Most are unmarried and have primary responsibility for the care of their children (Forsyth, 1995). Whether or not they themselves have HIV disease, a majority of women with infected children rely on public assistance to survive.

As mothers, infected women are central to providing care for their infected and uninfected children. Women in general are more likely than men to care for their children, spouses, friends, and elderly relatives (Baines, Evans, & Neysmith, 1991). Women are found providing informal HIV/AIDS care in their roles as mothers, grandmothers, wives, daughters, sisters, and aunts (Richardson, 1988; Stephens, 1989). The traditional role of mother as caregiver and nurturer is often highlighted in the presence of HIV disease (Sherr, 1995).

Age is a critical variable in a discussion of informal AIDS caregiving. Younger women who are infected themselves must confront the physical and emotional needs of their chronically ill partners and dependent children at the same time as they try to cope with their own illness. Older women who are mothers and grandmothers must deal with the uncertainties of caring for their chronically ill children and dependent grandchildren (Kurth, 1993). Women may have to become caregivers at times in their lives when these demands were not anticipated.

Most studies of informal caregiving have focused on the care given to people with cancer or Alzheimer's disease and to the elderly (Wardlaw, 1994). Studies of elder care have found that most of it is provided by the family rather than by the health care system even in those countries with extensive health care systems. The caregivers are most often women – daughters, daughters-in-law, wives, and other female relatives (Crystal & Sambamoorthi, 1996).

AIDS presents a different situation for caregivers compared to cancer and elder care. Quite often, the caregiver to someone with AIDS is ill with the disease as well. An infected child in the family almost always means that the mother is infected, and perhaps the father too.

The impact of illness thus is shifted from the individual to the entire family unit.

Mothers are accustomed to sharing with each other their knowledge about childhood diseases, but they are not always comfortable doing so when the disease is HIV/AIDS because of the stigma it carries. The result is that the demands of caregiving in HIV-infected families can often be extremely isolating. In fact, most caregivers function in isolation (Simpson & Williams, 1993). Stigma and the related need for secrecy are among the primary concerns expressed by families with HIV disease (Wissow, Hutton, & McGraw, 1996). They often surpass the families' concerns about obtaining health care and other support services. Families with HIV disease frequently live in constant fear of disclosure or of loss of support of friends and family.

Infected women are often affected by HIV/AIDS both as caregivers and as needers of care. Women are more likely than men to be living with other infected family members (Crystal & Sambamoorthi, 1996), and the burden of caring for others often delays infected women in seeking care for themselves (Simpson & Williams, 1993). As caregiving mothers, infected women often have a difficult time tending to their own needs. Many women become so involved with the health of their children that they fail to be compliant in their own care (Sunderland & Holman, 1993). They follow treatment regimens for their children thoroughly and at the expense of their own health. The result is that a woman's health might deteriorate while her child's health stabilizes (Ibid.). When women finally seek treatment, many find that their disease is in an advanced stage (Smith, 1996). Because of the demands of caregiving, these women had not been able to benefit from early intervention with drug therapy.

Sick children cause anxiety for others, particularly mothers, because children are supposed to be healthy (Andiman, 1995). HIV-infected children need special attention and care from birth. It is heartening and provides some balance to the demands of caregiving that their caring for children can also have a positive effect on infected women's own health (Wissow, Hutton, & McGraw, 1996). This is true despite the numerous obstacles women encounter in caregiving. Mothers comment that caring for their infected children gives them a sense of purpose in life and helps them maintain hope for the future (Ibid.).

Through caregiving, they feel useful and have a position in society that they ordinarily might not occupy. If transportation to medical care is available, caring for sick children can help women relieve their isolation. These women can be drawn into activities and support networks through their child's medical care by having the opportunity to meet other women in a supportive environment. This setting may also provide them with the chance to share advice and even material resources. In addition, the caregiving woman may make contacts that will help her learn more about her own illness and encourage her to seek care for herself.

Another way in which caring for children can benefit their mothers is that it sometimes helps them to overcome strained relations within their families (Ibid.). Especially if a mother's condition deteriorates, the family may need to unite to care for her surviving children. Children can be a motivating force reuniting relatives who otherwise would remain estranged. It may also be easier for an ill mother to ask her family for help for her children rather than for herself.

Caregiving can be cathartic, but many mothers still must cope with the loss of a child. AIDS breaks the rules of dying because it affects predominantly the young, not the old (Geballe, Gruendel, & Andiman, 1995). Children tend to be young because of the age distribution of HIV disease among adult women (Sherr, 1995). The median age of death for women with AIDS is 33 years (Wissow, Hutton, & McGraw, 1996). Children who die before their parents represent a disruption in the natural life process in which parents are expected to die before their children.

Estimates are that between 93,000 and 112,000 uninfected children will be born to infected women in the decade between 1992 and 2002 (Ibid.). It is also estimated that 125,000 children in the United States will lose their mothers to HIV disease by the end of this decade (as cited in Forsyth, 1995). AIDS is rapidly approaching the same status for women that it has for men as the leading cause of death in the child-rearing years. The high degree of mortality associated with the disease makes it important to recognize its impact on the family unit, including the role of the father in leaving orphaned children. Soon more children in the United States will lose parents to AIDS than to any other cause of death (Geballe, Gruendel, & Andiman, 1995). The magnitude of this loss for children is obvious.

In times of peace and prosperity children are usually shielded from death. They are buffered by two beliefs – that their parents will always be there and that only old people die (Wissow, Hutton, & McGraw, 1996). In families with HIV disease, however, both of these defenses are threatened.

Children who lose parents to HIV/AIDS will often lose not just their parents but also their neighborhoods, friends, and schools – their sense of community. Their feelings of loss and dislocation are therefore often intense. One study of outcomes for orphaned children upon a mother's death found that 75% of these children moved (cited in Levine, 1996). A national study of children in the United States found repeated family relocation to be associated with an increased risk of children's failing a grade in school and having four or more behavioral problems that occur frequently (Ibid.). Children feel helpless in dealing with a parent's death or with other events that are beyond their control. As a result, a significant change in their environment will generally have a negative impact on their adjustment to both their parents' death and their new environment (Ibid.). This change may create additional stress for orphaned children. Furthermore, these children not only must deal with their loss but also with society's indifference to their plight (Andiman, 1995).

In some families, children may lose more relatives than just their parents. In families where there are multiple infections, children may also lose brothers, sisters, aunts, and uncles. They thus must deal with multiple loss.

There is a growing literature on bereavement and AIDS. However, it pertains almost exclusively to white gay men and their families, partners, and friends (Levine, 1996). Most work on bereavement has focused on those gay men who are themselves infected and/or who have lost partners and friends to HIV/AIDS and has primarily dealt with the impact of multiple loss (Siegel & Gorey, 1994). Only recently has attention to survivors expanded to include children. Even so, the literature on the impact of parental death from AIDS is limited (Levine, 1996; Siegel & Gorey, 1994).

Infected mothers must plan for the welfare of their children after their own deaths. These women are not only bereaved from losing a shared future with children but also from the additional burden of knowingly leaving orphaned children (Sherr, 1995). Some women may refuse care for themselves in an attempt to deny their own illness (Wissow, Hutton, & McGraw, 1996), or they may perceive their child's illness as prefiguring their own fate.

One study that examined caregiving to children born to infected mothers found that barely over one-half (56%) of these children were living with their biological parents. Twenty-seven percent were living in foster homes, 10% with relatives, 3% with adoptive parents, and 4% in group settings or with other caregivers (as cited in Forsyth, 1995). There was some geographic variation. For example, in New York City, only 42% of children were living with a biological parent compared to Texas, where 70% were. Injection drug use by the mother was the most important factor associated with whether children lived with other caregivers. In all locations, and for all racial and ethnic groups, a newborn whose mother used injection drugs was more likely to be placed with someone other than the mother. Only 6.3% of the mothers in this study were deceased.

The study just cited is significant because it examined a critical evolving situation. Future projections suggest that caregiving will continue to be a pressing issue, as more parents are certain to die. As indicated by the data already presented, children whose family units are affected by AIDS are often placed in informal kinship care settings.

Kinship Care. A study conducted by the New York Division of AIDS Services examined the outcome in 43 AIDS cases that were closed shortly after the mother's death. The study found that approximately half (58%) of the children went to live with their grandmothers or aunts (as cited in Levine, 1995). In a study of 72 infected mothers in Chicago, 21 of them indicated that they would like their mothers to take their children upon their own death; 9 designated their sisters; and 22 designated other relatives. Twenty of the women were not able to designate anyone. Both studies suggest that informal kinship care is an important provider of care for children of infected mothers.

The kinship parent plays a key role in families in which the mother can no longer care for her children. In most states, when the biological parent with HIV/AIDS is not able to take care of a child, the child will be placed in the home of a relative (Boland, Czarniecki, & Haiken, 1992). The kinship parent may be a grandmother, aunt, or older sibling (Simpson & Williams, 1993), although in most families it is the grandmother or aunt who assumes care (Boland, Czarniecki, & Haiken, 1992; as cited in Levine, 1996).

The phenomenon of children being raised by grandmothers is referred to as "skip-generation parenting" (Levine, 1995). Skip-generation parenting actually did not start with the advent of AIDS. It became a more common practice because of drug use, particularly the use of crack cocaine in the 1980s. Skip-generation parenting is especially noticeable in African American communities because of the crack cocaine epidemic (Ibid.). The number of African American children living with grandmothers in some urban areas is quite high. For example, the percentage of African American children living with grandmothers ranges between 30% and 70% in some parts of Detroit and New York (Ibid.). Now AIDS is another reason why skip-generation parenting has become more common.

Kinship families often learn of an infected family member's HIV diagnosis at the same time as they are requested to become kinship parents (Simpson & Williams, 1993). This situation requires them to adjust and to respond to both sets of information at once. The emotional impact of an HIV diagnosis on kinship families has not been examined in depth. For example, there is little research on grandmothers' emotional response to the impending loss of both a child and a grandchild (Nehring, Malm, & Harris, 1993).

The socioeconomic situation of most kinship parents reflects that of their infected family member. That is, these persons often have low incomes and few assets or resources (Ibid.). In many families, kinship parents endure a lengthy financial crisis as a direct consequence of their childcare commitment (Ibid.). Kinship parents of children with HIV have many complex needs. Interventions that have been successful in kinship situations involving children sick with other serious diseases, such as children who have cancer, have not been as effective with kinship families dealing with HIV/AIDS (Ibid.). These families appear to have special support needs because of the social stigma they often face, their lack of resources, and the burden of multiple infections in a single family (Ibid.).

Although kinship families have special needs, they often resist the involvement of local children's social service agencies (Ibid.). These families choose to be independent of formal social services, despite the potential financial benefit to them of these services. Kinship families may view official social services as an intrusion and a threat to their autonomy. They may resent any government agency judging their suitability to care for their own kin. As a result, it is common to find informal foster care situations in which family members receive no assistance for care provided to children over an extended period of time (Ibid.). In fact, whereas foster parents can receive between $900 and $1,200 per month to care for an HIV-infected child, kinship parents typically get no financial assistance (Boyd-Franklin & Boland, 1995).

Even before the AIDS epidemic, kinship families constituted the first potential source of caregiving in many minority communities in which HIV disease is prevalent (Wissow, Hutton, & McGraw, 1996). However, the pool of available family members may be reduced for many reasons. Some caregivers are already stretched to their capacities. Some of the grandmothers and aunts who take over the care of children whose mothers are ill or have died from HIV/AIDS have additional responsibilities and must care for their own children, partners, elderly parents or other relatives. Some of them will not be able to continue as kinship parents because of the great physical and emotional strain it entails.

Often grandmothers who are skip-generation parenting are not in good health themselves. One study of African American grandparents found that they tended to ignore their own health needs because the needs of their grandchildren took priority (as cited in Levine, 1996). Their own fairly serious health problems included diabetes, hypertension, back problems, and low energy. Many of the grandparents saw their own illness and death as their only escape from a burdensome situation. The caregiving grandparents and infected mothers are similar in their tendency to put the needs of the children before their own. When these grandmothers are no longer able to care for their grandchildren, or when they die, these children will experience the loss of a caregiver for the second time.

An additional outcome of skip-generation parenting is that because of the mothers' death, there will be fewer grandmothers to replace this generation's (Levine, 1996). The current lost generation of mothers will become a lost generation of grandmothers. The impact of this loss is significant: It represents a break in family continuity for children whose lives are already fragile and unstable.

There is another type of skip-generation parenting that involves the younger generation. In this version the teenagers and young adults in the family take over the care of younger children (Ibid.). Although this is less common than kinship care by grandparents, it is found in some families, particularly in those in which older relatives cannot assume care of the children. It is expected that by the year 2000 the number of young adults over 18 whose mothers die from HIV/AIDS will reach 64,000 (Ibid.). In some families, the teenagers and young adults also take care of their mother until her death. This skip-generation parenting phenomenon involving young people has been referred to as the "parentification" of youth (Ibid.). Clearly it has important implications for the futures of these young people as well as for their younger siblings.

From this discussion, it is evident that women in various roles have assumed difficult caregiving tasks in families with HIV disease. This caregiving role has a significant impact on these women as well as on their families.

The Caregiving Role

To understand the caregiving role in families with HIV, it is important to recognize the specific ways that women have come to perceive their identity as women. Historically, the role of caregiver has been overwhelmingly ascribed to women on the basis of their presumed natural ability (Wilson, 1992). Caregiving is considered to be an important and necessary activity for the healthy functioning of society. But although it is seen as important, it is usually thought of as separate from the mainstream activities of men (Ibid.). Thus, as Jean Baker Miller maintains in *Towards a New Psychology of Women* (1986), women acting "in" the world are often recorded as a supportive element for the men who are acting "upon" and changing the world. The caring role of women is deemed secondary to the primary, the "producing" role of men. This assumption has important implications for how both women and men view their work. Women often describe what they do as less useful or less important than what men do (Wilson, 1992). When women internalize such a devalued sense of their role, their self-esteem and self-worth necessarily suffer.

Conversely, when men internalize a valued sense of their role, their self-esteem and self-worth are enhanced. Unlike women, men have concentrated on the care and manipulation of the material world (Bennett, Casey, & Austin, 1996). Thus men can evaluate themselves on the basis of their achievements, which are usually external, concrete, and easily measured (Wilson, 1992). Accordingly, their identity and self-worth are often shaped by their successes.

By devaluing their role, women deny the importance and significance of their own experience and activities, not only for themselves as individuals but for other women as well. Women tend to evaluate themselves on the quantity and quality of caregiving that they provide their families. The problem is that caregiving is less visible, less easily measured, and less valued by society than are the activities pursued by men. Miller (1986) argues that the relegation of caregiving to a peripheral role creates a double bind for many women. Even though their caregiving activities are seen as secondary to the "real work" that men perform, if women do not fulfill these caregiving responsibilities they will be fiercely criticized. Yet women are still expected to feel as though they are fully valued in society.

Clearly, the implications of this situation for women in families with HIV disease are far-reaching. Particularly when they themselves are ill, women who are caregivers enter an arena full of demands, suppressed needs, and conflicting priorities (Wilson, 1992). It can be overwhelming. Such pressure makes women vulnerable and often destabilizes their lives.

Some families with HIV disease have special needs. These families include those of mothers who are IDUs and those of hemophiliacs. Both populations of families face unique issues and circumstances in the context of HIV disease.

Families of Mothers Who Are IDUs. Families headed by mothers who are IDUs must be discussed because of the close relationship between injection drug use and pediatric AIDS. An overwhelming majority of children under 13 with HIV/AIDS have parents who use injection drugs (Williams & O'Connor, 1995). Nevertheless, little is known about the family relationships of injection drug users (Stowe et al., 1995). However, the vast literature on social support suggests the importance of family relationships to a person's mental health and well-being.

Children are an important personal and emotional connection in the lives of women who use drugs. Motherhood provides these women with an opportunity for personal fulfillment because it is a role that is sanctioned by their own community of drug users as well as by the larger society. Women who use drugs are often deeply involved with their children and take pride in being good mothers, although how they define "good mothering" may vary. In their families lavishing gifts on the children may alternate with detachment. But a woman who takes care of her children, despite her drug habit, is respected in the drug subculture (Simpson & Williams, 1993). Rosenbaum (1981) found for women who use heroin that their role as a mother is their source of self-esteem. Moreover, their concern for a child's well-being is often a strong motivator for women to quit using drugs (Williams & O'Connor, 1995).

The demands of motherhood, however, often conflict with the demands of drug dependence, causing additional stress for female IDUs. Drug dependency creates a need for large sums of money for drugs, which can lead the addict into illegal activities that carry a risk of arrest and imprisonment. Sometimes small children are present when drugs are traded and used, placing the children in physical danger. Sometimes small children are simply left alone at home without adequate supervision. These situations often catch the attention of child protective services, and a drug-using mother might lose custody of her children. This consequence is devastating for these women particularly when their children are then placed with strangers.

A majority (at least 75%) of women who are current or former IDUs have children in state-sponsored foster care (Smith, 1996). These mothers are usually required to complete parenting classes in order to be granted visitation rights to see their children. These women often find themselves in a double bind in custody situations. To get custody of their children, they must undergo drug treatment. However, most drug treatment centers will not accept children if they regain custody. Even for those women who have completed drug treatment, regaining custody is not usually immediate. In addition, these women must grapple with other problems first, such as getting a job or finding a place to live. Finally, when infected women seek expanded custody over or visitation with their children in foster care, the parental right to bond with one's child is weighed against the state's right to insure that parents who use drugs are rehabilitated and are able to provide for their children (Ibid.).

Children who test positive for drugs at birth may be separated from their mothers. Drug-addicted and HIV-infected children are especially difficult to place in foster homes because of their special needs and also because foster parents prefer healthy children. When these children must remain in the hospital awaiting placement they are referred to as "boarder babies" (Ibid.). Some boarder babies were abandoned at birth in the hospitals (Boyd-Franklin & Boland, 1995). The cost of caring for boarder babies is high because of their special needs.

In reality, motherhood presents a paradox for women who use drugs. These women take pride in their child-rearing skills, but that pride is severely undermined by guilt when their addiction interferes with their ability to take care of their children (Ibid.). Thus women often feel the most pride in themselves as well as the most guilt in their activities as mothers.

Women who use drugs usually have few close relationships. Often, they are estranged from their families (Williams & O'Connor, 1995). Those women who do have contact with their families, however, tend to be closest to their mothers. Mothers are especially likely to maintain the relationship with their daughters when there are young children who require care. Addicted women frequently send their children to live with members of their extended family, often their mother or another older female relative (Ibid.). Sometimes relatives take in the children because they are being abused or have been abandoned.

Women who use drugs commonly experience feelings of multiple loss (Denenberg, 1995). Sometimes a partner or a child has died from HIV/AIDS. Or a woman may have lost custody of her children. These women often live in poor communities and may have experienced losses because of crime or drugs (Ibid.). To cope with loss, some women even become pregnant to replace those of their children who have died or who have been lost to foster care (Ibid.). The effect of their multiple losses is to leave these women with a sense of profound grief.

It is encouraging that some agencies have developed special, culturally sensitive programs that respond to the needs of infected drug-using mothers. For example, the Mom's Project in Boston seeks to help women recover from drug use and maintain family integrity (Ibid.). The project works with women to address their most pressing concerns, including housing, food, addiction, abuse, violence, and legal or custody issues. In Culver City, California, Prototypes' "WomensLink" offers a 12-Step Narcotics Anonymous Program in both English and Spanish (Sharon Hammer, personal communication, 1996). The program is developing a workshop on life skills that will deal with parenting and domestic violence, among other issues. (The program found that 95% of its participants had experienced domestic violence in the form of rape or battery.) Additional projects are being developed in response to needs identified by the program participants. Womens-Link also sponsors a legacy project in which infected women are helped to make a videotape or an audio cassette to leave to their children when they are gone. The use of legacy or memory projects in preserving family histories is discussed in the next chapter.

Hemophiliac Families. Families infected as a result of hemophilia do not constitute as large a group as families infected from injection drug use. However, it is an important group, and its special needs have not been given very much attention in the AIDS epidemic. Most of the attention paid to hemophiliac families has involved society's reaction to the school attendance of infected hemophiliac children. Two well-known cases – that of Ryan White in Indiana and of the three Ray brothers in Florida – were heavily covered in the media. As an age group, adult hemophiliacs have not received as much notice.

A high proportion of adult men with hemophilia are in the 40–49-year-old age group and are living in intact families (Greenblat, 1995). Hemophiliac families were dramatically affected by the changes in treatment for hemophilia in the 1970s. Before that time, men with the disease suffered from life-threatening, unpredictable bleeding episodes. These episodes required immediate medical attention, and thus hemophiliac men were frequently visitors to clinics and emergency rooms. In addition, hemophiliac men faced a shortened life expectancy and various psychological problems.

Children with hemophilia often had long absences from school and as a result, felt isolated and lonely (Wilkie, 1990). Overprotection of hemophiliac children has been a long-standing problem in many of their families (Wicklund & Jackson, 1992). A majority of affected children come from families in which hemophilia has been present for many generations (Ibid.). Girls in these families were often uncertain about their potential as carriers of this hereditary disease and concerned about having to explain their condition to a future partner.

Because of the complex issues associated with the disease, many hemophiliac families relied heavily on the medical care system as well as on support from the National Hemophilia Foundation.

The introduction of factor concentrate that could be administered at home had a tremendous impact on the lives of families affected by hemophilia. Because medical care could be managed at home, the number of clinic visits declined substantially. Psychosocial needs changed as well, as men with hemophilia could now look forward to a normal life expectancy. Affected families had less of a need for support groups to help them deal with the psychosocial issues of hemophilia. Many chapters of the National Hemophilia Foundation came to exist in name only. The "talking" approach favored as a way of coping by hemophiliac families in support groups also declined in use (Greenblat, 1995). Although hemophilia continued as a chronic illness in their lives, these families were able to function much more independently than before the concentrate was available.

Against this background, HIV entered the lives of hemophiliacs through tainted blood products in the 1980s. Suddenly, HIV was added to their hemophilia as another chronic, life-threatening illness. Because of their HIV disease, hemophiliacs once again were forced to be heavily dependent upon the medical system. Hemophiliacs held the health care system responsible for their HIV infection, and the atmosphere between them and hospital staff became highly charged (Tsiantis et al., 1995). The trust that hemophiliac families had once had in the medical system was seriously eroded (Wicklund & Jackson, 1992).

HIV disease also added greatly to the medical costs of hemophiliac families. Costs of factor concentrate for severe hemophiliacs range from $70,000 to $100,000 per year (Ibid.). With the additional medical costs of treating HIV, many hemophiliacs have exceeded the lifetime medical cap on their insurance policies.

A majority of hemophiliac children are infected with HIV perinatally, which means that both parents are infected (Ibid.). There are, however, children and adolescents who were infected directly from contaminated factor concentrate. In hemophiliac families, mothers may feel guilt about passing on a hereditary disease to their children. That many families blame the mother for her child's condition only adds to this guilt (Ibid.). Some mothers feel even more guilty because they were involved in administering infusions to their children at home and thus feel personally responsible for administering the contaminated factor concentrate (Wilkie, 1990).

Hemophilia combined with HIV has a complex ripple effect in families. Because hemophilia is a sex-linked hereditary disease, mothers often must deal not only with their sons' hemophilia and HIV but also with their fathers' and brothers'. Numerous families have more than one infected member. The mother in one such family had seven infected brothers as well as a son who was infected (Greenblat, 1995).

Hemophilia together with HIV in one family disturbs family equilibrium. Sometimes past conflicts are revived (Tsiantis et al., 1995). Unaffected children can feel neglected because of the attention given to their HIV-infected siblings, particularly because these same children, as hemophiliacs, had long been the focus of the family.

The threat of HIV infection comes at a critical time in the lives of hemophiliac adolescents. Because of the media coverage that surrounded the school attendance of Ryan White and the Ray brothers, young hemophiliacs often feel isolated in their schools. The factor concentrate introduced in the 1970s had allowed them to be involved in physical activities from which they had formerly been excluded because of the risk of injury (Kolata, 1988). Some factor concentrate was contaminated with HIV, however, and many adolescent hemophiliacs no longer trusted that the concentrate would be free of all virus. As a result, they restricted their use of it to control known or suspected bleeding (Wicklund & Jackson, 1992).

HIV-infected hemophiliac children and adolescents entering puberty must deal with complex sexuality issues. Infected adolescent boys often describe feelings of confusion about their sexuality. They are not sure whether to date at all and if they do date, whether to have sex (Kolata, 1988). They also express distress over whether to disclose their hemophilia and HIV seropositivity to their female partners (Miller et al., 1989). Adolescent hemophiliacs have expresseed concerns about not being able to form meaningful relationships and not being able to marry and have children because of their disease. These concerns appear to be greater and more real to them than fears about a premature death (Jones, 1995).

Adolescence is often filled with various types of risk taking, including sexual risk taking. Adolescents with hemophilia experience the same peer pressure, same sense of invulnerability and immortality, and same need to become independent of their parents as other adolescents (Olson, Huszti, & Chaffin, 1992). In addition, they may feel a need to prove that they are normal in spite of their inherited chronic illness. Sexual activity is often an important vehicle for them to establish their normality and masculinity, especially because they have been prevented from engaging in contact sports by the risk of personal injury (Ibid.). These youth may also use sex as a way to rebel against the limits imposed by their disease and by a childhood of parental overprotection (Ibid.). Additionally, sexual activity may be a way for them to gain acceptance from their peers.

Adolescent hemophiliacs have been particularly difficult to induce to change their sexual behavior (Valdiserri, 1989). Adolescent hemophiliacs tend to be similar to unaffected adolescent males in their tendency to engage in risk-taking behavior (Ibid.). Barriers to risk reduction by adolescent hemophiliacs include denial, decreased feelings of masculinity and sociability, and inheritance of a stigmatized chronic disease (Ibid.).

Infected hemophiliac adult men are often in denial or are willing to discuss their situations only one-to-one with medical professionals (Greenblat, 1995). Women, in contrast, have been more interested in participating in support groups. These groups often include not just the wives but also the mothers, sisters, daughters, and female friends of hemophiliac men (Ibid.). Women have also expressed more interest than have hemophiliac men in understanding the physical and psychological impact of HIV (Ibid.). They have made more of an attempt to encourage communication in the family about HIV.

It is clear from the preceding discussion that hemophiliac families have many unmet needs. One program, known as ENCOUNTERS, which began in 1989, attempts to assist women in developing family communication skills through the use of simulations and support groups (Ibid.). An indirect measure of the success of this approach is that hemophiliac men have become more interested in participating (Ibid.). As a result, a set of simulations for men was developed and is currently used in training and counseling by the National Hemophilia Foundation.

That one of the first programs to meet the needs of hemophiliac families concentrated on the responsibility of women to promote family communication and to ease family stress for men is significant. In a way, these goals may actually feed a mother's guilt by encouraging her to believe that the family's emotional adjustment is her responsibility.

Barriers to Care

Families face tremendous barriers in accessing care for members with HIV disease. Their isolation and invisibility are often the only factors that are common to women with HIV disease (Gorna, 1996). Women's experience thus differs from that of gay men, for whom the impact of HIV disease is a communal experience. AIDS affects the pre-existing gay communities. Thus what makes AIDS so tragic for gay men is also what gives them their cultural identity and the possibility of peer support (Ibid.). Of course, these circumstances do not in any way lessen the tragedy felt by the gay community. In contrast, infected women do not have this sense of community when they meet other women with HIV disease. Often all they share is the virus itself.

An HIV/AIDS diagnosis has a different impact for a woman than it does for a gay man. Gay men who are diagnosed often know other gay men who are also seropositive. Similarly, men with hemophilia who receive an HIV/AIDS diagnosis may know other hemophiliacs with this disease. These men also have links through their preexisting relationship with the health care system because of their hemophilia. Women do not share such preexisting links or connectedness (Ibid.). Their social networks are more dispersed.

The male model upon which support services are based causes barriers for women seeking care. Some of these involve practical constraints. Women may be unable to take advantage of services because they have transportation or child care problems. In addition, many women do not like to attend support group meetings that are held in the evening because they fear being out after dark.

Most AIDS agencies use support groups. However, not all women find comfort in these groups. Often racial, ethnic, and class differences keep poor women from participating in available services (Springer, 1992). Women of different socioeconomic backgrounds may get varying degrees of comfort in group-therapy settings. Compared with middle-class women, poor women are not always able to "talk it out" endlessly and may not find much relief in this therapeutic approach (Gross, 1987).

Some families with HIV disease have sought help from organizations that provide services and support for families coping with other chronic diseases but have not always found these agencies receptive to their particular needs (Baker, 1992). These agencies are sometimes "disease specific" and will not extend themselves to help families with HIV/AIDS.

Families dealing with HIV/AIDS often keep it a secret that remains within the family because of the social stigma surrounding the disease. Mothers, in particular, are concerned about confidentiality because they fear the impact of AIDS stigmatization on their children's well-being (Gorna, 1996). Protecting a secret about HIV/AIDS within the family takes a psychological toll. Negative experiences that follow disclosure of HIV disease may lead families to become excessively secretive and mistrustful of the few community supports available to them (Simpson & Williams, 1993). As happens with other secrets, families may become dysfunctional when they are organized around protecting the secret (Baker, 1992). When asked about their reactions to having a brother or sister with HIV disease, siblings reported that either they did not tell anyone at all or they told only those who they believed would understand (Nehring, Malm, & Harris, 1993). In some instances, families have lied to others outside the home by attributing a member's illness to a disease other than HIV/AIDS (Andiman, 1995).

The medical needs of women and their children may require that they make frequent visits to various agencies. In addition, a family with HIV disease may have to apply for services at many different agencies. One study found that care can involve as many as 12 to 16 different agencies (Cohen & Kelly, 1995). Because HIV-infected children require so many medical, mental health, and social services, the task of coordinating their care is complex. A child or family may have as many as 12 case managers within different clinics and agencies (Boyd-Franklin & Boland, 1995). Care becomes especially fragmented when women have both younger and older children because the older children cannot be seen in pediatric clinics (Sunderland & Holman, 1995). This is why it is essential that care be family centered. Also patient satisfaction and treatment adherence are more likely to be achieved through coordinated care.

Family-centered care is comprehensive, coordinated, continuous, and accessible (Cohen & Kelly, 1995). In contrast, pediatric and maternal health care systems are rarely coordinated (Patton, 1994), and mothers are thus forced to choose between two poorly coordinated systems. It is especially important that appointments for women and their children be linked (Kurth, 1993). Family-centered care involves the idea that the mother's needs and the child's needs are not in conflict (Ibid.). Indeed, the HIV/AIDS services that are most successful in reaching women are those based on the premise that the women are best engaged when their concerns about their children are addressed (Sunderland & Holman, 1993). For example, some infectious disease programs have a gynecologist available to mothers who bring their children to pediatric clinics (Rodriguez-Trias & Marte, 1995). These programs recognize that many women put their children's needs first and are more likely to go to a pediatric clinic than to a clinic that treats women.

A few demonstration models of multiservice clinics have been created (Ibid.). These comprehensive clinics offer one-stop health care to women and children by providing a range of social services. These include drug treatment, legal advice, and mental health care. The first comprehensive women-centered HIV clinic, the Women's and Children Project at Cook County Hospital in Chicago, was created in 1988 in direct response to the unmet needs of HIV-infected women (Ibid.). It began as a small service that offered peer-support groups and medical care to drug-addicted HIV-infected women. It evolved into a comprehensive, women-centered, program. Many of its services were developed in response to the needs articulated by the women themselves (Ibid.). Thus one service it provides is to be an advocate for its clients with the city's child welfare department. This comprehensive women-centered program has proven to be a successful model, one worthy of replication.

As stated earlier, the type of care needed by women and children is different from that needed by men. Women often require transportation, day care, or on-site child care services. Continuity of care means that the delivery of services is planned in such a way that women are able to care both for themselves and for their families (Holzemer, Rothenberg, & Fish, 1995).

Home care is also important because of its potential for keeping women and children together as a family. Services aimed at keeping the family intact may reduce the need for foster care and group housing (Ibid.). Such services include drug treatment, shelters, respite services, homemaking services, day care, and parenting classes. Respite care is especially critical for reducing the stress and fatigue of the caregiver. Under this arrangement, the family identifies a relative, friend, or neighbor who is paid to provide services to relieve the primary caregiver of relentless caregiving demands (Simpson & Williams, 1993). Respite care may allow a child to remain at home nd avoid expensive hospitalizations, particularly stays in the hospital that are socially driven rather than medically necessary (Ibid.). In addition, respite care has the potential to help a family avoid having children placed in foster care, which is expensive and psychologically disruptive.

Kinship foster families are often in greater need of respite care because they have no one to rely on for assistance. Grandmothers, particularly, need respites because of their age and their own health status (Baker, 1992). Respite care is among the most valuable and, unfortunately, least available support services (Brown, 1991).

Although women are usually the primary caregivers in families with HIV, men sometimes serve as primary or secondary caregivers (Mellins et al., 1996). Clearly, services that support female caregivers are needed, but these same services must be available to men who play significant caregiving roles in families with HIV. As will be discussed in Chapter 7, policies that penalize poor families when fathers are present in the household are detrimental to the welfare of these families.

Young survivors placed in alternative living situations have special needs. Children's social service organizations have therefore found it necessary to offer special support, training, and financial incentives to recruit foster families for children with HIV/AIDS (Boland, Czarniecki, & Haiken, 1992). One example is Baby Moms, a project in San Francisco serving HIV-infected children. To be eligible, foster parents must not themselves have children under 6 and are limited to caring for 2 children from the Baby Moms project. The foster parent allows the natural parent to visit the child and work toward family reunification. The project pays high reimbursement rates, between $1,300 and $1,800, and $350 for respite care in order to attract providers. The program also provides foster parents with monthly training, a support network of caregivers, and 50 hours of paid respite care (Ibid.). Like Chicago's Women's and Children Project, this project is also one worth emulating.

Some foster parents have tried to adopt HIV-infected children but have run into legal obstacles in doing so. Adoption can be a lengthy process lasting several years (Baker, 1992). But time is of the essence in adopting HIV-infected children, as illustrated by the family that got approval to adopt a child one day after the child had died (Ibid.).

Both kinship and other foster parents sometimes feel that they have been given responsibility without being given authority. These parents have a difficult time being the primary caretaker of a child, particularly an infected child, because they lack the legal standing to make decisions about the child's care (Baker, 1992). Although these parents bear the burden of the child's daily care, they have no power to make major decisions about the child's medical care. This is a critical issue in foster care situations because HIV-infected children often need emergency treatment (Boyd-Franklin & Boland, 1995). Among the decisions that foster care parents cannot legally make is that of "do not resuscitate." This decision and others must be made by the natural parent, if that parent is still alive, or by a children's social services agency (Boland, Czarniecki, & Haiken, 1992). When natural parents and children's social services are involved, differences of opinion regarding appropriate care can arise (Boyd-Franklin & Boland, 1995). Decisions about medication, participation in clinical trials, and prophylactic treatments all require the consent of several parties (Ibid.). This process can consume a great deal of time, especially if the natural parents are unavailable or disagree with medical recommendations.

An additional barrier to care for an infected child is that child custody laws may not correspond to the kinship family's vision of how its members are related (Wissow, Hutton, & McGraw, 1996). Children in many African American families are routinely raised by relatives other than their parents. However, the courts may interpret the law as giving noncustodial parents a stronger claim than the grandmother who has actually been raising the child (Ibid.).

In some families, no relative is able to assume caregiving responsibilities for the children of mothers with HIV/AIDS, putting increased pressure on the child welfare system to place the child in an alternative setting. If further disruption of children's lives is to be avoided, society must give more support to the foster care system, and family social services must demonstrate greater flexibility and creativity in meeting the complex needs of families with HIV disease.

HIV disease has changed the family in many ways. It has altered family size, roles, and relationships. HIV disease has also stretched the coping and caring skills of caregivers and has tested the endurance of many families. These families will need to be empowered to deal with the multiple challenges of HIV disease.

7

WOMEN, FAMILIES, AND HIV/AIDS

Five weeks ago I started with this 6-month study and it's showing great results. My viral load was 33,700 on the first tests, and today is showing 27,000. It's great news for me. Praise God.

I've been going through some grieving time. I have an appointment to legally sign guardianship with my sister. That really hit me hard. Today I had an appointment at 8 A.M. with Larry, the official from court. He came to investigate the family. He's one of the persons working on the legal guardianship or joint custody of my children. He stayed a couple of hours and asked to see my children's bedrooms, etc. I'm surprised of the details he went through. I guess it's just the normal thing to do. After all, it's my children's custody. Giving up my children, it's not that I'm giving them up at present but it reminds me. I have the feeling that I have been cheated because my children are so special to me – the ones that I hold on to.

– Leticia

I got to see my kids last week for the first time in 6 months. I got to spend 2 hours with them. My ex-husband is deteriorating real fast with this disease. He told the DCS worker that he wanted to put them in foster care and have them adopted out. She says that as soon as he dies, I will get my kids back with no strings attached.

– Denise

The man at Voc Rehab asked me to fill out this form. It was a crazy form. When I gave it back to him, he said that I hadn't filled it out right. So I read it again and said, "I know I'm not crazy. I think I followed the instructions." Then he looked at it again and said that I was right and that he was wrong.

I know I'm a drug user but that doesn't mean I'm crazy. Now I'm eligible for SSI only because of my HIV not because of my drug use.

– Louann

I've stopped using drugs; I've stopped drinking, and I've changed my whole way of thinking. You see, I'm not scared to die anymore. I understand my circumstances and realize that I could have died for any other reason. Many of my friends have died of overdose or gang fights, etc., and me, I'm still alive, living with HIV and dealing with it, in the most positive way I possibly can.

Death is something that happens to every living being. HIV is not death but a situation that I got myself into by my own actions. And now I am responsible to see that I can take care of myself today.

– Loretta

I go pick up the food I need. I go to the support groups for the families or for the fathers – single fathers. I go to five support groups in L.A. and Long Beach. There we find people with the same problem. I know that we are not alone. We demonstrate there that one can live being infected with HIV or sick with AIDS. We give the best we can give to the person who is ill with support and advice.

– Jose

I did not take my methadone today because the bus did not come. I started crying when I called the methadone clinic. I felt a little bad today.

I went to the doctor and he had good news for me. He said that I only have a little virus in me and I was so glad that I kept on shouting out that I am going to live a long time. I kept singing out loud.

– Eunice

But it's helped a lot to go to support groups and to talk about it. I think it's harder for those people who just kind of suck it in themselves and sit at home and wait for the worst to happen without letting anybody else know.

When a position came up, I started getting more involved – more involved time-wise – volunteering to do things. My life personally has just completely switched around. Now I work in the field which was something that I never saw myself doing. I try to help other parents. I'm out in the field. I help organize support groups. I have four different support groups. They're all Latino families, all mostly monolingual. They speak Spanish.

It's nice to see that people are coming out to look for help but at the same time, it's sad to find out that our groups keep growing and growing. Every month they grow and we add people to it. We lose people. Unfortunately we don't lose them because they're getting well. Some of our family members die but lately we've been growing more than losing which is good.

– Mariana

Since I found out, my life has been different. Thanks to my family's support which has always been there. My siblings give me a lot of support. My parents – They have come to see me.

Now the more I see, it is something wonderful what the doctors can do. Well, I am very happy. Everything is normal and good. My parents and my family are very happy because they have seen that I have a great desire to live and I want to continue taking my medicines and doing everything the doctors tell me because I want to live.

I don't want to be left behind and it is what I wish for everyone, to continue ahead, to continue to follow their treatment, not to give in to the illness because it is sad and painful for those, for those that leave us and sad for the children because they suffer more than we do. And what we wouldn't give so that they could be better. The support I receive from my siblings and my parents is something that motivates me to go forward and also other people in the hospital and other places that I have met in my groups.

– Juana

AIDS SERVICE DELIVERY

The large number of women involved in caregiving as professionals demonstrates women's strong commitment to this type of work. If anything, women tend to be overrepresented in professional caregiving roles (Baines, Evans, & Neysmith, 1991; Fraser & Jones, 1995). Seventy percent of social workers are women (Baines, 1991). They are usually concentrated in the lower-paying direct service jobs, whereas men dominate in the more lucrative leadership positions (Ibid.).

In medical settings, women comprise most nurses (97%) as well as a significant proportion of nurses aides, home health care workers, and medical clerical staff. An increasing number of physicians are also women (Durham & Douard, 1993; Stoller, 1995). In addition, women are well represented in the public health field, particularly in health education. Although women comprise a majority of professional care-givers, there has been scant research on the roles that these women have played in the HIV/AIDS epidemic, and little is known about the contribution of women working as caregivers in the community (Squire, 1993). A few personal accounts and how-to books were written fairly early in the epidemic (e.g. Lester, 1989; Moffat, 1987; Peabody, 1987), but most early information on professional caregivers, particu-larly nurses, involved disease-transmission issues (Durham & Douard, 1993). Most later work on HIV/AIDS caregiving focused on issues of burnout (Gillman, 1996). From the beginning of the epidemic, nurses have played a central role in AIDS caregiving.

Nurses. Because HIV/AIDS is a disease with no cure, it involves caring and is thus appropriately a nursing disease (Fox, Aiken, & Messi-komer, 1991). Although nurses have been providing care to HIV/AIDS patients since the beginning of the epidemic, the media has paid little attention to them (Ibid.). Whereas AIDS is a high profile disease, nurses have been given a low profile. Many physicians have had a lot of media exposure throughout the epidemic. They have often been interviewed about the AIDS crisis and about patient care issues. Nurses, despite being in the trenches of medical service delivery, have rarely been inter-viewed (Ibid.). They have been relatively invisible despite their dedica-tion (Ibid.; Fraser & Jones, 1995).

The crisis of HIV disease affects all aspects of the health care system. Its most direct impact is felt by nurses, however, because nurses pro-vide personal care for people with the disease (McGarrahan, 1994). The shifts of nurses are spent entirely on patient care (College of Pub-lic and Community Service and Multicultural AIDS Coalition, 1992). Nurses are the most constant providers of continual care to patients.

The gap in communication between people and science is bridged by nurses who explain medicine to patients and patients to other med-ical practitioners. In this sense, nurses often find themselves in the tra-ditional female role of being in the middle (Fraser & Jones, 1995). The nurse's role has always been one of translating the rigors of a treatment regimen to a patient so that the regimen will succeed and the patient will get well. New treatments with combination therapies involve complex regimens and make the nurse's role in HIV/AIDS care all the more critical.

The physical complications of HIV disease tend to be multiple, concurrent, unpredictable, and often confusing. There is a great deal of ambiguity and uncertainty in providing care to persons with HIV disease. In addition to opportunistic infections, these persons suffer from secondary cancers, changing nutritional deficits, various motor weaknesses, sensory and perceptual deficits, and quick alterations in fluid volumes (Callahan & Powell, 1994). These symptoms require continual monitoring and constant decision making about physical care.

HIV/AIDS puts tremendous responsibility on nurses because of their patients' potential multisystem failures and the resultant heavy use of intensive care. Patients are often in intense pain, and neurological problems may make them anxious, angry, and depressed. They also may be demanding, noncompliant, and difficult to care for. An additional factor adding to the burden of nurses caring for persons with HIV/AIDS is that these persons are often placed in floors that are already among the busiest in hospitals, specifically, the general medical and surgical units (Ibid.).

In addition to the patients' demands on nurses, families with HIV disease require a great deal of nursing care. Family dramas are sometimes played out in hospital rooms. As a result, nurses become keepers of family secrets (Fraser & Jones, 1995). Nurses are sometimes confidantes in a patient's suicide plan. A nurse is also often the person who spends the final hours with a patient or who finds a patient dead. In addition, nurses may serve as surrogate family for patients who have been abandoned (College of Public and Community Service and Multicultural AIDS Coalition, 1992). Some patients would die alone were it not for the presence of nurses.

The role of nurse draws on traditional nurturing and service models (Stoller, 1995). Although nurses can be involved in decision making, they often must defer to physicians and administrators. They have little authority and are not involved in budgetary or planning decisions (Fraser & Jones, 1995). In this sense, they have been called "handmaidens" (Callahan & Powell, 1994; Fraser & Jones, 1995).

Although women have taken the central role as nurses in mainstream health care delivery, HIV/AIDS units have often been staffed primarily with men (Bennett, Casey, & Austin, 1996). In one study, gender and sexual preference were seen by health care providers as the determinants of a nurse's right and ability to work in the HIV/AIDS field (Ibid.). As nurses, gay men had created a working environment accepting of gays, one that gay nurses had not experienced before. As a result, the entry of heterosexual women into HIV/AIDS nursing may have been perceived by gay nurses as a threat to their working environment. Thus, in some work settings, tension may exist.

Today, many nurses have a raised feminist consciousness as a result of the women's movement (Fox, Aiken, & Messikomer, 1991). In fact, the profession has attracted women committed to fighting for social justice and equality (Fraser & Jones, 1995). These women have been active in bringing about change to the nursing profession. The recent addition of more men to the nursing profession has also helped change the concept of nursing as "women's work." However, nurses still encounter a male hierarchy in their profession that has not changed because of the HIV/AIDS epidemic (Baines, 1991).

Volunteer Caregiving

The definition of AIDS volunteerism is not always clear because much unpaid work on behalf of persons with HIV disease takes place in the context of kinship or other personal relationships (Jonson & Stryker, 1993). Volunteers provide people with HIV/AIDS ongoing assistance and sustained support by offering potentially costly help without obligation. They do work that others are unable or unwilling to do. Although volunteers comprise an important part of AIDS caregiving, there has been little research on their contribution (Omoto & Synder, 1995). Nor is there much information on the money saved by using volunteers (Jonson & Stryker, 1993).

Most of the attention to social support from volunteer caregiving has been on gay men. In the early years of the epidemic, the most common situations involved gay men (often partners) caring for other gay men (e.g., McCann & Wadsworth, 1994; Monette, 1988; Omoto & Crain, 1994; Shelby, 1992, 1995; Williams, 1988).

Women also comprise an important sector of volunteer caregivers. White, middle-class, educated heterosexual women make up the majority of volunteers in AIDS service organizations (Maslanka, 1993;

Squire, 1993). These women have a history of caregiving that started long before the AIDS epidemic (Cf. Baines, 1991).

The profile of the AIDS volunteer has changed over the years. Women initially became involved in the AIDS epidemic because they were the mothers, sisters, or friends of gay men. Many women continue to be involved in this way. However, a change has occurred in that infected women themselves are now involved as volunteers. And many of these women have children.

Lesbian women have also made a considerable contribution to voluntary caregiving, particularly in the care of gay men. Much of this caregiving activity grew out of the gay rights movement in the 1970s. Many AIDS service agencies would not exist today had it not been for the organizing done by gay men and lesbians during that decade (Altman, 1994). Thus the political organization was already in place when the epidemic occurred.

Lesbians and gay men united in fighting the AIDS crisis. However, there has been some tension in the alliance between gay men and lesbians over women's issues. Both lesbians and straight women have provided support and nurturing to gay men during the AIDS crisis (Stoller, 1995). Yet these women have not always found gay men's support to be reciprocal. They have observed an absence of gay men volunteering to help in women's agencies such as women's shelters or rape crisis centers (Burkett, 1995). In addition, gay men's lack of interest in and concern about women's health problems (such as breast cancer) have been noted. This issue has created a difficult test of loyalties for some lesbians involved in AIDS caregiving who have been criticized for tending to the needs of gay men rather than devoting their energies to women's causes (Gorna, 1996). There is also the feeling among some women that the gay community is already well resourced because of its early and sustained response to the epidemic. As a result, some women have chosen to work in smaller community-based organizations more oriented toward women (Squire, 1993).

Despite progress, society still has some way to go in recognizing women's contribution to AIDS service delivery. Women's nurturing skills have been recognized by many AIDS service organizations; however, their organizational skills have received much less acknowledgment (Stoller, 1995). Although women occupy leadership positions at some agencies, their contributions are underreported and underrated.

Women have encountered a "glass ceiling" in the AIDS industry (Gorna, 1996), and as a result, their AIDS work often lacks visibility.

As health care systems become overwhelmed with HIV/AIDS cases, the burden of care is shifted to the community. In reality, the term "community" is a euphemism for the unremunerated (and often unrecognized) care provided by women – mostly by mothers (Sherr, 1995). The roles of female caregivers become subsumed under the rubric of "community care" and the sacrifices made by these women are still not recognized. For example, needs assessment surveys that examine utilization and financing of services usually disregard the informal care provided by women (Schiller, 1993). There is profound silence on the subject of women's informal caregiving (Ibid.).

This silence on women's informal caregiving is reflected in the absence of coverage given to it at international AIDS conferences. The Ninth International Conference on AIDS held in Berlin in 1993 featured 329 abstracts on professional caregivers (Ankrah, Schwartz, & Miller, 1996). Topics included infection risks, burnout, stress, and support needs, among others. But there was only one abstract on informal caregivers. As discussed in Chapter 4, the class and racial dimensions of informal caregiving are especially poignant in that a disproportionate amount of AIDS care falls on poor minority women, whose contribution is not recognized.

Barriers in Service Delivery

The oldest community-based AIDS support service organizations, such as the Gay Men's Health Crisis and AIDS Project Los Angeles, were established by and for gay men (Baker, 1992). These organizations grew out of gay men's health concerns and focused mainly on white single men. Typically, caregivers reflect the same demographic characteristics as client populations. Thus some of these organizations may feel ambivalent about helping members of the heterosexual community that traditionally rejected them (Ibid.). More recently, however, some of these groups have tried to reach out to women and children, although the services they provide to families are often inadequate (Ibid.).

Whether professionals or volunteers, caregivers have been aiding a client population that has changed over time. Initially, clients were generally white, middle-class gay men (Fraser & Jones, 1995). However, the HIV/AIDS client population has grown to include poor, minority families as well. As a result, caregivers are increasingly affected by poverty associated with HIV disease (Ibid.). Their poor and minority clients are among the most alienated and compromised by the system's inequities and inefficiencies (Ibid.). Caregivers must respond sensitively to the complex needs of this population. Caregivers have had to address differences in drug use history, socioeconomic status, and race between themselves and their clients (Squire, 1993). Although these differences are relevant to service delivery, little research has been conducted on them (Ibid.). There is also an increasing need for organizations to reflect the demographics of their client population.

Through AIDS activism, gay men created new health care alternatives for themselves. However, the resources that poor women bring to living with HIV disease are strikingly different (Ward, 1993). The strongest source of support for HIV-infected poor women is from feminists who had organized around reproductive rights and economic empowerment before the advent of AIDS. Yet infected women are often alienated by the feminist model for women's groups (Gorna, 1996).

As clients, women have more complex socioeconomic, legal, and medical issues than gay men (Jonson & Stryker, 1993). Programs too often see their clients as isolated individuals rather than as persons upon whom others are dependent (Rubin, 1996), which sometimes increases the burdens on those very persons the programs are trying to help. Doubts have been expressed that organizations will be able to meet the complex needs of an increasingly diverse AIDS population (Ibid.). At issue is whether the needs of this population can be addressed by these groups in ways that replicate the services of the more affluent and organized gay community from which the volunteer movement arose.

An evaluation of the Gay Men's Health Crisis found that its female clients were satisfied with services they received and believed that these services were culturally sensitive (Schaffzin, 1997). Nevertheless, female clients were less integrated within the organization's client community. They used fewer services and fewer hours of service than their gay male counterparts. However, the evaluation acknowledged the difficulty of prioritizing women's needs because of the urgent health needs of men who have sex with men and of substance-abusing men along with the agency's limited resources and close identification with the gay male community (Ibid.).

One study of the services provided by the AIDS Action Committee, an agency in Massachusetts, evaluated differences by gender in the needs expressed by clients (as cited in Patton, 1994). Women asked for concrete services to help them with finances, housing, and child care. Men asked for money and more emotional support. In particular, men who did not have families expressed a need for emotional support and domestic assistance. In contrast, women needed less personal support but more support so that they could provide traditional domestic and maternal services. In response, the agency designed a "lay caregiver" project to address the needs of caregivers by supporting family members other than just the infected member. More projects for caregivers modeled after this one are critically needed.

Another survey comparing infected women to infected men found that the experience of living with HIV/AIDS was different for the women (Crystal & Sambamoorthi, 1996). Although support groups were a major source of help for the men, they were not for the women. The women and men were equally interested in participating in support groups, but the women had less access to groups appropriate to their needs and concerns. It appears that women could benefit from social support networks if they had access to them.

It also appears that caregivers may be poorly informed about the needs of infected women. A study of how student nurses perceived these needs found that a majority considered the needs of infected women to be no different than those of infected men (Bennett, Casey, & Austin, 1996). Such perceptions could, of course, affect the type of care they deliver to infected women.

In a survey of providers of HIV/AIDS services to youth in Los Angeles and their recipients, societal denial and indifference were reported to undermine the ability of providers and clients alike to confront AIDS-related issues (Division of Adolescent Medicine, 1996). Specifically, both groups commented on the community's hushed and moralistic responses to the topics of adolescent sexuality and HIV/AIDS. Sexism, racism, and homophobia were also described as barriers to the delivery and reception of HIV/AIDS prevention services to youth.

Fragmentation of health services affects the health of both women and men. HIV/AIDS service providers have failed to forge links with agencies that promote reproductive health as well as with those that offer STD services (Chavkin, 1995). It has been suggested that to improve women's health, reproductive health services and STD services be integrated (Fox et al., 1995). This integration would also be a way to include men in health services, particularly family planning. As discussed in Chapters 2 and 5, there is a serious need to address the marginalization of men in health services. The inclusion of men must start early in their lives.

As stated in the last chapter, a real need exists for comprehensive programs to assist families with HIV disease. Professional caregivers must often negotiate a wide array of services for their clients, and some caregivers observe their clients falling through the cracks because of the fragmentation in services (Land, 1996). Programs that focus only on HIV have little relevance to people living in communities pervaded by poverty, unemployment, violence, alcohol and drug use, unsafe sex, elevated school dropout rates, and high rates of unplanned pregnancies (Guinan & Leviton, 1995). It is especially important to forge connections between HIV services and drug treatment because it is drug use that is driving the heterosexual epidemic (Chavkin, 1995). Ending the fragmentation of health services must be a goal in formulating new AIDS prevention and service delivery strategies.

FAMILY POLICY
Caregiving and Provider Roles

Gender inequality must be addressed as a central issue affecting families in the formulation of a rational policy on HIV/AIDS. This policy must recognize that gender inequality takes many forms. It is found in women's occupational segregation in the labor force, in the generally unequal division of labor in homes, in patterns of domestic violence, and in the lack of provisions for child care (Currie & Skolnick, 1997). HIV disease is deeply rooted in these structural conditions affecting families.

Official disregard for the family and, particularly, for the caregiver role of HIV-infected and -affected women will continue to have social costs unless reversed (Rodriguez-Trias & Marte, 1995). For many families, HIV disease initiates a financial and social slide downward. Staff in clinics or social service agencies watch clients lose their jobs and income because of frequent medical appointments and HIV-induced crises (Ibid.). Indeed, many service providers at the 1997 National Conference on Women and HIV describe having had this experience.

The government has contributed to poor people's risk for HIV through changes in antipoverty programs that affect health and well-being (Connors, 1996). Federal cuts in Medicaid, the nation's health care program for the poor, is one example of how the government has ignored the link between poverty and risk of HIV disease (Ibid.).

Welfare is another area in which government policy has had an impact on HIV risk factors. Massive welfare reform legislation in 1996 put a work requirement on recipients as well as a lifetime cap on benefits (Rivera, 1996). Yet welfare reform as it now exists does not have any provision for job training or any assurance of a job (Smith, Johnson, & O'Reilly, 1997). The idea that welfare undermines the family is at the center of the efforts to reform the system (Currie & Skolnick, 1997). But as Currie and Skolnick argue, the welfare state in the United States is among the least developed of any advanced society, and it is this underdevelopment that is responsible for the problems of many poor families (Ibid.).

Changes in welfare eligibility requirements not only have devastating consequences for poor families but also continue to promote the idea that poverty is an individual matter. In fact, the 1996 legislation is known as the Personal Responsibility and Work Opportunity Act of 1996. The plight of the poor is seen as their own fault, the result of poor personal choices (Connors, 1996). Thus poverty and HIV disease share in that both are seen as matters of personal responsibility.

The ideology of social irresponsibility is rooted in the belief that individual families should handle their own problems with a minimum of outside help (Currie & Skolnick, 1997). This ideology is apparent in the lack of available social supports (such as child care programs) to help people cope with shifts in the labor market or in their family's composition.

Historically, minority women have had to rely on public assistance because the fathers of their children were unemployed or underemployed and unable to support them. Such assistance was based on the agreement that these fathers could not live with their families, an agreement that has worked to the serious detriment of the urban nuclear family (Simpson & Williams, 1993). This welfare policy, combined with the absence of minority men because of drug use, incarceration, violence, homicide, and AIDS, has had the effect of intensifying the matriarchal presence in urban settings (Ibid.). Such a matriarchal system characterizes caregiving in urban minority AIDS populations.

Recent cuts in prenatal care will have a devastating impact on women at risk for HIV (Rodriguez-Trias, 1997). These cuts will affect immigrant women particularly (Ibid.). With the denial of prenatal care a host of other services are also denied women at risk. For example, as discussed in Chapter 2, most women get tested for HIV during prenatal care so the lack of access to prenatal care can be a barrier to the early detection and treatment of HIV in women. It also has consequences for HIV prevention in controlling future transmission. Women have used HIV services when these services are available to them. They have had high acceptance rates when testing and AZT therapy have been offered (Rogers, 1997). The cuts in prenatal care then have serious implications for delivery of these services as well.

Still, there is a strange irony in the relationship between poverty and HIV disease. HIV disease has given the infected poor access to services that they might not otherwise receive (Wissow, Hutton, & McGraw, 1996). This irony speaks to the level of poor people's disenfranchisement. In these times of serious budgetary cutbacks, every last safety net is being pulled out from under the poor suffering from HIV disease. This elimination of the safety nets was confirmed at the 1997 National Conference on Women and HIV. Many of the service providers at that conference stated that those persons with HIV disease that they have assisted over the years have nevertheless continued to grow poorer, and more desperate.

Similar comments have been made by service providers from the CARE Program and Project AHEAD, two community-based organizations serving families with HIV disease in Long Beach, California. Many of their clients had underlying problems prior to their HIV diagnosis. These problems persist, despite marked improvement in the clients' health, often attributable to new combination therapies. Service providers at these agencies describe some clients as suffering from dual diagnoses – drug and/or alcohol addiction and mental illness. Many clients are homeless. Thus, although clients are in better physical health, their original problems have not in any sense gone away and often seem insurmountable. These clients' lives are not stable, and their burdens continue to be heavy ones.

Drug Policy. In the criminal justice system, mandatory minimum sentences for drug-related charges target poor urban communities almost exclusively. One out of three young African American men are involved with the justice system in some way – awaiting trial, in prison, or on probation (Connors, 1996). This has important implications for the family: Children must live without their fathers, and fewer families are stable. Society also pays a high price in the cost of incarcerating these men and supporting their families. Drug policies that work to the detriment of those men who are providers must be reversed.

Another aspect of drug policy, the criminalization of drug abuse during pregnancy, also creates a barrier to treatment. Women who use drugs and who are HIV infected or at risk of infection may not seek medical treatment for fear that they will be convicted as criminals or that they will lose their children (Alemán et al., 1995). Twenty-four states have prosecuted women for ingesting drugs while they were pregnant and, if their child died, for murder (Connors, 1996). The majority of women who were prosecuted were poor and African American, and the number of these prosecutions tripled from 1990 to 1992 (Ibid.). Many women in recovery following drug treatment spend years trying to regain custody of their children and reunite their families.

Many HIV-infected drug-dependent persons are treated punitively by social service agencies that criminalize their behaviors rather than provide them with the social supports that would allow them to restore their families (Rodriguez-Trias & Marte, 1995). An example of society's punitive response to drug use is the federal legislation on Social Security Income (SSI) eligibility.

Since 1974, drug- and alcohol-addicted persons had been eligible for SSI based on a disability status. In 1994, however, the original legislation was reformed. Under this reformed legislation, drug- and alcohol-addicted persons could not receive benefits unless they were in a treatment program, and the amount of time these persons could receive benefits was limited to 36 months (Ellis, 1996). The most recent legislation on SSI, in 1997, was approved separately from the massive welfare reform package that also took effect in 1997. It was enacted in response to a philosophical debate about addiction. The concern was that addicted persons on SSI would use the money to support their addiction. This economic concern was coupled with another that involved the skyrocketing costs of the SSI program itself (Ibid.).

The law that took effect in 1997 disqualified anyone from receiving SSI if the claim was based solely on an addiction (Ellis, 1996). Individuals receiving SSI had been given until the end of 1996 either to file an appeal requesting a continuation of their benefits based on a disability other than an addiction or to find work. Of course, drug users quite often have more than one disabling condition. Thus users with HIV who had claimed a disability based on their addiction could reapply for benefits based on their HIV status. Some HIV-infected drug users had originally been approved for SSI based on their HIV status, and for them benefits continued. The vignette by Louann is a telling illustration of the results of this contradiction in policy.

Also under the new legislation, drug users who do not have other disabling conditions will lose not only their SSI income but also their medical insurance and access to drug treatment. There is a concern that these changes will result in an increase in crime and a higher rate of sexually transmitted diseases, including AIDS (Ibid.).

Clearly, this law further disenfranchises the addicted poor, who are already politically marginal. It targets those persons who are the most dysfunctional and socially disruptive and leaves them with fewer resources.

There have been additional cuts in drug treatment funding separate from those caused by changes in SSI. As a result of these cuts, we can expect to see more cases of HIV among drug users, particularly because these cuts are combined with a refusal to support needle-exchange programs (Brown, 1997). To control the HIV/AIDS epidemic, policy should be aimed at enabling and empowering drug users to reduce their risk for HIV disease rather than prohibiting and penalizing their behaviors.

Children and Youth

Agencies providing services to children and youth have been overwhelmed by the volume and complexity of family issues surrounding HIV disease. The vignettes provided by Leticia, Denise, and Louann illustrate this complexity. In Newark, New Jersey, where there are high rates of perinatal infection, over 50% of children treated for HIV disease become involved with the child welfare system at some point (Wissow, Hutton, & McGraw, 1996).

The sweeping changes made in the massive overhaul of the welfare system effective in 1997 also affect skip-generation grandparents. Grandparents may come under the same work requirement as other adults under the new policy (Rivera, 1996). That this work requirement may discourage some grandparents from assuming responsibility for their grandchildren is a concern. Also, under the new law, states could actually force grandparents to obtain legal custody of the children in their care as a condition for welfare assistance (Ibid.).

The child welfare system has historically had difficulty finding sufficient permanent placements for minority children (Gruendel & Anderson, 1995). Because a majority of HIV-infected and -affected children are minority children, their growing numbers further contribute to this problem. Older children from any group are also difficult to place in permanent foster homes (Levine, 1995).

An additional problem is to find permanent placements for all of the siblings in a family. Siblings are sometimes separated because it is not possible to place all of them with relatives or with one foster family. This is a particular problem in placing children from large families. Some siblings even end up in different states (Smith, 1996). Because orphaned children are often grieving about their parents, subsequent separation from their siblings only compounds their feelings of loss. Some children who are difficult to place because of their special needs never find permanent foster homes and simply emancipate, or "age-out," at age 18.

In most families, grandparents and aunts usually become the new caregivers for orphaned children (Taylor-Brown, 1998). But it is easy for these children to fall through the cracks. In situations in which parents have designated guardians, little information on the actual outcomes for orphaned children may exist. The only known follow-up study found that most of the families had more than one child and that in over half of these families the siblings were separated after their parents' death. Of 15 families that had made permanency plans, none of the children was still with the designated caregiver after one year (as cited in Taylor-Brown, 1998).

Child welfare agencies sometimes become involved with families because of concerns about a child's neglect while parents are still living but in failing health. Although children's protective services are designed to help children and families in need, some of these families may see these agencies as punitive and intrusive. There is a gray area in child welfare law involving the difference between parents guilty of criminal neglect of a child and parents stretched to the limits of their caregiving capabilities (Wissow, Hutton, & McGraw, 1996). Medical and other social services usually cannot meet all the needs of families with HIV disease. In many communities, children's protective services have priority access to these resources (Ibid.). However, some families may be unwilling to accept these services because of an agency's perceived intrusiveness.

Sometimes a mother may not want to relinquish custody of her child. In most states, assigning guardianship requires that the parent give up custody (Smith, 1996). The exceptions here would be those states that have standby guardianship provisions. For some HIV-infected mothers, their maintaining custody represents the hope that at some future time they again will be able to care for their child (Nehring, Malm, & Hein, 1993).

That the child welfare system does not have provisions for parents to make legally binding choices about guardianship for their children is a major inadequacy. Ten states, including New York, Florida, and California, have enacted standby guardianship laws, although their provisions vary (McGovern, 1997). These laws allow parents while they are still competent to make placement decisions and even to initiate a shift in custody prior to their death (Ibid.). Unlike traditional guardianship, these laws do not require the parent to relinquish custody of the child until that parent is unable to provide care. Standby guardianship allows the parent to offer insights about the best care plan for the child. But because most states do not have standby guardianship provisions, their family courts intervene routinely after a parent's death and reassign guardianship (Wissow, Hutton, & McGraw, 1996). These cases are decided on custody law or as a result of a hearing involving the parties contending.

In 1988, a number of states made an effort to keep children together in families by passing legislation that favored family preservation over foster care placement. However, conservatives who consider HIV-infected women to be unfit mothers are trying to change these laws (McGovern, 1997). This effort has made it especially difficult for HIV-infected mothers to get their children back from foster care. The number of child neglect issues involving infected mothers may have risen because of the current direction toward mandatory testing of pregnant women and newborns in many states (Ibid.).

Some AIDS orphans will ultimately be placed in foster care, but foster care systems are plagued by systemic problems such as inadequate funding; burgeoning, complex caseloads; and an insufficient number of placement alternatives appropriate to a child's needs (Geballe, 1995). Many children in foster care simply drift from one temporary placement to another until they age out of the system. Children who are at most risk of being orphaned by AIDS are also at risk for "foster care drift" (Ibid.). This risk is increased once the children become orphans because they have no parents to challenge the state's decisions. Such children are at risk of becoming orphans in the legal system as well.

The child welfare system is not equipped to handle the complexity of HIV-related family issues (Wissow, Hutton, & McGraw, 1996). Courts lack the resources to provide legal representation to children and surviving family members. Thus far, no public policy has addressed the needs of AIDS orphans (Rodriguez-Trias & Marte, 1995).

In most states, youth are emancipated from foster care at age 18, but many actually have no place to go. Seventy-five percent do not have high school diplomas, and 60% have no job experience at all (Nazario, 1993). As a result, many become homeless. Nationally, 25% of youth emancipated from foster care end up living on the street, and more than 25% of youth at homeless shelters arrive directly from foster care (Nazario, 1993).

When foster care is no longer able to accommodate HIV-infected and affected children, other types of institutional care will have to be found. Young survivors placed in these settings will endure the emotional impact of having to deal with their loss while living in an institutional setting. The harder-to-place youth, such as older AIDS orphans, will be those in most need of institutional care. One suggested approach to helping troubled youth is to remove them from dangerous environments in their communities and place them in group homes (Levine, 1995). Some of these group homes for teens exist today, and many orphaned adolescents are already in these placements. However, overall there has been little attention to the special needs of these youth (Ibid.).

Unless AIDS orphans are taken in by their friends, family members, or the foster care system, they will likely join the ranks of homeless children. Street youth often gravitate toward coastal cities with higher prevalences of HIV infection. Uninfected youth orphaned by AIDS who are forced to make their own way may engage in survival sex to support themselves (Geballe, 1995). Ironically, the same behavior that allows them to survive puts them at great risk for HIV/AIDS (Sondheimer, 1992). In this way, currently uninfected AIDS orphans may represent a future HIV/AIDS population. Perinatal transmission also becomes relevant because girls living on the streets have high rates of pregnancy (Roan, 1994). More than one-half of homeless female adolescents become pregnant while on the streets (Sondheimer, 1992).

Adolescents are not a well-defined group in other statistical reporting or clinical care (Sondheimer, 1992). They are frequently grouped with younger children or with adults, blurring their distinctive characteristics and making comparison of data difficult (Ibid.). The CDC's surveillance report classifies AIDS cases for adolescents and adults under 25 into two categories: 13–19 years and 20–24 years. These age divisions somewhat obscure the impact of the epidemic on adolescents. Age divisions are problematic because adolescence is not a period that can be strictly defined by age (Cohn & Futterman, 1995). For example, for some adolescents, the developmental process extends past age 22. Most HIV/AIDS educational programs have not responded to these developmental considerations (Wilcox, 1990).

Males (1996) points out an additional issue in that adolescence is often defined as a developmental period characterized by problems. In this way, adolescence becomes medicalized into a condition that is inherently pathological. Society's response has been to test, treat, and control adolescents.

Adolescents take risks to achieve goals appropriate to their developmental growth (Denenberg, 1995). These risks include asserting a sexual identity, choosing partners, becoming independent from their family, and deciding to have children. This growth process can be positive in that it can allow for healthy development and the potential for forming healthy social bonds with others outside the family. However, for many youth, this growth process is not positive and takes place in an unsafe environment, one scarred by poverty, drugs, and violence (Ibid.).

In 1959, children were 1.4 times more likely than adults to live in poverty. By 1969, reflecting the positive impact of the War on Poverty enacted during the Johnson administration, the child-adult poverty ratio bottomed out at 1.2. (Males, 1996). This success was shortlived, however. Many youth poverty programs were dismantled in the 1970s and 1980s during which time the number of children living in poverty rose to 6 million. By the late 1980s, children born into poverty in the 1970s were reaching adolescence. The rise in poverty among youth paralleled a rise in crime among this age group (Ibid.). By 1992, children were 2.1 times more likely than adults to live in poverty. This disparity was larger than any in previous decades.

The figures just cited suggest that the needs of youth were being neglected. This neglect started even before the time of AIDS. Children have long lacked access to resources they need because of poverty, community disruption, and minority status (Novick, 1995). Impoverished, displaced children have been evident in the inner city since the 1950s (Ibid.). Yet little has been done to respond to their needs with appropriate support services.

Youth of today face many risks and dangers – neglect, abuse, exploitation, poverty, homelessness, drugs, and violence. These risks make them vulnerable to HIV disease. In this way, HIV is added to an already formidable list of risks and dangers. The increasing rate of HIV disease among young women will eventually lead to an increase in the number of children born to infected mothers. These young women will face the same difficult issues about the custody of their children that were faced by older cohorts of women, some of whom may be relatives (Levine, 1996).

Adolescents became part of the national AIDS agenda late in the epidemic. The limited research that has been done on adolescents has usually studied either seroprevalence or knowledge, attitudes, and behaviors related to HIV/AIDS. This research has largely ignored the complex, multiple issues that HIV/AIDS presents for youth.

The first national conference on pediatric HIV/AIDS was held in 1984. The first plenary session for adolescents, however, was not delivered until the 1991 national conference (Rotheram-Borus, Koopman,

& Ehrhardt, 1991). Not only has the attention given to adolescents been late, it has also been piecemeal.

In addition, adolescents have been neglected as research participants in clinical trials. Until 1991, youth between 13 and 17 could not participate in national clinical trials as there were no established protocols for this age group (Hein et al., 1993). Adolescents' underenrollment in clinical trials is also because of age-based stereotypes. Some researchers perceive adolescents as difficult to reach and noncompliant with treatment regimens (Barnhart, 1997). However, there is actually no data that suggest that adolescents are less compliant with treatment regimens than other populations (Ibid.).

Adolescents are also neglected in HIV/AIDS service delivery. Community-based organizations are not typically designed for adolescents (Rotheram-Borus, 1997a), and it is estimated that although there are almost 9,000 HIV-infected adolescents in the United States, fewer than 1,000 are linked to services (Rotheram-Borus, 1997b). The AIDS program at Montefiore Hospital in New York City estimates that only 5% of the city's infected adolescents are in care (as cited in Barnhart, 1997). HIV is often diagnosed late in the course of illness. Fifty percent of infected adolescents learn of their infection just one year before they are diagnosed with AIDS (Ibid.).

The exclusion of adolescents from services is due to a number of barriers, including ability to pay for care, need for consent, confidentiality, disenfranchisement, and a lack of providers trained in adolescent medicine (Barnhart, 1997). These barriers are sometimes interlinking. For example, issues of consent and confidentiality intersect with the problem of paying for care. Payment and disclosure are intricately linked because health insurance plans usually cover adolescents as dependents, making it difficult for young people to receive services without their parents' knowledge or consent.

The political context of social policy aimed at addressing youth's needs has important implications for HIV/AIDS prevention. Despite the looming HIV epidemic among adolescents, many involved in the teenage sexuality debate will continue to object to laws and policies aimed at facilitating control by adolescents over their own sexuality. In this view, a growing openness about sex and increased availability of family planning services are seen as indicators of a pervasive permissiveness that is undermining family life (Currie & Skolnick, 1997).

Although these objectors may be aware of the devastating impact of the HIV/AIDS epidemic on youth, they still may weigh family values and government restraint more highly (King, 1996). These values are reflected in policies that favor traditional family values over adolescent needs.

In contrast to their European counterparts, young people in the United States are at increasing risk for HIV infection because of our culture-based fear of adolescent sexuality and the limited scope of prevention messages (Rotheram-Borus, 1997a). Abstinence has been the dominant HIV prevention message to youth in the United States (Ibid.). These young people would be better served if more attention were paid to the impact of policies on their health and well-being than to family values or parental or governmental authority (King, 1996). This goal can best be accomplished through empowering youth by providing them with information about HIV/AIDS and with access to services necessary to prevent transmission of the disease.

Little federal legislation has focused on adolescents and HIV disease (Wilcox, 1990). Most policy discussions involving adolescents have pertained to school attendance cases (Ibid.). Although clearly important, these cases are somewhat removed from other realities facing adolescents with HIV disease. Moreover, many infected adolescents are in high-risk groups and are unlikely even to attend school (Ibid.). Thus these adolescents are not served by policy on this issue.

A National AIDS Policy. The grassroots advocacy efforts of the white gay male community, though controversial, have had some success. Most notably, significant gains have been made in AIDS research and treatment because of the well-developed lobbying efforts of an educated and articulate gay community. In contrast, it has been difficult for families with HIV to advocate for themselves because they are so disenfranchised. There is a striking absence of a unified national advocacy effort for the pediatric, adolescent, and family HIV/AIDS community (Harvey, 1995). In particular, there is no advocacy effort that draws on the policy delivery role of clinicians as well as the direct experiences of families, including children and adolescents, who are living with HIV disease (Ibid.). Children and youth typically lack a spokesperson for other issues, including past epidemics, that affect them as well (Novick, 1995). HIV now contributes to this lack of political voice.

Most national policy discussions involving adults and HIV have centered around mandatory testing, confidentiality, and disclosure. With the promising results of the 076 study, discussed in Chapter 2, came the hope of eradicating perinatal transmission. This hope, however, had important political implications. Immediately after the findings of the 076 study were released, discussions of coercive measures involving mandatory testing of pregnant women and newborns began. These discussions took place even though voluntary testing of pregnant women was working (Hansen, 1997). Moreover, the preventative value of mandatory testing is questionable. Yet this coercive response was seen in many states, including New York, where legislation mandating testing of newborns (and thereby identifying infected mothers) was passed in 1996.

Also in 1996, authorization of the Ryan White Health Care Act, to be phased in over four years, included an amendment permitting, actually encouraging, mandatory testing of newborns (Ibid.). This law represents a culmination of a federal effort to mandate HIV testing of pregnant women and/or newborns. (However, plans are underway to try again to mandate testing at the federal level [Ibid.]).

In 1995 an attempt to mandate testing was defeated in California (Ibid.). Instead, the state passed legislation making voluntary testing and counseling available to pregnant women. This policy is consistent with the CDC's recommendations. It makes health care providers responsible for offering testing and counseling and gives women the choice to accept or reject these services.

Proponents of coercive testing depict mothers (often, poor minority women) as a danger to their children (Bergman, 1997). Women who resist coercive testing are seen as selfish. Ironically, policies that surveille mothers and punish them by removing their children are based on the ideology of "family preservation." Yet a policy in keeping with the interests of families would be one that united family members rather than separated them.

To date, society has done little to formulate policy that would ease the tremendous burdens placed upon families living with HIV disease. The lack of family policy is not in any way specific to HIV disease, however. The absence of policy in other areas that affect the well-being of families has been evident for some time (Blum, 1993). Laws reflecting policies on sex education, family planning, abortion, foster care, maternal and child health, child support, and welfare demonstrate a similar lack of commitment to family well-being. It is clear that families are still not a national priority. A national AIDS policy for families would have to encompass research, care, and prevention.

The present is a critical time for families with HIV disease. It is a time of hope. This hope can be seen in the accounts of Leticia, Eunice, and Juana, who describe improvements in their health from new drug therapies. Yet the promise of new drugs and new combination therapies is counterbalanced by difficult therapeutic regimens, uncertainties about length of benefit, and failure of some persons to benefit. Early detection of HIV and early intervention are now more important than ever.

The contribution that social scientists can make to policy is in explaining the structural conditions, such as poverty and gender inequality, that put poor families, particularly poor women, at risk and keep them there. HIV/AIDS policy needs to be sensitive to the socio-cultural context in which families conduct their daily lives. Social scientists must take an active role in formulating a national social policy that will empower families with HIV disease.

WOMEN, FAMILIES, AND HIV/AIDS

The social impact of HIV/AIDS extends far beyond the family. The cumulative effect of generational losses from the urban-based epidemic on social, cultural, and economic life is substantial (Levine, 1996). Because of HIV/AIDS society is losing the productivity potential of a generation of young people who will not be able to contribute to their family's and community's income and welfare.

One response to generational loss is the memory art that some families with HIV disease have created. This art is made to ensure that children will have memories of their parents and knowledge of their family history and cultural heritage. With the assistance of HIV/AIDS service agencies, families are producing and saving videotapes, audiotapes, photographs, letters, keepsakes, and documents of important family events (Kloser & Craig, 1994). A program in England uses a "memory store," a colorful box with a book for recording family history and compartments to hold items that can help children learn about and remember their parents. The Child Welfare League of

America also publishes the *Parents' Planning Guide*, which includes a worksheet for parents to document their personal history (Merkel-Holguin, 1994).

The accounts of persons living with HIV/AIDS at the opening of each chapter demonstrate the many ways in which HIV/AIDS has affected individuals and families. These accounts may help other parents recognize the need to protect themselves and their children from HIV/AIDS. They may also show how the family can be a motivating force in the future prevention of HIV/AIDS. Mothers and fathers have key responsibilities in the socialization of their children. They guide their children's development and the direction of their lives by providing them with a safe environment in which to grow up. Thus parents have an important role in prevention by communicating information about HIV/AIDS to their children. Education within families is one of the few ways the epidemic can be controlled. The role of families in ensuring healthy future generations is critical. Families must be empowered to deal with the epidemic.

Throughout this book you have read the accounts of eleven persons living with HIV disease. (Their biographies appear in Appendix B.) These individuals courageously relate how they have learned to cope with their own illness or with the illness of family members or with both. They describe the daily realities of HIV disease, and their diverse family situations form a complex story. These individuals have contributed immeasurably to this book. Their accounts help provide "A Sociological Perspective on the Epidemic in America."

This book identifies areas of research that merit further investigation. Among these is how adolescent gender role socialization, gender power relations, and heterosexual male identity put women at elevated risk for HIV disease. The impact of HIV disease on the family, particularly on women, is another important area for future study.

This book has also raised critical issues regarding service delivery to families with HIV disease. With the recent promising results in treatment from combination therapies, it is even more crucial that persons with HIV disease be linked to care immediately upon diagnosis. The current fragmented system of care must improve and provide services that are coordinated, continuous, and comprehensive. At present the quality of care that many persons with HIV disease receive is inferior, and there are no available aftercare services to help bereaved families cope with the loss of a family member. Pressure to improve standards of care must be placed on service providers.

I hope that the information in this book will be helpful to service providers who want to improve standards of care for those with HIV disease. It is also my wish that this book will be of value to families living with HIV disease and that the people with the disease who contributed so much to this book will find benefit from reading it and that in some way their lives will be improved.

APPENDIX A:
METHOD OF INQUIRY

I conducted in-depth interviews with members of two support groups for persons living with HIV disease that meet in Long Beach, California. Five women – Denise, Eunice, Loretta, Louann, and Naomi – from a weekly support group for HIV-infected women in recovery from drug and alcohol addiction provided interviews as well as four women and two men from a Spanish-speaking support group for families with HIV disease. Ed, Jose, Juana, Leticia, Mariana, and Rosemary were from that group, which meets bimonthly. Each person who was interviewed was also asked to keep a diary of her or his experiences living with HIV.

I attended weekly meetings with the women in recovery for 10 weeks during the summer of 1996. All of the women are in this particular Narcotics' Anonymous group as a condition of their treatment. Only HIV-infected women are members. Some of the chapter-opening quotations come from these group meetings. Besides participating in an individual and/or a group interview, several of the women also kept diaries.

I did not attend meetings of the Spanish-speaking support group. Interviews were conducted at the members' homes. Each person provided an individual interview, and some also kept diaries. Unless otherwise indicated in the individual biographies in Appendix B, their interviews were conducted and diaries were written in English.

For the diaries, the participants received notebooks that included carbon paper and were instructed to make a copy of every entry. Entries could include thoughts and feelings as well as daily happenings. When they had completed their diaries at the end of the summer, I took the copies, and the diarists kept the originals. Not all of the participants kept diaries. Of those who did, most did not write in them every day.

Appendix A: Method of Inquiry

An effort was made to gather demographic information on each person. Participants were encouraged to tell about themselves in addition to answer demographic questions. As follow-up, interviewees were asked to verify the accuracy of their biographies and to update their situations.

APPENDIX B:
BIOGRAPHIES OF PERSONS
LIVING WITH HIV DISEASE

DENISE

Denise, a 28-year-old white woman who is bisexual, was infected by her former husband. She used crystal and drank alcohol for 5 years. She now belongs to a Women in Recovery group. She has been living with HIV disease and in recovery for 11 months.

Denise is divorced and has two children, ages 6 and 8 years. She has a high school education and has worked as a professional vocalist. Her source of income is General Relief.

ED

Ed is a 34-year-old infected man who was born in the United States but grew up in Spain. He believes he was infected through heterosexual transmission in the United States but does not know the source of his infection. Ed has been living with HIV disease since December 1995.

Ed, who is separated from his wife (who is not infected), is raising his 2½-year-old daughter. He was recently hospitalized but is now managing his illness at home.

Ed has an eighth-grade education and has work experience in the military. His source of income is SSI. Ed belongs to a Spanish-speaking support group in Long Beach and finds comfort in its meetings.

EUNICE

Eunice, a 37-year-old infected African American woman, has been living with HIV disease for 8 years. She used heroin for 22 years, and has been in recovery for one year, and is now on methadone maintenance. For many years Eunice engaged in prostitution to support her drug habit. She is currently single, although she has plans to marry her partner, James. Eunice has one child, who does not live with her. She has a seventh-grade education and her source of income is General Relief.

JOSE

Jose, a 32-year-old immigrant from Mexico, has been living in the United States for 7 years and living with HIV disease for 3 years. He was infected by his wife, who died in 1994 at age 22. (She was originally from Honduras and had been infected there by her second husband.)

Jose now raises his 3-year-old, HIV-infected daughter, who is often ill and requires frequent hospitalizations. Jose's mother and father came to help him but have since returned to their native Mexico.

Jose has a high school education and at one time worked in a refinery doing insulation work. His current source of income is SSI.

Jose, who is Catholic, belongs to several support groups and finds comfort in their meetings. He provided his interview in English and his diary in Spanish.

JUANA

Juana is a 26-year-old infected woman from the state of Hildalgo in Mexico. She has been in the United States for 5 years during which time she has been living with HIV disease. Juana's husband, Alfonso, died from HIV disease in 1996. At that time, they were living in New York, but he died in Mexico. Juana subsequently moved to Long Beach and now raises their 6-year-old daughter, who was infected after birth through breast-feeding.

Juana, who has a ninth-grade education, has Medi-Cal insurance but no other state or county support. Her source of income is her sister, with whom she lives. She has frequent contact with her parents and other members of her extended family in Mexico.

Though she was recently hospitalized, she remains hopeful about her health. Both she and her daughter are on AZT and protease inhibitor therapy. Juana is especially encouraged by her daughter's health. Her daughter has been free of medical problems since birth and is considered a long-term child survivor.

Juana is Catholic and derives great comfort from her belief in God. She belongs to a Spanish-speaking HIV support group and finds comfort in its meetings. Juana provided both her interview and her diary in Spanish.

LETICIA

Leticia, a 34-year-old infected woman from Guatemala, has been in the United States for 20 years and has been living with HIV disease for 7 years. Her husband, Bobby, was from Puerto Rico and started using drugs after he came to the United States. He used cocaine and heroin for 21 years and spent 6 years in recovery. Bobby died from HIV disease in 1996. Their son, Marvin, was born infected and died when he was 19 months old in 1993. Leticia now raises their two uninfected children, 8 and 9 years old. Leticia has a high school education, and until 1990, she worked as a waitress. Her current source of income is SSI. Leticia's mother came from Guatemala to help her and the children 2 years ago. She has remained here, and they all live with Leticia's brother and nephew.

Leticia is Baptist and is active in her church. She gives much credit to Jesus for her good health. Leticia is getting good results from her current medications and is encouraged about her health. Leticia belongs to a Spanish-speaking HIV support group in Long Beach. She is also active in speaking to various groups about her experiences as a person living with HIV disease.

LORETTA

Loretta, 37 years old, is a lesbian-identified Latina who has been living with HIV disease for 8 years. She has three children, ages 14, 19, and 20 years, who do not live with her.

Loretta, who used drugs, including heroin, cocaine, and alcohol, for 28 years, has been in recovery for 8 months. She has a GED and is currently enrolled in a junior college. She does not have an income and volunteers as a community outreach assistant. Loretta feels positive about her drug treatment program and school work and believes she is progessing in making a new life for herself.

LOUANN

Louann, a 35-year-old infected African American woman, has been living with HIV disease for 2 years. She has 4 children, ages 3, 8, 14, and 20 years, none of whom live with her at present.

Louann, who used drugs, including heroin, cocaine, and alcohol, for 16 years, has been in recovery for 15 months. She has a 10th-grade education and has worked variously as a mail clerk, nursing assistant, and waitress. Her current source of income is SSI. Louann gains sustenance from the weekly meetings of her Women in Recovery group and also gets support from her sister.

MARIANA

Mariana, a 29-year-old uninfected Latina mother, is married and has three children, ages 2 months, 4 years, and 11 years. Her 11-year-old son was infected when he was 14 months during a family vacation in Mexico in 1986 when he was given three blood transfusions during emergency surgery. Her son has never been hospitalized and remains in good health. He is now on protease inhibitor therapy.

Mariana, who has completed one year of college, is now employed as a family advisor for Los Angeles Pediatric AIDS Network (LAPAN) and does outreach to families living with HIV disease. She leads Spanish-speaking support groups in Los Angeles and Long Beach and finds comfort in helping other families cope with HIV disease.

NAOMI

Naomi was a member of the Women in Recovery group. Unfortunately, no additional biographical information about her is available. Naomi relapsed after the first group meeting from which interview data were collected.

ROSEMARY

Rosemary, a 28-year-old uninfected woman from Honduras, has been in the United States for 5 years. Her husband, who is also from Honduras, has been living with HIV disease for 6 years. They have three children, ages 10 months, 2 years, and 7 years.

Rosemary's husband was infected and learned of his diagnosis in the United States. She joined him here from Honduras and shortly thereafter became pregnant with their oldest child.

Rosemary has a sixth-grade education and is a housewife. Her husband's health continues to allow him to work and support the family. Rosemary belongs to a Spanish-speaking HIV support group and gains comfort from its meetings. Rosemary provided her interview in Spanish.

REFERENCES

CHAPTER 1

Aral, S. O., & Wasserheit, J. N. (1995). HIV, other STDs, socioeconomic status, and poverty: Interactions in women. Pp. 13–41 in A. O'Leary & J. S. Jemmott (eds.), *Women at Risk: Issues in the Primary Prevention of AIDS.* New York: Plenum.

Barnhart, K. (1997). Adolescent underrepresentation in clinical AIDS research. Pp. 74–85 in N. Goldstein & J. L. Manlowe (eds.), *The Gender Politics of HIV/AIDS in Women.* New York: New York University Press.

Brettle, R. P., & Leen, C. L. S. (1991). The natural history of HIV and AIDS in women. *AIDS,* 5, 1283–1292.

Burkett, E. (1995). *The Gravest Show on Earth: America in the Age of AIDS.* Boston: Houghton Mifflin.

Cameron, D., Simonsen, N., D'Costa, L. J., Ronald, A. R., Maitha, G. M., Gakinya, M. N., Cheang, M., Ndinya-Achola, J. O., Piot, P., Brunham, R. C., & Plummer, F. A. (1989). Female-to-male transmission of human immunodeficiency virus type 1: Risk factors for seroconversion in men. *Lancet,* 2, 403–407.

Caravano, K. (1991). More than mothers and whores: Redefining the AIDS prevention needs of women. *International Journal of Health Services,* 21, 131–142.

Centers for Disease Control. (1981). Follow-up on Kaposi's sarcoma and pneumocystis pneumonia. *MMWR,* 30, 409–410, August 28.

(1983a). Immunodeficiency among female sexual partners of males with acquired immune deficiency syndrome (AIDS) – New York. *MMWR,* 31, 697–698, January 7.

(1983b). Acquired Immunodeficiency Syndrome (AIDS). *Weekly Surveillance Report – United States,* December 12.

(1990). HIV-1 infection and artificial insemination with processed semen. *MMWR,* 39, 249–256.

References

(1993a). Update: Acquired Immunodeficiency Syndrome – United States 1992. *MMWR*, **42**, 547–557.

(1993b). 1993 revised classification system for HIV infection and expanded surveillance case definition of AIDS among adolescents and adults. *MMWR*, **41**, 1–23.

(1994). Update: Impact of the expanded AIDS surveillance case definition for adolescents and adults on case reporting – United States, 1993. *MMWR*, **43**, 160–161, 167–170.

(1995). Update: AIDS among women – United States, 1994. *Journal of the American Medical Association*, **273**, 767–768.

(1997a). *HIV/AIDS Surveillance Report.* Year-end edition, cases through December, **9**, 1–40.

(1997b). HIV/AIDS in women who have sex with women (WSW) in the United States, Update, April.

(1998). AIDS among persons aged ≥ 50 years – United States 1991–1996. *MMWR*, **47**, 21–26, January 23.

Chadwick, E. G. (1995). Pediatric HIV infection. *Improving the Management of HIV Disease*, **3**, 16–19.

Chaisson, M. A., Stoneburner, K. L., & Joseph, S. C. (1990). Human immunodeficiency virus transmission through artificial insemination. *Journal of Acquired Immune Deficiency Syndromes*, **5**, 850–852, 1992.

Chu, S. Y., Birchler, J. W., Fleming, P. L., & Berkelman, R. L. (1990). Epidemiology of reported cases of AIDS in lesbians, United States, 1980–89. *American Journal of Public Health*, **80**, 1380.

Cimons, M. (1997). AIDS deaths drop further, U.S. Reports. *Los Angeles Times*, pp. A1, 12, July 15.

Corea, G. (1992). *The Invisible Epidemic.* New York: Harper Perennial.

European Study Group on Heterosexual Transmission of HIV. (1992). Comparison of female-to-male and male-to-female transmission of HIV in 563 stable couples. *British Medical Journal*, **304**, 809–813.

Feingold, A. R., Vermund, S. H., Burk, R. D., Kelley, K. F., Schrager, L. K., Schreiber, K., Munk, G., Friedland, G. H., & Klein, R. S. (1990). Cervical cytologic abnormalities and papillomavirus in women infected with human immunodeficiency virus. *Journal of Acquired Immune Deficiency Syndromes*, **3**, 896–903.

Fischl, M., Fayne, T., & Flancga, S. (1988). Seroprevalence and risks of HIV infection in spouses of persons infected with HIV. Fourth International Conference on AIDS, Stockholm, Sweden.

Forsyth, B. W. C. (1995). A pandemic out of control: The epidemiology of AIDS. Pp. 19–31 in S. Geballe, J. Gruendel, & W. Andiman (eds.), *Forgotten Children of the AIDS Epidemic*. New Haven, CT: Yale University Press.

References

Guinan, M. E. & Leviton, L. (1995). Prevention of HIV infection in women: Overcoming barriers. *Journal of the American Medical Association, 50,* 74–77.

Haverkos, H. W., & Battjes, R. (1992). Female-to-male transmission of HIV. *Journal of the American Medical Association,* **268,** 1855.

Hirschhorn, L. R. (1995). HIV infection in women: Is it different? *The AIDS Reader,* 99–105, May/June.

Hoegsberg, B., Abulafia, O., Sedlis, A., Feldman, J., DesJarlais, D., Landesman, S., & Minkoff, H. (1990). Sexually transmitted diseases and human immunodeficiency virus among women with pelvic inflammatory disease. *American Journal of Obstetrics and Gynecology,* **163,** 1135–1139.

Inciardi, J. A., Lockwood, D., & Pottieger, A. E. (1993). *Women and Crack-Cocaine.* New York: Macmillan.

Kaplan, J. (1997). Prevention of opportunistic infections. Antiretroviral therapy: Basic science, clinical care, and policy, Session No. 210, National Conference on Women and HIV, Pasadena, CA.

Kline, M. W. (1995). Long-term survival in vertically acquired HIV infection. *The AIDS Reader,* 153, Sept./Oct.

Laga, M. (1993). STD control for prevention. Ninth International Conference on AIDS. Berlin, Germany.

Legg, J. J. (1993). Women and HIV. *The Journal of American Board of Family Practice,* **6,** 367–377.

Males, M. A. (1996). *The Scapegoat Generation: America's War on Adolescents.* Monroe, ME: Common Courage Press.

Marmor, J., Weiss, L. R., Lyden, M., Weiss, S. H., Saxinger, W. C., Spira, T. J., & Feorino, P. M. (1986). Possible female-to-female transmission of human immunodeficiency virus. *Annals of Internal Medicine,* **105,** 969.

Martin, A. D. (1988). AIDS prevention and education with gay and lesbian adolescents. Pp. 379–395 in M. Quackenbush & M. Nelson (eds.), *The AIDS Challenge: Prevention Education for Young People.* Santa Cruz, CA: Network Publications.

McCombs, S. B., McCray, E., Wendell, P. A. Sweeney, P. A., & Onorato, I. M. (1992). Epidemiology of HIV-1 infection in bisexual women. *Journal of Acquired Immune Deficiency Syndromes,* **5,** 850–852.

Mofenson, L. M. (1997). Global overview of perinatal transmission trials. Pregnant women and HIV in this new era of anti-HIV therapy, Session No. 204, National Conference on Women and HIV, Pasadena, CA.

Monzon, O. T., & Cappelan, J. M. (1987). Female-to-female transmission of HIV. *Lancet,* **2,** 40–41.

National Institute of Allergy and Infectious Diseases (NIAID). (1997a). Women and HIV, April 1–7.

References

(1997b). NIAID resources for studying HIV/AIDS in women, April 1–4.

Office of National AIDS Policy. (1996). Youth and HIV/AIDS: An American Agenda. Washington, DC, March 1–17.

Padian, N. (1991). Epidemiology of AIDS and heterosexually transmitted HIV in women. *AIDSFILE*, 5, 1–2.

(1995). Heterosexual partners study and the rise of infection in women. Oral presentation, Conference on Women and HIV: A Call to Action, University of California, Santa Cruz, CA, April 30.

Padian, N., Marquis, L., Francis, D. P., Anderson, R. E., Rutherford, G. W., O'Malley, P. M., & Winkelstein W. (1987). Male-to-female transmission of human immunodeficiency virus. *Journal of the American Medical Association*, 258, 788–790.

Padian, N. S. (1987). Heterosexual transmission of acquired immunodeficiency syndrome: International perspectives and national projections. *Review of Infectious Diseases*, 9, 947–960.

Padian, N. S., Shiboski, S. C., & Jewel, N. P. (1989). The effect of number of exposures on the risk of heterosexual HIV transmission. *Journal of Infectious Diseases*, 161, 883–887.

Patton, C. (1994). *Last Served? Gendering the HIV Pandemic*. New York: Taylor & Francis.

Perry, S., Jacobsberg, L., & Fogel, K. (1989). Orogenital transmission of human immunodeficiency virus (HIV). *Annals of Internal Medicine*, 111, 951–952.

Provencher, D., Valme, B., Averette, H. E., Ganjei, P., Donato, D., Penalver, M., & Sevin, B. U. (1988). HIV status and positive papanicolaou screening: Identification of a high-risk population. *Gynecological Oncology*, 31, 184–190.

Reback, C. J. (1997). *The social construction of a gay drug: Methamphetamine use among gay and bisexual men in Los Angeles*. Los Angeles.

Rogers, M. F. (1997a). Epidemiology of HIV/AIDS in women and children in the U.S.A. *Acta Paediatric Supplement*, 421, 15–16, June.

(1997b). The challenges of implementing recommendations for the prevention of perinatal transmission: How have we done so far? Pregnant women and HIV in this new era of anti-HIV therapy, Session No. 204, National Conference on Women and HIV, Pasadena, CA.

Rothenburg, R., Woelfel, M., Stoneburner, R., Milberg, J., Parker, R., Truman, B. (1987). Survival with the acquired immunodeficiency syndrome. *New England Journal of Medicine*, 317, 1297–1302.

Rotheram-Borus, M. J. (1997a). Annotation: HIV prevention challenges – realistic strategies and early detection programs. *American Journal of Public Health*, 87, 544–546.

References

(1997b). Adolescents and AIDS. Behavioral and prevention science track, Session No. 101, National Conference on Women and HIV, Pasadena, CA.

Sabo, C. E., & Carwein, V. L. (1994). Women and HIV/AIDS. *Journal of the Association of Nurses in AIDS Care*, 5, 15–21.

Safrin, S., Dattel, B. J., Hauer, L., & Sweet, R. L. (1990). Seroprevalence and epidemiologic correlates of human immunodeficiency virus infection in women with acute pelvic inflammatory disease. *Journal of Obstetrics and Gynecology*, 75, 666–670.

Schraeger, L. K., Friedland, G. H., Maude, D., Schreiber, K., Adachi, A., Pizzuti, D. J., Koss, L. G., & Klein, R. S. (1989). Cervical and vaginal squamous cell abnormalities in women infected with human immunodeficiency virus. *Journal of Acquired Immune Deficiency Syndromes*, 2, 570–575.

Semprini, A. E. (1993). Insemination of HIV-negative women with processed semen of HIV-positive partners. *Lancet*, 321, 1343–1344.

Semprini, A. E., Levi-Setti, P., Bozzo, M., Ravizza, M., Taglioretti, A., & Sulpizio, P. (1992). Insemination of HIV-negative women with processed semen of HIV-positive partners. *Lancet*, 340, 1317–1319.

Shearer, W. T., Quinn, T. C., LaRussa, P., Lew, J. F., Mofenson, L., Almy, S., Rick, K., Handelsman, E., Diaz, C., Pagano, M., Smeriglio, V., & Kalish, L. A., for the Women and Infants Transmission Study Group (1997). Viral load and disease progression in infants infected with human immunodeficiency virus type 1. *New England Journal of Medicine*, 336, 1337–1342.

Siegel, K. Raveis, V. H., & Gorey, E. (1997). Barriers and motivating factors impacting delaying seeking medical care among HIV-infected women. Health services utilization and policy, Session No. 108, National Conference on Women and HIV, Pasadena, CA.

Sperling, R. S., Freidman, F., Joyner, M., Brodman, M., & Dottino, P. (1991). Seroprevalence of human immunodeficiency virus in women admitted to the hospital with pelvic inflammatory disease. *Journal of Reproductive Medicine*, 36, 122–124.

Stein, Z. A. (1995). More on women and the prevention of HIV infection (editorial). *American Journal of Public Health*, 85, 1485–1488.

Stewart, G. J., Tyler, J. P. P., Cunningham, A. L., Barr, T. A., Driscoll, G. L., Gold, J., & Lamont, B. J. (1985). Transmission of human t-cell lymphotropic virus type 3 by artificial insemination by donor. *Lancet*, 2, 581–584.

Stine, G. J. (1998). *AIDS Update 1998*. Upper Saddle River, NJ: Prentice-Hall.

St. Louis, M. E., Conway, G. A., Hayman, C. R., Miller, C., Peterson, L. R., Dondero, T. J. (1991). Human immunodeficiency virus infection in

References

disadvantaged adolescents. Findings from the U.S. Job Corps. *Journal of the American Medical Association,* 266, 2387–2391.

Stoneburner, R. L., DesJarlais, D. C., Benezra, D., Gorelkin, L., Sotheran, J. L., Friedman, S. R., Schultz, S., Marmor, M., Mildvan, M., & Maslansky, R. (1988). A larger spectrum of severe HIV-1 related disease in intravenous drug users in New York City. *Science,* 242, 916–919.

Stuntzner-Gibson, D. (1991). Women and HIV disease: An emerging social crisis. *Social Work,* 26, 22–28.

Treichler, P. (1988). AIDS, gender, and biomedical discourse: Current contests for meaning. Pp. 190–266 in E. Fee & D. M. Fox (eds.), *AIDS, The Burdens of History.* Berkeley: University of California Press.

Vermund, S. H., Kelley, K. F., Klein, R. S., Feingold, A. R., Schreiber, K., Munk, G., Burk, R. D. (1991). High risk of human papillomavirus and cervical squamous intraepithelial lesions among women with symptomatic human immunodeficiency virus infection. *American Journal of Obstetrics and Gynecology,* 165, 392–400.

Wasser, S. C., Gwinn, M., & Fleming, P. (1993). Urban-nonurban distribution of HIV infection in childbearing women in the United States. *Journal of Acquired Immune Deficiency Syndromes,* 6, 1035–1042.

Weissman, G. B., Sowder, B., & Young, P. (1990). The relationship between crack cocaine use and other risk factors among women in a national AIDS prevention program. Sixth International Conference on AIDS, San Francisco.

Williams, A. B. (1992a). The epidemiology, clinical manifestations, and health-maintenance needs of women infected with HIV. *Nurse Practitioner,* 17, 27–44.

    (1992b). Women in the HIV epidemic. *Critical Care Nursing Clinics of North America,* 4, 437–445.

Wofsy, C. (1987). Human immunodeficiency virus infection in women. *Journal of the American Medical Association,* 257, 2074–2076.

Wofsy, C. B., Padian, N. S., Cohen, J. B., Greenblatt, R., Coleman, R., & Korvick, J. A. (1992). Epidemiology of AIDS in women and heterosexually transmitted HIV. Pp. 303–328 in P. Volberding & M. A. Jacobson (eds.), *AIDS Clinical Review.* New York: Marcel Dekker.

Wolfe, M. (1997). Who's "The Cure" for? Defining a national AIDS Policy: Research, health service, and prevention, Session No. 303, National Conference on Women and HIV, Pasadena, CA.

Worth, D. (1989). Sexual decision-making and AIDS: Why condom promotion among vulnerable women is likely to fail. *Studies in Family Planning,* 20, 297–307.

Wortley, P. M., Chu, S. Y., & Berkelman, R. L. (1997). Epidemiology of

References

HIV/AIDS in women and the impact of the expanded 1993 CDC surveillance definition of AIDS. Pp. 3–14 in D. Cotton & D. H. Watts (eds.), *The Medical Management of AIDS in Women*. New York: Wiley-Liss.

Wortley, P. M., & Fleming, P. L. (1997). AIDS incidence in women: Recent trends. Epidemiology of HIV and AIDS in women, Session No. 106, National Conference on Women and HIV, Pasadena, CA.

CHAPTER 2

Andiman, W. (1995). Medical aspects of AIDS: What do children witness? Pp. 32–49 in S. Geballe, J. Gruendel, & W. Andiman (eds.), *Forgotten Children of the AIDS Epidemic*. New Haven, CT: Yale University Press.

Bentley, M., & Herr, K. (1996). Contextualizing the development of adolescent girls: The missing piece in HIV education. Pp. 147–162 in M. K. Moore & M. L. Forst (eds.), *AIDS Education: Reaching Diverse Populations*. Westport, CT: Praeger.

Berrebi, A., Kobuch, W. E., Puel, J., Tricoire, J., Herne P., Grandjean, H., & Pontonnier, G. (1990). Influence of pregnancy on human immunodeficiency virus disease. *European Journal of Obstetrics and Gynecology and Reproductive Biology*, 37, 211–217.

Brettle, R. P., Raab, G. M., Ross, A., Fielding, K. L., Gore, S. M., & Bird, A. G. (1995). HIV infection in women: Immunological markers and influence of pregnancy. *AIDS*, 9, 1177–1184.

Brossard, Y., Aubin, J. T., Mandelbrot, L., Bignozzi, C., Brand, D., Chaput, A., Roume, J., Mulliez, N., Mallet, F., Agut, H, Barin, F., Brechot, C., Goudeau, A., Huraux, J.-M., Barrat, J., Blot, P., Chavinie, J., Ciraru-Vigneron, N., Engelman, P., Herve, F., Papiernik, E., & Henrion, R. (1995). Frequency of early *in utero* HIV-1 infection: A blind DNA polymerase chain reaction study of 100 fetal thymuses. *AIDS*, 9, 359–366.

Brown, G. R., & Rundell, J. R. (1990). Prospective study of psychiatric morbidity in HIV-seropositive women without AIDS. *General Hospital Psychiatry*, 12, 20–35.

Bryson, Y. J. (1996). Perinatal HIV-1 transmission: Recent advances and therapeutic interventions. *AIDS*, 10, S33–S42.

Cates, W., & Stone, K. M. (1992). Family planning, sexually transmitted diseases, and contraceptive choice: A literature update. *Family Planning Perspectives*, 24, 75–84, 122–128.

Cates, W. J., Stewart, F. H., & Trussell, J. (1992). The quest for women's prophylactic methods – Hopes vs. science (commentary). *American Journal of Public Health*, 81, 1479–1482.

References

Centers for Disease Control. (1982). Unexplained immunodeficiency and opportunistic infections in infants – New York, New Jersey, California. *MMWR*, **31**, 665–667, December 17.

   (1995). U.S. Public Health Service recommendations for Human Immunodeficiency Virus counseling and voluntary testing for pregnant women. *MMWR*, **44**, No. RR-7, 1–15.

   (1997). *HIV/AIDS Surveillance Report.* Year-end edition, cases through December, **9**, 1–40.

Cohn, J., & Futterman, D. (1995). Adolescents and HIV. Pp. 133–148 in P. Kelly, S. Holman, R. Rothenberg, & S. P. Holzemer (eds.), *Primary Care of Women and Children with HIV Infection.* Boston: Jones & Bartlett.

Connor, E. M., Sperling, R. S., Gelber, R., Kiselev, P., Scott, G., O'Sullivan, M. J., VanDyke, R., Bey, M., Shearer, W., Jacobson, R. L., Jimenez, E., O'Neill, E., Bazin, B., Delfraissy, J., Culnane, M. S., Coombs, R., Elkins, M., Moye, J., Stratton, P., & Balsley, J., for the Pediatric AIDS Clinical Trials Group Protocol 076 Study Group. (1994). Reduction of maternal-infant transmission of human immunodeficiency virus type 1 with zidovudine treatment. *New England Journal of Medicine*, **331**, 1173–1180.

De Bertolini, C., Scarso, C. Andreetto, U., Bertuzzo, P., Milan, E., Favero, E., Cadrobbi, P., Cattelan, A. M., Rupolo, G. P. (1996). Risk-related sexual behavior: Differences between HIV-positive heterosexual males and females. Abstract No. Mo.D. 1891, Eleventh International Conference on AIDS, Vancouver, Canada.

Denenberg, R. (1995). Special concerns of women with HIV and AIDS. Pp. 115–135 in W. Odets & M. Shernoff (eds.), *The Second Decade of AIDS: A Mental Health Practice Handbook.* New York: Hatherleigh Press.

   (1997). HIV does not erase desire: Addressing the sexual and reproductive concerns of women with HIV/AIDS. Pp. 323–336 in N. Goldstein & J. L. Manlowe (eds.), *The Gender Politics of HIV/AIDS.* New York: New York University Press.

De Vincenzi, I., for the European Study Group on Heterosexual Transmission of HIV. (1994). A longitudinal study of human immunodeficiency virus transmission by heterosexual partners. *New England Journal of Medicine*, **331**, 341–146.

Dickover, R. E., Garratty, E. M., Herman, S. A., Sim, M.-S., Plaeger, S., Boyer, P. J., Keller, M., Deveikis, A., Stiehm, E. R., & Bryson, Y. J. (1996). Identification of levels of maternal HIV-1 RNA associated with risk of perinatal transmission: Effect of maternal zidovudine treatment on viral load. *Journal of the American Medical Association*, **275**, 599–605.

References

Duliege, A. M., Amos, C. I., Felton, S., Biggar, R. J., the International Registry of HIV-Exposed Twins, & Goedert, J. J. (1995). Birth order, delivery route, and concordance in the transmission of human immunodeficiency virus type 1 from mothers to twins. *The Journal of Pediatrics*, **126**, 625–632.

Dunn, D. T., Newell M. L., Ades A. E., & Peckham, C. (1992). Risk of human immunodeficiency virus type 1 transmission through breastfeeding. *Lancet*, **340**, 585–588.

Dunn, D. T., Newell, M. L., Mayaux, M. J., Kind, C., Hutto, C., Goedert, J. J., Andiman, W., & Perinatal AIDS Collaborative Transmission Studies. (1994). Mode of delivery and vertical transmission of HIV-1: A review of prospective studies. *Journal of Acquired Immune Deficiency Syndromes*, **7**, 1064–1066.

Elias, C. J., & Heise, L. L. (1994). Challenges for the development of female-controlled vaginal microbicides. *AIDS*, **8**, 1–9.

European Collaborative Study (1992). Risk factors for mother-to-child transmission of HIV-1. *Lancet*, **339**, 1007–1012.

——— (1994). Caesarean section and risk of vertical transmission of HIV-1 infection. *Lancet*, **343**, 1464–1467.

Faden, R. R., Chwalow, A. J., Quaid, K., Chase, G. A., Lopes, C., Leonard, O., & Holtzman, N. A. (1987). Prenatal screening and pregnant women's attitudes toward the abortion of defective fetuses. *American Journal of Public Health*, **77**, 288–290.

Fischl, M. A., Dickinson, G. M., Scott, G. B., Klimas, D., Fletcher, A., & Parks, W. (1987). Evaluation of heterosexual partners, children, and household contacts of adults with AIDS. *Journal of the American Medical Association*, **257**, 640–644.

Garcia, P. (1995). HIV disease in women. *Improving the Management of HIV Disease*, **3**, 7–9.

Haney, D. Q. (1997). Major studies aim to protect babies from AIDS virus. *Press Telegram*, p. A5, January 27.

Hankins, C. (1993). Women and HIV infection. Pp. 20–40 in L. Sherr (ed.), *AIDS and the Heterosexual Population.* Chur, Switzerland: Harwood.

Hankins, C. A., and Handley, M. A. (1992). HIV disease and AIDS in women: Current knowledge and research agenda. *Journal of Acquired Immune Deficiency Syndromes*, **5**, 957–971.

Hirschhorn, L. R. (1995). HIV infection in women: Is it different? *The AIDS Reader*, 99–105, May/June.

Hutchinson, M., & Shannon, M. (1993). Reproductive health and counseling. Pp. 47–65 in A. Kurth (ed.), *Until the Cure: Caring for Women with HIV.* New Haven, CT: Yale University Press.

References

Jason, J. B., Evatt, L., & Hemophilia AIDS Collaborative Study Group (1990). Pregnancies in human immunodeficiency virus-infected sex partners of hemophiliac men. *American Journal of the Diseases of Children*, **144**, 485–490.

Johnstone, A. M., Brettle, R. P., MacCallum, L. R., Mok, J., Peutherer, J. F., & Burns, S. (1990). Women's knowledge of their antibody state: Its effect on their decision whether to continue the pregnancy. *British Medical Journal*, **300**, 23–24.

King, P. A. (1996). Reproductive choices of adolescent females with HIV/AIDS. Pp. 345–366 in R. R. Faden & N. E. Kass (eds.), *HIV, AIDS, and Childbearing, Public Policy, Private Lives*. New York: Oxford University Press.

Kline, W., Lewis, D. E., Hollinger, B., Reuben, J. M., Hanson, C., Kozinetz, C. A., Dimitrov, D. H., Rosenblatt, H. M., & Shearer, W. T. (1994). A comparative study of human immunodeficiency virus culture, polymerase chain reaction, and anti-human immunoglobulin A antibody detection in the diagnosis during early infancy of vertically acquired human immunodeficiency virus infection. *Pediatric Infectious Diseases*, **13**, 90–94.

Krivine, A., Firtion, G., Cao, L., Francoual, C., Henrion, R., & Lebon, P. (1992). HIV replication during the first weeks of life. *Lancet*, **339**, 1187–1189.

Kuhn, L., & Stein Z. A. (1995). Mother-to-infant HIV transmission: Timing, risk factors, and prevention. *Paediatric and Perinatal Epidemiology*, **9**, 1–29.

Kuhn, L., Stein, Z. A., Thomas, P. A., Singh, T., & Tsai, W. (1994). Maternal-infant HIV transmission and circumstances of delivery. *American Journal of Public Health*, **84**, 1110–1115.

Kurth, A. (1993). Reproductive issues, pregnancy and childbearing in HIV-infected women. Pp. 104–133 in F. L. Cohen & J. D. Durham (eds.), *Women, Children, and HIV/AIDS*. New York: Springer.

Kurth, A., & Hutchinson, M. (1990). Reproductive health policy and HIV: Where do women fit in? *Pediatric AIDS and HIV infection: Fetus to adolescent*, **1**, 121–133.

Kurth, A., & Minkoff, H. L. (1995). Pregnancy and reproductive concerns of women with HIV infection. Pp. 59–87 in P. Kelly, S. Holman, R. Rothenberg, & S. P. Holzemer (eds.), *Primary Care of Women and Children with HIV Infection*. Boston: Jones and Bartlett.

Legg, J. J. (1993). Women and HIV. *The Journal of American Board of Family Practice*, **6**, 367–377.

Luzuriaga, K., Bryson, Y., McSherry, G., Robinson, J., Stechenberg, B.,

References

Scott, G., Lamson, M., Cort, S., & Sullivan, J. L. (1996). Pharmacokinetics, safety, and activity of nevirapine in human immunodeficiency virus type-1 infected children. *The Journal of Infectious Diseases*, 174, 713–721.

Males, M. A. (1996). *The Scapegoat Generation: America's War on Adolescents.* Monroe, ME: Common Courage Press.

Mandelbrot, L., & Henrion, R. (1993). Does pregnancy accelerate disease progression in HIV-infected women? Pp. 157–171 in M. A. Johnson & F. D. Johnstone (eds.), *HIV Infection in Women.* New York: Churchill Livingstone.

Mano, H., & Chermann, J. C. (1991). Fetal HIV-1 infection of different organs in the second trimester. *AIDS Research on Human Retroviruses*, 7, 83–88.

Marteau, T. M. (1989). Psychological costs of screening. *British Medical Journal*, 299, 527.

Maugh, T. H. (1998). New therapy may cut AIDS in newborns. *Los Angeles Times*, pp. A1, 23, June 30.

Mayaux, M. J., Blanche, S., Rouzioux, C., Le Chenadec, J., Chambrin, V., Firtion, G., Allemon, M.-C., Vilmer, E., Vigneron, N. C., Tricoire, J., Guillot, F., Courpotin, C., & the French Pediatric HIV Infection Study Group. (1995). Maternal factors associated with perinatal HIV-1 transmission: The French cohort study: 7 years of follow-up observation. *Journal of Acquired Immune Deficiency Syndromes and Human Retrovirology*, 8, 188–194.

Mitchell, J. L. (1988). Women, AIDS, and public policy. *AIDS and Public Policy Journal*, 3, 50–52.

——— (1992). HIV and women: Current controversies and clinical relevance. *Journal of Women's Health*, 1, 35–39.

——— (1993). Pregnancy-related transmission of HIV to women and infants. Pp. 71–88 in M. Berer & S. Ray (eds.), *Women and HIV: An International Resource Book.* London: Pandora.

Mofenson, L. M. (1997). Global overview of perinatal transmission trials. Pregnant women and HIV in this new era of anti-HIV therapy, Session No. 204, National Conference on Women and HIV, Pasadena, CA.

Patton, C. (1994). *Last Served? Gendering the HIV Pandemic.* New York: Taylor & Francis.

Peckham, C. (1993). Mother-to-child transmission of HIV: Risk factors and timing. Ninth International Conference on AIDS, Berlin, Germany.

Pediatric AIDS Foundation. (1997). *Progress Report*, summer.

Pies, C. (1995). AIDS, ethics, reproductive rights: No easy answers. Pp. 322–334 in B. E. Schneider & N. E. Stoller (eds.), *Women Resisting*

References

AIDS, Feminist Strategies of Empowerment. Philadelphia: Temple University Press.

Pivnick, A., Mulvihill, M., Jacobsen, A., Hsu, M. A., Eric, K., & Drucker, E. (1991). Reproductive decisions among HIV-infected drug-using women: The implications of mother-child coresidence. *Medical Anthropology Quarterly,* 5, 153–169.

Rogers, M. F. (1997). The challenges of implementing recommendations for the prevention of perinatal transmission: How have we done so far? Pregnant women and HIV in this new era of anti-HIV therapy, Session No. 204, National Conference on Women and HIV, Pasadena, CA.

Rotheram-Borus, M. J. (1997). HIV prevention challenges – realistic strategies and early detection programs (annotation). *American Journal of Public Health,* 87, 544–546.

Rotheram-Borus, M. J., Jemmott, L. S., & Jemmott, J. B. (1995). Preventing AIDS in female adolescents. Pp. 103–129 in A. O'Leary & L. S. Jemmott (eds.), *Women at Risk: Issues in the Primary Prevention of AIDS.* New York: Plenum.

Schneider, B. E. (1989). Women and AIDS: An International Perspective. *Futures,* 72–88, February.

Selwyn, P. A., & Antoniello, P. (1993). Reproductive decision-making among women with HIV infection. Pp. 173–185 in M. A. Johnson & F. D. Johnstone (eds.), *HIV Infection in Women.* New York: Churchill Livingstone.

Selwyn, P. A., Carter, R. J., Schoenbaum, E. E., Roberston, V. J., Klein, R. S., & Rogers, M. F. (1989). Knowledge of HIV antibody status and decisions to continue or terminate pregnancy among intravenous drug users. *Journal of the American Medical Association,* 261, 3567–3571.

Semprini, A. E., Castagna, C., Ravizza, M., Fiore, S., Savasi, V., Muggiasca, M. L., Grossi, E., Guerra, B., Tibaldi, C., Scaravelli, G., Prati, E., & Pardi, G. (1995). The incidence of complications after caesarean section in 156 HIV-positive women. *AIDS,* 9, 913–917.

Sherr, L. (1991). *HIV and AIDS in Mothers and Babies.* Oxford: Blackwell Scientific Publications.

(1993a). HIV testing in pregnancy. Pp. 42–68 in C. Squire (ed.)., *Women and AIDS: Psychological Perspectives.* London: Sage.

(1993b). Discordant couples. Pp. 83–102 in L. Sherr (ed.), *AIDS and the Heterosexual Population.* Chur, Switzerland: Harwood.

(1993c). Counselling around HIV testing in women of reproductive age. Pp. 17–35 in M. A. Johnson & F. D. Johnstone (eds.), *HIV Infection in Women.* New York: Churchill Livingstone.

(1996). Gender, psychology, and HIV infection. Pp. 16–45 in L. Sherr, C. Hankins, & L. Bennett (eds.), *AIDS as a Gender Issue: Psychological Perspectives*, London: Taylor & Francis.

Sherr, L., & Quinn, S. (1993). Testing, counselling, and behaviour. Pp. 180–197 in L. Sherr, (ed.), *AIDS and the Heterosexual Population*. Chur, Switzerland: Harwood.

Siena Consensus Workshop II. (1995). Strategies for prevention of perinatal transmission of HIV infection. Report of a Consensus Workshop, Siena, Italy, June 3–6, 1993. *Journal of Acquired Immune Deficiency Syndromes and Human Retrovirology*, 8, 161–175.

Simonds, R. J., & Oxtoby, M. (1995). Epidemiology and natural history of HIV infection in children. Pp. 89–101 in P. Kelly, S. Holman, R. Rothenberg, & S. P. Holzemer (eds.), *Primary Care of Women and Children with HIV Infection*. Boston: Jones & Bartlett.

Soeiro, R., Rubenstein, A., Rashbaum, W. K., & Lyman, W. D. (1992). Maternofetal transmission of AIDS: Frequency of human immunodeficiency virus type 1 nucleic acid sequences in human fetal DNA. *Journal of Infectious Diseases*, 166, 699–703.

Sonnenberg-Schwan, U., Jaeger, H., Reuter, U., & Hammel, G. (1993). HIV-discordant couples: Artificial insemination with processed sperm – psychological and psychosocial implications. Ninth International Conference on AIDS, Berlin, Germany.

Sprecher, S., Soumenkoff, G., Puissant, F., & Deguelde, M. (1986). Vertical transmission of HIV in 15-week fetus (letter). *Lancet*, 2, 288–289.

Stein, Z. (1990). HIV prevention: The need for methods women can use. *American Journal of Public Health*, 80, 460.

(1993). HIV prevention: An update on the status of methods women can use. *American Journal of Public Health*, 83, 1379–1382.

(1995). More on women and the prevention of HIV infection (editorial). *American Journal of Public Health*, 85, 1485–1488.

St. Louis, M. E., Kamenga, M., Brown, C., Nelson, A. M., Manzila, T., Batter, V., Behets, F., Kabagabo, V., Ryder, R. W., & Oxtoby, M. (1993). Risk for perinatal HIV-1 transmission according to maternal immunologic, virologic, and placental factors. *Journal of the American Medical Association*, 269, 2853–2859.

Sunderland, A. (1990). Influence of human immunodeficiency virus infection on reproductive decisions. *Obstetrics and Gynecology Clinics of North America*, 17, 585–594.

Sunderland, A., Minkoff, H. L., Handle, J., Moroso, G., & Landesman, S. (1992). The impact of HIV serostatus on reproductive decisions of women. *Obstetrics and Gynecology*, 7, 1027–1031.

References

Wagner, K., & Cohen, J. (1993). Programs and policies for prevention. Pp. 228–238 in A. Kurth (ed.), *Until the Cure: Caring for Women with HIV*. New Haven, CT: Yale University Press.

WHO/Global Programme on AIDS. (1992). Consensus statement from the WHO/UNICEF consultation on HIV transmission and breastfeeding. WHO/GPA/Inf./92.1

Williams, A. B. (1992). Women in the HIV epidemic. *Critical Care Nursing Clinics of North America*, 4, 437–445.

Worth, D. (1989). Sexual decision-making and AIDS: Why condom promotion among vulnerable women is likely to fail. *Studies in Family Planning*, 20, 297–307.

CHAPTER 3

Albert, A. A., Warner, D. L., Hatcher, R. A., Trussell, J., & Bennett, C. (1995). Condom use among female commercial sex workers in Nevada's legal brothels. *American Journal of Public Health*, 85, 1514–1520.

Alemán, J. del C., Kloser, P., Kreibick, T., Steiner, G. L., & Boyd-Franklin, N. (1995). Women and HIV/AIDS. Pp. 90–111 in N. Boyd-Franklin, G. L. Steiner, & M. G. Boland (eds.), *Children, Families, and HIV/AIDS, Psychsocial and Therapeutic Issues*. New York: Guilford Press.

Alexander, P. (1995). Sex workers fight against AIDS: An international perspective. Pp. 99–123 in B. E. Schneider & N. E. Stoller (eds.), *Women Resisting AIDS: Feminist Strategies of Empowerment*. Philadelphia: Temple University Press.

Amaro, H. (1995). Love, sex, and power: Considering women's realities in HIV prevention. *American Psychologist*, 50, 437–447.

Barnard, M., & McKeganey, N. (1996). Prostitutes and peer education: Beyond HIV. Pp. 103–117 in T. Rhodes & R. Hartnoll (eds.), *AIDS, Drugs, and Prevention: Perspectives on Individual and Community Action*. New York: Routledge.

Barth, R. P. (1993). Shared family care: Child protection without parent-child separation. Pp. 272–295 in R. P. Barth, J. Pietrzak, & M. Ramler (eds.), *Families Living with Drugs and HIV: Intervention and Treatment Strategies*. New York: Guilford Press.

Bayer, R. (1989). *Private Acts, Social Consequences*. New York: Free Press.

Becker, M. H., & Joseph, J. G. (1988). AIDS and behavioral change to reduce risk: A review. *American Journal of Public Health*, 78, 394–410.

Bellis, D. J. (1993). Reduction of AIDS risk among 41 heroin addicted female street prostitutes: Effects of free methadone maintenance. *Journal of Addictive Diseases*, 12, 7–23.

References

Brandt, A. M. (1987). No Magic Bullet: *A Social History of Venereal Disease in the United States Since 1880*. New York: Oxford University Press.

Brown, V., & Weissman, G. (1993). Women and men injection drug users: An updated look at gender differences and risk factors. Pp. 173–194 in B. Brown & G. Beschner (eds.), *Handbook on Risk of AIDS: Injection Drug Users and Sexual Partners*. Westport, CT: Greenwood Press.

Campbell, C. A. (1990). Prostitution and AIDS. Pp. 121–137 in D. G. Ostrow (ed.), *Behavioral Aspects of AIDS*. New York: Plenum.

Carmen, A., & Moody, H. (1985). *Working Women: The Subterranean World of Street Prostitution*. New York: Harper & Row.

Centers for Disease Control. (1983). Immunodeficiency among female partners of males with acquired immune deficiency syndrome (AIDS) – New York. *MMWR*, **31**, 697–698, January 7.

——— (1987a). Antibody to human immunodeficiency virus in female prostitutes. *MMWR*, **36**, 157–161, March 27.

——— (1987b). Human immunodeficiency virus infection in the United States: A review of current knowledge. *MMWR*, **36**, 1–48, December 18.

——— (1987c). Public Health Service guidelines for counseling and antibody testing to prevent HIV infection and AIDS. *MMWR*, **36**, 509–515.

——— (1992). Operational Research Section. *What We Have Learned from Community Demonstration Projects*. June 15.

Chaisson, M., Stoneburner, R., Hildebrandt, D., Ewing, W. E., Telzak, E. E., & Jaffe, H. W. (1991). Heterosexual transmission of HIV-1 associated with the use of smokable freebase cocaine (crack). *AIDS*, **5**, 1121–1126.

Chickwem, J. O., & Gashau, W. (1988). Impact of health education on prostitutes' awareness and attitudes to acquired immune deficiency syndrome (AIDS). *Public Health*, **102**, 439–445.

Clumeck, N., Robert-Guroff, M., Van de Perre, P., Jennings, A., Sibomana, J., De Mol, P., Cran, S., & Gallo, R. C. (1985). Seroepidemiological studies of HTLV-III antibody prevalence among selected groups of heterosexual Africans. *Journal of the American Medical Association*, **254**, 2599–2602.

Cohen, B. (1980). *Deviant Street Networks: Prostitutes in New York City*. Lexington, MA: Lexington Books.

Cohen, J. B. (1987). Three years' experience promoting AIDS prevention among 800 sexually active high risk women in San Francisco. *NIMH/NIDA Research Conference on Women and AIDS*. Bethesda, MD.

Cohen, J. B., & Alexander, P. (1995). Female sex workers: Scapegoats in the AIDS epidemic. Pp. 195–218 in A. O'Leary & L. S. Jemmott (eds.), *Women at Risk: Issues in the Primary Prevention of AIDS*. New York: Plenum Press.

References

Cohen, J., Alexander, P., & Wofsy, C. (1988). Prostitutes and AIDS: Public policy issues. *AIDS and Public Policy*, 3, 16–22.

Connors, M. (1996). Sex, drugs, and structural violence: Unraveling the epidemic among poor women in the United States. Pp. 91–123 in P. Farmer, M. Connors, & J. Simmons (eds.), *Women, Poverty, and AIDS: Sex, Drugs, and Structural Violence*. Monroe, ME: Common Courage Press.

Corea, G. (1992). *The Invisible Epidemic: The Story of Women and AIDS*. New York: Harper Perennial.

Darrow, W. W. (1990). Prostitution, parenteral substance abuse, and HIV-1 in the United States. Pp. 18–40 in M. Plant (ed.), *AIDS, Drugs, and Prostitution*. London: Routledge.

Darrow, W. W., Bigler, W., Deppe, D., French, J., Gill, P., Potterat, J., Ravenholt, O., Schable, C., Sikes, R. K., & Wofsy, C. (1988). Antibody in 640 U.S. prostitutes with no evidence of intravenous (IV)-drug abuse. Fourth International Conference on AIDS, Stockholm, Sweden.

Day, S. (1988). Prostitute women and AIDS: Anthropology. *AIDS*, 2, 421–428.

Delacoste, F., & Alexander, P. (eds.). (1988). *Sex Work: Writings by Women in the Sex Industry*. San Francisco: Cleo Press.

Denenberg, R. (1995). Special concerns of women with HIV and AIDS. Pp. 115–135 in W. Odets & M. Shernoff (eds.), *The Second Decade of AIDS: A Mental Health Practice Handbook*. New York: Hatherleigh Press.

Des Jarlais, D. C. (1984). Heterosexual partners: A risk group for AIDS. *Lancet*, 2, 1346.

Des Jarlais, D. C., & Friedman, S. R. (1988). HIV infection among persons who inject illicit drugs: Problems and prospects. *Journal of AIDS*, 1, 267–273.

Dubler, N. N., & Sidel, V. W. (1992). AIDS and the prison system. Pp. 71–83 in D. Nelkin, D. P. Willis, & S. V. Parris (eds.), *A Disease of Society*. Cambridge: Cambridge University Press.

Dworkin, A. (1981). *Pornography: Men Possessing Women*. London: Women's Press.

Edlin, B. R., Irwin, K. L., Ludwig, D. D., McCoy, H. V., Serrano, Y., Word, C., Bowser, B. P., Faruque, S., McCoy, C. B., & Schilling, R. F. (1992). High-risk sex behavior among young street-recruited crack cocaine smokers in three American cities: An interim report. *Journal of Psychoactive Drugs*, 24, 363–371.

Friedman, S. R., Des Jarlais, D. C., Ward, T. P., Jose, B., Neaigus, A., & Goldstein, M. (1993). Drug injectors and heterosexual AIDS. Pp. 41–65 in L. Sherr (ed.), *AIDS and the Heterosexual Population*. Chur, Switzerland: Harwood.

Fumento, J. (1990). *The Myth of Heterosexual AIDS*. New York: Basic Books.

References

Gross, M., & Brown, V. (1993). Outreach to injection drug-using women. Pp. 445–463 in Brown, B. S., & Beschner, G. M. (eds.), *Handbook on Risk of AIDS: Injection Drug Users and Sexual Partners.* Westport, CT: Greenwood Press.

Guinan, M. E., & Leviton, L. (1995). Prevention in HIV infection in women: Overcoming barriers. *Journal of the American Medical Association,* 50, 74–77.

Inciardi, J. (1989). Trading sex for crack among juvenile drug users: A research note. *Contemporary Drug Problems,* 16, 689–700.

Inciardi, J. A., Lockwood, D., & Pottieger, A. E. (1993). *Women and Crack-Cocaine.* New York: Macmillan.

Institute of Medicine, National Academy of Sciences. (1986). *Confronting AIDS.* Washington, DC: National Academy Press.

James, J. (1976a). Prostitution and addiction: An interdisciplinary approach. *Addictive Diseases: An International Journal,* 2, 601–618.

(1976b). Prostitution: Arguments for change. Pp. 110–123 in S. Gordon & R. W. Libby (eds.), *Sexuality Today and Tomorrow.* North Scituate, MA: Duxbury Press.

Kane, S. (1991). HIV, heroin, and heterosexual relations. *Social Science and Medicine,* 32, 1037–1050.

Khoshnood, K., & Stephens, P. C. (1997). Can needle exchange better serve women? Pp. 357–372 in N. Goldstein & J. L. Manlowe (eds.), *The Gender Politics of HIV/AIDS.* New York: New York University Press.

Kreiss, J. K., Koech, D., Plummer, F. A., Holmes, K. K., Lightfoote, M., Piot, P., Ronald, A. R., Ndinya-Achola, J. O., D'Costa, L. J., Roberts, P., Ngugi E. N., & Quinn T. C. (1986). AIDS virus infection in Nairobi prostitutes. *New England Journal of Medicine,* 314, 414–418.

Leigh, C. (1988). Further violations of our rights. P. 180 in D. Crimp (ed.), *AIDS, Cultural Analysis, Cultural Activism.* Cambridge, MA: MIT Press.

Lewis, D. K., & Watters, J. K. (1991). Sexual risk behavior among heterosexual intravenous drug users: Ethnic and gender variations. *AIDS,* 5, 77–83.

Luthy, R., Ledergerber, B., Tauber, M., & Siegenthaler, W. (1987). Prevalence of HIV antibodies among prostitutes in Zurich, Switzerland. *Klinische Wochenschrift* 65, 287–288.

McCaul, M. E., Lillie-Blanton, M., & Svikis, D. S. (1996). Drug use, HIV status, and reproduction. Pp. 110–139 in R. R. Faden & N. E. Kass (eds.), *HIV, AIDS, and Childbearing.* New York: Oxford University Press.

Miller, H. G., Turner, C. F., & Moses, L. E. (eds.). (1990). *AIDS: The Second Decade.* Washington, DC: National Academy Press.

National Institute on Drug Abuse (NIDA). (1990). AIDS prevention model: Reaching women at risk. Bethesda, MD: Nova Research.

References

Nevada Statewide AIDS Advisory Task Force. (1987). AIDS and Nevada: Policy recommendations. Report to Governor Richard Bryan and the Nevada State Board of Health, pp. 13–14, September 16.

Patton, C. (1994). *Last Served? Gendering the HIV Pandemic.* New York: Taylor & Francis.

Pearce, D. M. (1978). The feminization of poverty: Women, work, and welfare. *The Urban and Social Change Review,* 11, 28–36.

(1982). *The Poverty of Our Future: The Impact of Reagan Budget Cuts on Women, Minorities, and Children.* Washington, DC: Center for National Policy Review.

Pheterson G. (ed.). (1989). *A Vindication of the Rights of Whores.* Seattle: Seal Press.

Philpot, C. R., Harcourt, C., Edwards, J., & Grealis, A. (1988). Human immunodeficiency virus and female prostitutes, Sydney, 1985. *Genitourinary Medicine* 64, 193–197.

Piot, P., Quinn, T. C., & Taleman, H. (1984). Acquired immunodeficiency syndrome in a heterosexual population in Zaire. *Lancet,* 2, 65–69.

Polk, B. F. (1985). Female-to-male transmission of AIDS (letter). *Journal of the American Medical Association,* 254, 3177–3178.

Polych, C. (1992). Punishment within punishment: The AIDS epidemic in North American prisons. *Men's Studies Review,* 9, 13–17.

Population Reports. (1989). AIDS education – a beginning. *Issues in World Health,* Series L, 17–18.

Potterat, J. J., Muth, J. B., & Markewich, G. S. (1986). Serological markers as indicators of sexual orientation in AIDS virus-infected men (letter). *Journal of the American Medical Association,* 256, 712.

Potterat, J. J., Phillips, L., & Muth, J. B. (1987). Lying to military physicians about risk factors for HIV infections (letter). *Journal of the American Medical Association,* 257, 1727.

Quarterly HIV/AIDS Surveillance Summary. (1993). Carson City, NV: Nevada Department of Human Resources, Health Division.

Quina, K., Harlow, L. L., Morokoff, P. J., & Saxon, S. E. (1997). Interpersonal power and women's HIV risk. Pp. 188–206 in N. Goldstein & J. L. Manlowe (eds.), *The Gender Politics of HIV/AIDS.* New York: New York University Press.

Redfield, R. R., Markham, P. D., Salahuddin, S. Z., Wright, D. C., Sarngadharan, M. G., & Gallo, R. C. (1985). Heterosexually acquired HTLV-III/LAV disease (AIDS-related complex and AIDS): Epidemiologic evidence for female-to-male transmission. *Journal of the American Medical Association,* 254, 2094–2096.

Roberts, D. (1993). Child welfare services for drug-exposed and HIV-affected newborns and their families. Pp. 253–271 in R. P. Barth, J. Pietrzak, & M. Ramler (eds.), *Families Living with Drugs and HIV: Intervention and Treatment Strategies.* New York: Guilford Press.

Rosenbaum, M. (1981). *Women on Heroin.* New Brunswick, NJ: Rutgers University Press.

Rosenberg, M. J., & Weiner, J. M. (1988). Prostitutes and AIDS: A health department priority? *American Journal of Public Health, 78,* 418–423.

Schultz, S., Milberg, J. A., Kristal, A. R., & Stoneburner, R. L. (1986). Female-to-male transmission of HTLV-III (letter). *Journal of the American Medical Association, 255,* 1703–1704.

Shaw, N., & Paleo, L. (1986). *Women and AIDS.* Pp. 150–151 in L. McKusic (ed.), *What to Do about AIDS.* Berkeley: University of California Press.

Simpson, B. J., & Williams, A. (1993). Pp. 200–211 in A. Kurth (ed.), *Until the Cure: Caring for Women with HIV.* New Haven, CT: Yale University Press.

Smith, G. L., & Smith, K. F. (1986). Lack of HIV infection and condom use in licensed prostitutes (letter). *Lancet 2,* 1392.

Sogolow, E. D., Des Jarlais, D. C., & Strug, D. (1991). Heterosexual HIV risk reduction among women: The heterosexual AIDS transmission study (HATS). Seventh International Conference on AIDS, Florence, Italy.

Solomon, M. Z., & DeJong, W. (1989). Preventing AIDS and other STDs through condom promotion. *American Journal of Public Health, 79,* 453–458.

Springer, E. (1992). Reflections on women and HIV/AIDS in New York City and the United States. Pp. 32–40 in J. Bury, V. Morrison, & S. McLachian (eds.), *Working with Women and AIDS.* London: Tavistock.

Stein, M. A. (1987). Bordellos of Nevada try to lure patrons, banish AIDS. *Los Angeles Times,* 1, p. 3, June 8.

Sterk, C. E. (1989). *Living the Life: Prostitutes and Their Health.* Rotterdam, Holland: Erasmus University Press.

Sterk, C. E., Friedman, S. R., Sufian, M., Stepherson, B., & Des Jarlais, D. C. (1989). Barriers to AIDS interventions among sexual partners of IV-drug users. Fifth International Conference on AIDS, Montreal, Canada.

Tirelli, U., Vaccher, E., Sorio, R., Carbone, A., & Monfardini, S. (1986). HTLV-III antibodies in drug-addicted prostitutes used by U.S. soldiers in Italy (letter). *Journal of the American Medical Association, 256,* 711–712.

Turner, C. F., Miller, H. G., & Moses, L. E. (eds.). (1989). *AIDS, Sexual Behavior, and Intravenous Drug Use.* Washington, DC: National Academy Press.

University of California, Berkeley and San Francisco. (1993). *The public health impact of needle exchange programs in the United States and abroad.* Vol. 1. Atlanta: Centers for Disease Control.

References

University of California, San Francisco. (1996). What are sex workers' HIV prevention needs? In *HIV Prevention: Looking Back, Looking Ahead.* San Francisco: Center for AIDS Prevention Studies and Harvard AIDS Institute.

Van de Perre, P., Clumeck, N., Carael, M., Nzabihimana, E., Robert-Guroff, M., De Mol, P., Freyens, P., Butzler, J. P., Gallo, R., & Kanyamupira, J. P. (1985). Female prostitutes: A risk group for infection with Human-T-cell Lymphotropic Virus Type III. *Lancet,* 2, 524–527.

Wagner, K., & Cohen, J. (1993). Programs and policies for prevention. Pp. 228–238 in A. Kurth (ed.), *Until the Cure: Caring for Women with HIV.* New Haven, CT: Yale University Press.

Wallace, J. I., Porter, J., Weiner, A., & Steinberg, A. (1997). Oral sex, crack smoking, and HIV infection among female sex workers who do not inject drugs. *American Journal of Public Health,* 87, 470.

Weissman, G. (1991a). Working with women at risk: Experience from a National Prevention Research Program. Plenary address, Comprehensive HIV/AIDS Mental Health Education Program, Annual Training Institute, Detroit, MI.

——— (1991b). AIDS prevention for women at risk: Experience from a National Demonstration Research Program. *The Journal of Primary Prevention,* 12, 49–63.

Weissman, G., & Brown, V. (1995). Drug-using women and HIV: Risk-reduction and prevention issues. Pp. 175–193 in A. O'Leary & L. S. Jemmott (eds.), *Women at Risk: Issues in the Primary Prevention of AIDS.* New York: Plenum.

Williams, A., & O'Connor, P. G. (1995). Substance abuse issues. Pp. 217–238 in P. Kelly, S. Holman, R. Rothenberg, & S. P. Holzemer (eds.), *Primary Care of Women and Children with HIV Infection.* Boston: Jones & Bartlett.

Wilson, D. (1993). Preventing transmission of HIV in heterosexual prostitution. Pp. 68–81 in L. Sherr (ed.), *AIDS and the Heterosexual Population.* Chur, Switzerland: Harwood.

Wofsy, C. (1987). Human immunodeficiency virus in women. *Journal of the American Medical Association,* 257, 2074–2076.

Worth, D. (1989). Sexual decision-making and AIDS: Why condom promotion among vulnerable women is likely to fail. *Studies in Family Planning,* 20, 297–307.

——— (1990). Minority women and AIDS: Culture, race, and gender. Pp. 111–135 in D. Feldman (ed.), *Culture and AIDS.* New York: Praeger.

Worth, D., Drucker, E., Chabon, B., Pivnick, A., & Cochrane, K. (1989). An ethnographic study of high risk sexual behavior in 96 women using heroin, cocaine and crack in the South Bronx. Fifth International Conference on AIDS, Montreal, Canada.

Wykoff, R. F. (1986). Female-to-male transmission of HTLV-III (letter). *Journal of the American Medical Association,* 255, 1704–1705.

CHAPTER 4

Allen, S., Tice, J., Van de Perre, P., Serufilira, A., Hudes, E., Nsengumuremyi, F., Bogaerts, J., Lindan, C., & Hulley, S. (1992). Effect of serotesting with counseling on condom use and seroconversion among HIV discordant couples in Africa. *British Medical Journal.* 304, 1605–1609.

Amaro, H. (1995). Love, sex, and power: Considering women's realities in HIV prevention. *American Psychologist,* 50, 437–447.

Amaro, H., & Gornemann, I. (1992). *HIV/AIDS related knowledge, attitudes, beliefs, and behaviors among Hispanics: Report of findings and recommendations.* Boston: Boston School of Public Health and Northeast Hispanic AIDS Consortium.

Auerbach, J. D., Wypijewska, C., & Brodie, H. K. H. (eds.). (1994). *AIDS and Behavior: An Integrated Approach.* Washington, DC: National Academy Press.

Banks, T. L. (1996). Legal challenges: State intervention, reproduction, and HIV-infected women. Pp. 143–177 in R. R. Faden & N. E. Kass (eds.), *HIV, AIDS, and Childbearing, Public Policy, Private Lives.* New York: Oxford University Press.

Bentley, M., & Herr, K. (1996). Contextualizing the development of adolescent girls: The missing piece in HIV education. Pp. 147–162 in M. K. Moore & M. L. Forst (eds.), *AIDS Education: Reaching Diverse Populations.* Westport, CT: Praeger.

Brown, V., & Weissman, G. (1993). Women and men injection drug users: An updated look at gender differences and risk factors. Pp. 173–194 in B. Brown & G. Beschner (eds.), *Handbook on Risk of AIDS: Injection Drug Users and Sexual Partners.* Westport, CT: Greenwood Press.

Burkett, E. (1995). *The Gravest Show on Earth: America in the Age of AIDS.* Boston: Houghton Mifflin.

Bury, J. (1992). Education and prevention of HIV infection. Pp. 99–109 in J. Bury, V. Morrison, & S. McLachian (eds.), *Working with Women and AIDS.* London: Tavistock.

Campbell, C.A. (1979). Women, Work, and Welfare. Unpublished M.A. thesis, University of Colorado, Denver.

——— (1995). Male gender roles and sexuality: Implications for women's AIDS risk and prevention. *Social Science and Medicine,* 41, 197–210.

References

Carrier, J. M. (1989). Sexual behavior and spread of AIDS in Mexico. *Medical Anthropology*, 10, 129–142.

Carroll, J. C., Volk, K. A., & Hyde, J. S. (1985). Differences between males and females in motives for engaging in sexual intercourse. *Archives of Sexual Behavior*, 14, 131–139.

Centers for Disease Control. (1981). Follow-up on Kaposi's sarcoma and pneumocystis pneumonia. *MMWR*, 30, 409–410, August 28.

(1982a). Update on Kaposi's sarcoma and opportunistic infections in previously health persons – United States. *MMWR*, 294–301, June 31.

(1982b). Unexplained immunodeficiency and opportunistic infections in infants – New York, New Jersey, California. *MMWR*, 31, 665–667, December 17.

(1983). Immunodeficiency among female sexual partners of males with acquired immune deficiency syndrome (AIDS) – New York. *MMWR*, 31, 697–698, January 7.

(1987). Antibody to human immunodeficiency virus in female prostitutes. *MMWR*, 36, 157–161, March 27.

(1991). *America responds to AIDS*. Materials catalog, i–31, May.

(1992). 1993 revised classification system for HIV infection and expanded surveillance case definition for AIDS among adolescents and adults. *MMWR*, 41, 1–23.

(1993). *Catalog of HIV and AIDS education and prevention materials*, iii–43, January.

(1994). Update: Impact of the expanded AIDS surveillance case definition for adolescents and adults on case reporting – United States, 1993. *MMWR*, 43, 160–161, 167–170.

Cochran, S. D. (1989). Women and HIV infection: Issues in prevention and behavior change. Pp. 309–327 in V. M. Mays, G. W. Albee, & S. F. Schneider (eds.), *Primary Prevention of AIDS: Psychological Approaches*. Newbury Park, CA: Sage.

Cohn, J., & Futterman, D. (1995). Adolescents and HIV. Pp. 133–148 in P. Kelly, S. Holman, R. Rothenberg, & S. P. Holzemer (eds.), *Primary Care of Women and Children with HIV Infection*. Boston: Jones & Bartlett.

Cole, R., & Cooper, S. (1991). Lesbian exclusion from HIV/AIDS education: Ten years of low-risk identity and high-risk behavior. *Seicus Report*, December 1990 – January 1991.

Connors, M. (1996). Sex, drugs, and structural violence: Unraveling the epidemic among poor women in the United States. Pp. 91–123 in P. Farmer, M. Connors, & J. Simmons (eds.), *Women, Poverty, and AIDS: Sex, Drugs, and Structural Violence*. Monroe, ME: Common Courage Press.

References

Cook, J. A. (1997). The women's interagency HIV study (WIHS): Correlates of childhood sexual violence and HIV risk. Violence against women and HIV risk, Session No. 122, National Conference on Women and HIV, Pasadena, CA.

Corea, G. (1992). *The Invisible Epidemic: The Story of Women and AIDS*. New York: Harper Perennial.

Cotton, P. (1990a). Examples abound of gaps on medical knowledge because of groups excluded from scientific study. *Journal of the American Medical Association*, **263**, 1051, 1055.

——— (1990b). Is there still too much extrapolation from data on middle-aged white men? *Journal of the American Medical Association*, **263**, 1049–1050.

Currie, E., & Skolnick, J. H. (1997). *America's Problems, Social Issues, and Public Policy*. New York: Longman.

Dalton, H. (1989). AIDS in blackface: Living with AIDS, part II. *Daedalus, Proceedings of the American Academy of Arts and Sciences: Common Threads*, **118**, 205–225.

Denenberg, R. (1995). Special concerns of women with HIV and AIDS. Pp. 115–135 in W. Odets & M. Shernoff (eds.), *The Second Decade of AIDS: A Mental Health Practice Handbook*. New York: Hatherleigh Press.

——— (1997). HIV does not erase desire: Addressing the sexual and reproductive concerns of women with HIV/AIDS. Pp. 323–336 in N. Goldstein & J. L. Manlowe (eds.), *The Gender Politics of HIV/AIDS*. New York: New York University Press.

Flaskerud, J. H., Uman, G., Lara, R., Romero, L., & Taka, K. (1996). Sexual practices, attitudes, and knowledge related to HIV transmission in low income Los Angeles Hispanic women. *The Journal of Sex Research*, **33**, 343–353.

Frieze, I. H., Parsons, J. E., & Johnson, P. E., Ruble, D. N., & Zellman, G. L. (1978). *Women and Sex Roles*. New York: Norton.

Fumento, M. (1990). *The Myth of Heterosexual AIDS*. New York: Basic Books.

Gilmore, S., DeLamater, J., & Wagstaff, D. (1996). Sexual decision making by inner city Black adolescent males: A focus group study. *The Journal of Sex Research*, **33**, 363–371.

Glassman, C. (1970). Women and the welfare system. Pp. 102–115 in R. Morgan (ed.), *Sisterhood Is Powerful*. New York: Random House.

Goldstein, N. (1997). Introduction. Pp. 1–72 in N. Goldstein & J. L. Manlowe (eds.), *The Gender Politics of HIV/AIDS in Women*. New York: New York University Press.

Gomez, C., & Marin, B. (1993). Can women demand condom use? Gender and power in safer sex. Ninth International Conference on AIDS, Berlin, Germany.

References

Gorna, R. (1996). *Vamps, Virgins, and Victims: How Can Women Fight AIDS?* New York: Cassell.

Gould, R. E. (1988). Reassessing news about AIDS: A doctor tells you why *you* may not be at risk. *Cosmopolitan*, 146–147, 204, January 1.

Gross, A. E. (1978). The male role and heterosexual behavior. *Journal of Social Issues*, 34, 87–107.

Guinan, M. E., & Hardy, A. (1987). Human immunodeficiency virus infection in women. *Journal of the American Medical Association*, 257, 2039–2042.

Hampton, D. (1996). AIDS gets a bad rap. *Poz*, 74–77, 101, October.

Hirschhorn, L. R. (1995). HIV infection in women: Is it different? *The AIDS Reader*, 99–105, May/June.

Iglitzen, L. (1977). A case study in patriarchal politics: Women on welfare. Pp. 96–112 in M. Githens (ed.), *A Portrait of Marginality*. New York: David McKay.

Kamenga, M., Ryder, R., Jingu, M., Mbuyi, N., Mbu, L., Behets, F., Brown, C., & Heyward, W. (1991). Evidence of marked sexual behaviour change associated with low HIV 1 seroconversion in 149 married couples with discordant HIV 1 serostatus-experience at an HIV counseling center in Zaire. *AIDS*, 5, 61–67.

King, D. (1990). "Prostitute as pariah in the age of AIDS": A content analysis of coverage of women prostitutes in the *New York Times* and *Washington Post*, September 1985–April 1988. *Women and Health*, 16, 3–4.

King, P. A. (1996). Reproductive choices of adolescent females with HIV/AIDS. Pp. 345–366 in R. R. Faden & N. E. Kass (eds.), *HIV, AIDS, and Childbearing: Public Policy, Private Lives*. New York: Oxford University Press.

Kurth, A. (1993). An overview of women and HIV disease. Pp. 1–18 in A. Kurth (ed.), *Until the Cure: Caring for Women with HIV*. New Haven, CT: Yale University Press.

Legg, J. J. (1993). Women and HIV. *Journal of American Board of Family Practitioners*, 6, 367–377.

Levine, O. H., Britton, P. J., James, T. C., Jackson, A. P., Hobfall, S. E., & Levin, J. P. (1993). The empowerment of women: A key to HIV prevention. *Journal of Community Psychology*, 21, 320–334.

Magaña, J. R., de la Rocha, O., & Amsel, J. L. (1996). Sexual history and behaviors of Mexican migrant workers in Orange County, California. Pp. 77–93 in S. I. Mishra, R. F. Conner, & J. R. Magaña (eds.), *AIDS Crossing Borders: The Spread of HIV among Migrant Latinos*. Boulder, CO: Westview.

Males, M. A. (1996). *The Scapegoat Generation: America's War on Adolescents*. Monroe, ME: Common Courage Press.

References

Marin, G. (1989). AIDS prevention among Hispanics: Needs, risk behaviors, and cultural attitudes. *Public Health Reports*, **104**, 411–415.

Maticka-Tyndale, E. (1992). Social construction of HIV transmission and prevention among heterosexual young adults. *Social Problems*, **39**, 238–252.

Mays, V. M., & Cochran, S. D. (1988). Issues in the perception of AIDS risk and risk reduction activities by Black and Hispanic/Latina women. *American Psychologist*, **48**, 949–957.

McGovern, T. M. (1997). Legal issues affecting women with HIV. Pp. 389–412 in D. Cotton & H. D. Watts (eds.), *The Medical Management of AIDS in Women*. New York: Wiley-Liss.

McGuire, J. F. (1997). The meaning is in the women: Gendered aspects of research participation. Clinical trials, research, and access to therapy: Implications for women, Session No. 227, National Conference on Women and HIV, Pasadena, CA.

Miller, H. G., Turner, C. F., & Moses, L. E. (eds.) (1990). *AIDS: The Second Decade*. Washington, DC: National Academy Press.

Miller, J. B. (1986). *Toward a New Psychology of Women*. Boston: Beacon Press.

Mitchell, J. L., Tucker, J., Loftman, P. O., & Williams, S. B. (1992). HIV and Women: Current controversies and clinical relevance. *Journal of Women's Health*, **1**, 35–39.

Morrow, K. M. (1995). Lesbian women and HIV/AIDS: An appeal for inclusion. Pp. 237–256 in A. O'Leary & L. S. Jemmott (eds.), *Women at Risk: Issues in Primary Prevention of AIDS*. New York: Plenum.

Murrain, M. (1995). Women of color and AIDS: Gender, race, class and science. Pp. 145–154 in G. E. Thomas (ed.), *Race and Ethnicity in America: Meeting the Challenge in the Twenty-first Century*. New York: Taylor & Francis.

Norwood, C. (1990). *Media Coverage of Women and AIDS: Bias, Negative Imagery, and Exclusion of Women's Experts and Sources*. Washington, DC: Center for Women Policy Studies.

O'Leary, A., & Jemmott, L. S. (1995). General issues in the prevention of AIDS in Women. Pp. 1–12 in A. O'Leary & L. S. Jemmott (eds.), *Women at Risk: Issues in the Primary Prevention of AIDS*. New York: Plenum.

O'Leary, A. Jemmott, L. S., Suarez-Al-Adam, M., Alroy, C., & Fernandez, M. I. (1993). Women and AIDS. Pp. 173–192 in S. Matteo (ed.), *American Women in the 1990s: Today's Critical Issues*. Boston: Northeastern University Press.

Padian, N. S., O'Brien, T. R., Chang, Y., Glass, S., & Francis, D. P. (1993).

References

Prevention of heterosexual transmission of human immunodeficiency virus through couple counseling. *Journal of Acquired Immune Deficiency Syndromes,* **6,** 1043–1048.

Patton, C. (1994). *Last Served? Gendering the HIV Pandemic.* New York: Taylor & Francis.

Pearce, D. (1993). Something old, something new: Women's poverty in the 1990s. Pp. 79–97 in S. Matteo (ed.), *American Women in the 1990s: Today's Critical Issues.* Boston: Northeastern University Press.

Peterson, J. L., & Marin, G. (1988). Issues in the prevention of AIDS among Black and Hispanic men. *American Psychologist,* **43,** 871–877.

Rhatigan, J., Connors, M., & Rodriguez, W. (1996). Rereading public health. Pp. 207–243 in P. Farmer, M. Connors, & J. Simmons (eds.), *Women, Poverty, and AIDS: Sex, Drugs, and Structural Violence.* Monroe, ME: Common Courage Press.

Richardson, D. (1994). Inclusions and exclusion: Lesbians, HIV, and AIDS. Pp. 159–170 in L. Doyle, J. Naidoo, & T. Wilton (eds.), *AIDS, Setting a Feminist Agenda.* London: Taylor & Francis.

Roan, S. (1995). A sign of the times. *Los Angeles Times,* pp. E1, 3, July 9.

Rodriguez-Trias, H., & Marte, C. (1995). Challenges and possibilities: Women, HIV, and the health care system in the 1990s. Pp. 301–321 in B. E. Schneider & N. E. Stoller (eds.), *Women Resisting AIDS: Feminist Strategies of Empowerment.* Philadelphia: Temple University Press.

Rotheram-Borus, M. J. (1997). Annotation: HIV prevention challenges – realistic strategies and early detection programs. *American Journal of Public Health,* **87,** 544–546.

Rotheram-Borus, M. J., Jemmott, L. S., & Jemmott, J. B. (1995). Preventing AIDS in female adolescents. Pp. 103–129 in A. O'Leary & L. S. Jemmott (eds.), *Women at Risk: Issues in the Primary Prevention of AIDS.* New York: Plenum.

Rotheram-Borus, M. J., Koopman, C., & Bradley, J. (1989). Barriers to successful AIDS prevention programs with runaway youth. Pp. 35–55 in J. O. Woodruff, D. Doherty, & J. G. Athey (eds.), *Troubled Adolescents and HIV Infection: Issues in Prevention and Treatment.* Washington, DC: Georgetown University.

Sacks, V. (1996). Women and AIDS: An analysis of media representations. *Social Science and Medicine,* **42,** 59–73.

Schneider, B. (1991). Women, children, and AIDS: Research suggestions. Pp. 134–148 in R. Ulack & W. F. Skinner (eds.), *AIDS and the Social Sciences: Common Threads.* Lexington: University Press of Kentucky.

Sherr, L. (1993). Discordant couples. Pp. 83–102 in L. Sherr (ed.), *AIDS and the Heterosexual Population.* Chur, Switzerland: Harwood.

(1995). Psychological aspects of providing care for women with HIV infection. Pp. 107–123 in H. Minkoff, J. A. DeHovitz, & A. Duerr (eds.), *HIV Infection in Women.* New York: Raven Press.

Sobo, E. J. (1995). *Choosing Unsafe Sex: AIDS–Risk Denial among Disadvantaged Women.* Philadelphia: University of Pennsylvania Press.

Stevens, E. P. (1973). Machismo and marianismo. *Transaction Society,* 10, 57–63.

Stevens, P. E. (1993). Lesbians and HIV: Clinical, research, and policy issues. *American Journal of Orthopsychiatry.* 63, 289–294.

Strebel, A. (1995). Whose epidemic is it: Reviewing the literature on women and AIDS. *South African Journal of Psychology,* 25, 12–20.

(1996). Prevention implications of AIDS discourses among South African women. *AIDS Education and Prevention,* 8, 352–374.

Travers, M., & Bennett, L. (1996). AIDS, women and power. Pp. 64–77 in L. Sherr, C. Hankins, & L. Bennett (eds.), *AIDS as a Gender Issue: Psychological Perspectives.* London: Taylor & Francis.

Treichler, P. (1988). AIDS, gender, and biomedical discourse: Current contests for meaning. Pp. 190–266 in E. Fee & D. M. Fox (eds.), *AIDS: The Burdens of History.* Berkeley: University of California Press.

Verbrugge, L. M. (1989). The twain meet: Empirical explanations of sex differences in health and mortality. *Journal of Health and Social Behavior,* 30, 282–304.

Weiser, B. S. (1997). Where's the data? Challenges in creating responsive multi-disciplinary health services for lesbian, bisexual, and transgendered women. HIV prevention strategies for women who have sex with women, Session No. 115, National Conference on Women and HIV, Pasadena, CA.

Weissman, G. (1991). AIDS prevention for women at risk: Experience from a National Demonstration Research Program. *The Journal of Primary Prevention,* 12, 49–63.

Wells, K. (1980). Gender role identity and psychological adjustment in adolescence. *Journal of Youth and Adolescence,* 9, 59–73.

Wermuth, L., Ham, J., & Robbins, R. L. (1992). Women don't wear condoms: AIDS risk among sexual partners of IV drug users. Pp. 72–93 in J. Huber & B. Schneider (eds.), *The Social Context of AIDS.* Newbury Park, CA: Sage.

Wingood, G. M., & DiClemente, R. J. (1995). The role of gender relations in HIV prevention research for women. *American Journal of Public Health,* 85, 592.

Wofsy, C. (1987). Human immunodeficiency virus infection in women. *Journal of the American Medical Association,* 257, 2074–2076.

Wolfe, M. (1997). Who's "The Cure" for? Defining a national AIDS Policy: Research, health service and prevention, Session No. 303, National Conference on Women and HIV, Pasadena, CA.

Worth, D. (1989). Sexual decision-making and AIDS: Why condom promotion among vulnerable women is likely to fail. *Studies in Family Planning*, 20, 297–307.

——— (1990). Minority women and AIDS: Culture, race, and gender. Pp. 111–135 in D. Feldman (ed.), *Culture and AIDS*. New York: Praeger.

Worth, D., & Rodriquez, R. (1987). Latina women and AIDS. *Radical America*, 20, 63–67.

Wyatt, G. (1997). Redefining the balance of power in relationships. Behavioral and Prevention Science Track, Session No. 201, National Conference on Women and HIV, Pasadena, CA.

CHAPTER 5

Alexander, P. (1995). Sex workers fight against AIDS: An international perspective. Pp. 99–123 in B. E. Schneider & N. E. Stoller (eds.), *Women Resisting AIDS: Feminist Strategies of Empowerment*. Philadelphia: Temple University Press.

Allen, S., Serufilira, A., Bogaerts, J., Van de Perre, P., Nsengumuremyi, F., Lindan, C., Carael, M., Wolf, W., Coates, T., & Hulley, S. (1992). Confidential HIV testing and condom promotion in Africa: Impact of HIV and gonorrhea rates. *Journal of the American Medical Association*, 268, 3338–3343.

Allen, S., Tice, J., Van de Perre, P., Serufilira, A., Hudes, E., Nsengumuremyi, F., Bogaerts, J., Lindan, C., & Hulley, S. (1992). Effect of serotesting with counseling on condom use and seroconversion among HIV discordant couples in Africa. *British Medical Journal*, 304, 1605–1609.

Anson, O., Carmel, S., & Levin, M. (1991). Gender difference in utilization of emergency department services. *Women and Health*, 17, 91–104.

Avins, A. L, Woods, W. J., Lindan, C. P., Hudes, E. S., Clark, W., & Hulley, S. B. (1994). HIV infection and risk behaviors among heterosexuals in alcohol treatment programs. *Journal of the American Medical Association*, 271, 515–518.

Berer, M., & Ray, S. (eds.), (1993). *Women and HIV/AIDS: An International Resource Book*. London: Pandora.

Bhattacharya, S., Chowdhury, K., & Chakraborty, S. (1996). Sexual health intervention program targeting male clients: An approach through socioeconomic mapping and outlets. Abstract No. Tu.C. 452. Eleventh International Conference on AIDS, Vancouver, Canada.

References

Blackwell, B. L. (1967). Upper middle class adult expectations about entering a sick role for physical and psychiatric dysfunctions. *Journal of Health and Human Behavior*, 8, 83–95.

Blum, R. (1993). Critical issues for the family research agenda and their use in policy formulation. Pp. 110–112 in G. E. Hendershot & F. B. LeClere (eds.), *Family Health: From Data to Policy*. Minneapolis, MN: National Council on Family Relations.

Boles, J., Elifson, K., Sweat, M. (1989). Self-reported bisexuality among male prostitutes. Presented at CDC Workshop on Bisexuality and AIDS, Atlanta, GA.

Bosk, C. L., & Frader, J. E. (1992). AIDS and its impact on medical work. Pp. 150–171 in D. Nelkin, D. P. Willis, & S. V. Parris (eds.), *A Disease of Society*. Cambridge: Cambridge University Press.

Boulton, M., Evans, Z. S., Fitzpatrick, R., & Graham, H. (1991). Bisexual men: Women, safer sex, and HIV transmission. Pp. 65–78 in P. Aggleton, G. Hart, & P. Davies (eds.), *AIDS: Responses, Interventions and Care*. London: Falmer Press.

Breitman, P., Knutson, K., & Reid, P. (1987). *How to Persuade Your Lover to Use a Condom and Why You Should*. Rocklin, CA: Prima Publications and Communications.

Brewer, T. F., & Derrickson, J. (1992). AIDS in prison: A review of epidemiology and preventive policy. *AIDS*, 6, 623–628.

Brown, B. (1988). Creative acceptance: An ethics for AIDS. P. 230 in I. Corless & M. Pittman-Lindeman (eds.), *AIDS: Principles, Practices and Politics*. New York: Hemisphere.

Carroll, J. C., Volk, K. A., & Hyde, J. S. (1985). Differences between males and females in motives for engaging in sexual intercourse. *Archives of Sexual Behavior*, 14, 131–139.

Center for Women Policy Studies (1993). *The Guide to Resources on Women and AIDS*. Washington, DC: Center for Women Policy Studies.

Centers for Disease Control. (1997). *HIV/AIDS Surveillance Report*. Year-end edition, cases through December, 9, 1–40.

Chu, S. Y., Peterman, T. A., Doll, L. S., Buehler, J. W., & Curran, J. W. (1992). AIDS in bisexual men in the United States: Epidemiology and transmission to women. *American Journal of Public Health*, 82, 220–224.

De Bertolini, C., Scarso, C., Andreetto, U., Bertuzzo, P., Milan, E., Favero, E., Cadrobbi, P., Cattelan, A. M., & Rupolo, G. P. (1996). Risk-related sexual behavior: Differences between HIV-positive heterosexual males and females. Abstract Mo.D. 1891, Eleventh International Conference on AIDS, Vancouver, Canada.

De Vincenzi, I. (1994). A longitudinal study of human immunodeficiency virus transmission by heterosexual partners. *New England Journal of Medicine*, **331**, 341–346.

Doll, L. S., & Beeker, C. (1996). Male bisexual behavior and HIV risk in the U.S.: Synthesis of research with behavioral interventions. *AIDS Education and Prevention*, **8**, 205–225.

Doll, L. S., Peterson, L. R., White, C. R., Johnson, E. S., Ward, J. W., & the Blood Donor Study Group. (1992). Homosexually and nonhomosexually identified men who have sex with men: A behavioral comparison. *Journal of Sex Research*, **29**, 1–14.

Dubler, N. N., & Sidel, V. W. (1992). AIDS and the prison system. Pp. 71–83 in D. Nelkin, D. P. Willis, & S. V. Parris (eds.), *A Disease of Society*. Cambridge: Cambridge University Press.

Edwards, S. R. (1994). The role of men in contraceptive decision-making. *Family Planning Perspectives*, **26**, 77–82.

Ehrhardt, A. A. (1992). Trends in sexual behavior and the HIV pandemic (editorial). *American Journal of Public Health*, **82**, 1459–1461.

Eighth International Conference on AIDS. (1992a). Conference summary report, 36, Amsterdam, The Netherlands.

(1992b) Session No. 110: Prevention programs for women; Session No. 185: Women's access to prevention and care; Session No. 235: Decreasing sexual transmission to women; and, Session No. 254: Empowering heterosexual women. Session No. 16: Changing male heterosexual attitudes and behavior, Amsterdam, The Netherlands, July 19–24.

Elifson, K. W., Boles, J., & Sweat, M. (1993). Risk factors associated with HIV infection among male prostitutes. *American Journal of Public Health*, **83**, 79–83.

Fadin, R., Geller, G., & Powers, M. (1991). *AIDS, Women, and the Next Generation*. Oxford: Oxford University Press.

Fasteau, M. F. (1975). *The Male Machine*. New York: Dell.

Fears, D. (1998). AIDS among black women seen as a growing problem. *Los Angeles Times*, pp. A1, 22, July 24.

Ferreros, C., Mivumbi, N., Kakera, K., & Price, J. (1990). Social marketing of condoms for AIDS prevention in developing countries. Abstract SC 697. Sixth International Conference on AIDS, San Francisco, CA.

Ford, K., & Wirawan, D. N. (1996). What makes an intervention effective? A multilevel analysis of data from female sex workers, pimps, and clients in Bali, Indonesia. Abstract No. Th.C. 4841, Eleventh International Conference on AIDS, Vancouver, Canada.

Forrest, K. A., Austin, D. M., Valdes, M. I., Fuentes, E. G., & Wilson, S. R. (1993). Exploring norms and beliefs related to AIDS prevention among California Hispanic men. *Family Planning Perspectives*, **25**, 111–117.

References

Freeborn, D. K., Pope, C. R., Davis, M. A., & Mulooley, J. P. (1977). Health status, socioeconomic status and utilization of outpatient services for members of a prepaid group practice. *Medical Care*, 115–128.

Gollub, E. L. (1995). Women-centered prevention techniques and technologies. Pp. 43–82 in A. O'Leary & L. S. Jemmott (eds.), *Women at Risk: Issues in the Primary Prevention of AIDS*. New York: Plenum.

Graham, H. (1984). *Women, Health, and Family*. Sussex, England: Wheatsheaf Books.

——— (1985). Providers, negotiators, and mediators: Women as the hidden carers. Pp. 25–52 in V. Olesen & E. Lewin (eds.), *Women, Health, and Healing*. New York: Tavistock.

Graham, S. (1957). Socio-economic status, illness, and the use of medical services. *Milbank Memorial Fund Quarterly*, **35**, 58–66.

Gross, A. E. (1978). The male role and heterosexual behavior. *Journal of Social Issues*, **34**, 87–107.

Guinan, M. (1992). HIV, heterosexual transmission, and women. *Journal of the American Medical Association*, **268**, 520.

Holland, J., Ramazanoglu, C., & Scott, S. (1990). AIDS: From panic stations to power relations, sociological perspectives, and problems. *Sociology*, **25**, 499–518.

Institute of Medicine, National Academy of Sciences. (1986). *Confronting AIDS*. Washington, DC: National Academy Press.

Japenga, A. (1992). Hidden dangers. *Los Angeles Times*, pp. E1, 12, May 21.

Juhasz, A. (1990). The contained threat: Women in mainstream documentary. *Journal of Sex Research*, **27**, 25–46.

Kamenga, M., Ryder, R., Jingu, M., Mbuyi, N., Mbu, L., Behets, F., Brown, C., & Heyward, W. (1991). Evidence of marked sexual behaviour change associated with low HIV 1 seroconversion in 149 married couples with discordant HIV 1 serostatus – experience at an HIV counseling center in Zaire. *AIDS*, **5**, 61–67.

Kaplan, H. S. (1987). *The Real Truth about Women and AIDS: How to Eliminate Risks without Giving Up Love and Sex*. New York: Simon & Schuster.

Kasprzyk, D., Montano, D. E., & Wilson, D. (1992). Beliefs, social norms, and other factors affecting condom use and monogamy in Zimbabwe. Oral Abstract ThD 1529, Eighth International Conference on AIDS, Amsterdam, The Netherlands.

Kolata, G. (1988). Hemophilia and AIDS: Silent suffering. *New York Times*, pp. A1, 13, May 16.

Kurth, A. (1993). An overview of women and HIV disease. Pp. 1–18 in A. Kurth (ed.), *Until the Cure: Caring for Women with HIV*. New Haven, CT: Yale University Press.

References

Leonard, T. L. (1990). Male clients of female street prostitutes: Unseen partners in sexual disease transmission. *Medical Anthropology Quarterly*, 4, 41–55.

Lever, J., Kanouse, D. E., Rogers, W. H., Carson, S., & Hertz, R. (1992). Behavior patterns and sexual identity of bisexual males. *Journal of Sex Research*, 29, 141–167.

Lifson, A. R. (1992). Men who have sex with men (editorial). *American Journal of Public Health*, 82, 166.

Long, L. D. (1996). Introduction: Counting women's experiences. Pp. 1–20 in L. D. Long & E. M. Ankrah (eds.), *Women's Experiences with HIV/AIDS: An International Perspective*. New York: Columbia University Press.

Mak, R. P., & Plum, J. R. (1991). Do prostitutes need more health education regarding sexually transmitted diseases and HIV infection? Experience in a Belgian city. *Social Science and Medicine*, 33, 963–966.

Marin, B. V., Gomez, C., Tschann, J., & Gregorich, S. (1996). Traditional gender role beliefs increase sexual coercion and lower condom use in U.S. Latino men. Abstract We.C. 3519, Eleventh International Conference on AIDS, Vancouver, Canada.

Markova, I., Wilkie, P. A., Naji, S. A., & Forbes, C. D. (1990). Knowledge of HIV/AIDS and behavioural change of people with haemophilia. *Psychology and Health*, 4, 125–133.

McCaul, M. E., Lillie-Blanton, M., & Svikis, D. S. (1996). Drug use, HIV status, and reproduction. Pp. 110–139 in R. R. Faden & N. E. Kass (eds.), *HIV, AIDS, and Childbearing*. New York: Oxford University Press.

Meininger, J. C. (1986). Sex differences in factors associated with use of medical care and alternative illness behaviors. *Social Science and Medicine*, 22, 285–292.

Miller, H. G., Turner, C. F., & Moses, L. E. (eds.). (1990). *AIDS, The Second Decade*. Washington, DC: National Academy Press.

Mills, S., & Fischer-Ponce, L. (1992). Media and Magic: The effects of Magic Johnson's HIV diagnosis on HIV antibody testing rates. Oral abstract MoCo060, Eighth International Conference on AIDS, Amsterdam, The Netherlands.

National Conference on Women and HIV. (1997). Innovation for care, policy, and prevention, Pasadena, CA.

Nelson, K. E., Celentano, D. D., Eiumtrakol, S., Hoover, D. R., Beyrer, C., Suprasert, S., Kuntolbutra, S., & Khamboonruang, C. (1996). Changes in sexual behavior and a decline in HIV among young men in Thailand. *New England Journal of Medicine*, 335, 297–303.

Norwood, C. (1987). *Advice for Life: A Woman's Guide to AIDS Risk and Prevention*. New York: Pantheon.

References

Panos Dossier (1990). *Triple Jeopardy: Women and AIDS*, Washington, Panos Institute, 1990.

Population Reports. (1986). *Men – New Focus for Family Planning Programs*. Series J, 879–919.

(1989). AIDS education – a beginning. *Issues in World Health*. Series L, 17–18.

Quina, K., Harlow, L. L., Morokoff, P. J., & Saxon, S. E. (1997). Interpersonal power and women's HIV risk. Pp. 188–206 in N. Goldstein & J. L. Manlowe (eds.), *The Gender Politics of HIV/AIDS*. New York: New York University Press.

Rapin, S. A. (1994). A private sector view of health, surveillance, and communities of color. *Public Health Reports*, **109**, 42–46.

Rapkin, B., Mantell, J. E., Tross. S., & Ortiz-Torres B. (1992). Do you believe in Magic? The public health consequences of Magic Johnson's announcement for inner-city women. Abstract No. ThD 1527, Eighth International Conference on AIDS, Amsterdam, The Netherlands.

Richardson, D. (1990). AIDS education and women: Sexual and reproductive issues. Pp. 168–179 in P. Aggleton, P. Davies, & G. Hart (eds.), *AIDS: Individual, Cultural and Policy Dimensions*. London: Falmer Press.

Rosenberg, M. J., & Weiner, J. M. (1988). Prostitutes and AIDS: A health department priority? *American Journal of Public Health*, **78**, 418–423.

Santos, B., & Author, M. J. (1992). As long as men have sexual power: The sexual behavior and spreading of AIDS/STD. Poster D 5512, Eighth International Conference on AIDS, Amsterdam, The Netherlands.

Scheerhorn, D. (1990). Hemophilia in the days of AIDS: Communicative tensions surrounding "associated stigmas." *Community Research*, **17**, 842–847.

Schneider, B. E. (1988). Gender, sexuality and AIDS: Social responses and consequences. Pp. 15–36 in R. A. Berk (ed.), *The Social Impact of AIDS in the U.S.*. Cambridge: Abt Books.

(1989). Women and AIDS: An international perspective. *Futures*, 72–88, February.

Sepulveda, J., Fineberg, H., & Mann, J. (eds.) (1992). *AIDS Prevention through Education: A World View*. Oxford: Oxford University Press.

Shepherd, C. M. (1994). *HIV Infection in Pregnancy*. Cheshire, England: Books for Midwives Press.

Sherr, L. (1993). Discordant couples. Pp. 83–102 in L. Sherr (ed.), *AIDS and the Heterosexual Population*. Chur, Switzerland: Harwood.

(1995). Psychological aspects of providing care for women with HIV infection. Pp. 107–123 in H. Minkoff, J. A. DeHovitz, & A. Duerr (eds.), *HIV Infection in Women*. New York: Raven Press.

References

Shilts, R. (1987). *And the Band Played On.* New York: Penguin Books.

Soesbeck, K. H., & Tielman, R. A. P. (1992). Patterns of male bisexual behavior in the Netherlands: A qualitative research project. Poster D 5197, *Eighth International Conference on AIDS*, Amsterdam, The Netherlands.

Stein, Z. (1990). HIV prevention: The need for methods women can use. *American Journal of Public Health*, 80, 460.

—— (1996). Family planning, sexually transmitted diseases, and the prevention of AIDS – Divided we stand? (editorial). *American Journal of Public Health*, 86, 783–784.

Stine, G. (1993). *AIDS: Biological, Medical, Social, and Legal Issues.* Englewood Cliffs, NJ: Prentice-Hall.

Stokes, J. P., McKirnan, D. J., Doll, S., & Burzette, R. G. (1996). Female partners of bisexual men: What they don't know might hurt them. *Psychology of Women Quarterly*, 20, 267–284.

Strebel, A. (1995). Whose epidemic is it? Reviewing the literature on women and AIDS. *South African Journal of Psychology*, 25, 12–20.

—— (1996). Prevention implications of AIDS discourses among South African women. *AIDS Education and Prevention*, 8, 352–374.

Tielman, R., Hendriks, A., & Soesbeck, K. (1992). International comparative study on bisexuality and HIV/AIDS. Poster D 5200, *Eighth International Conference AIDS*, Amsterdam, The Netherlands, 1992.

Ulin, P. R. (1992). African women and AIDS: Negotiating behavioral change. *Social Science and Medicine*, 34, 63–73.

Wilkie, P. (1990). Haemophilia, AIDS, and HIV: Some social and ethical considerations. Pp. 34–40 in B. Almond (ed.), *AIDS: A Moral Issue.* New York: St. Martin's Press.

Wilson, D., Sibanda, B., Mboyi, L., Msimanga, S., & Dube, G. (1990). A pilot study for an HIV intervention program among commercial sex workers in Bulawayo, Zimbabwe. *Social Science and Medicine*, 31, 609–618.

Wilton, T., & Aggleton, P. (1991). Condoms, coercion, and control: Heterosexuality and the limits to HIV/AIDS education. Pp. 149–156 in P. Aggleton, G. Hart, & P. Davies (eds.), *AIDS: Responses, Interventions, and Care.* London: Falmer Press.

Wingood, G. M., & DiClemente, R. J. (1995). The role of gender relations in HIV prevention research for women. *American Journal of Public Health*, 85, 592.

Wolf, T. J. (1987). Group counselling for bisexual men. *Journal for Specialists in Group Work*, 12, 162–165, November.

Wolitski, R .J., Rietmeijer, C., & Goldbaum, G. (1996). Men's disclosure of HIV risk to their female partners. Abstract No. We.D. 3613, Eleventh International Conference on AIDS, Vancouver, Canada.

References

Wride, N. (1992). Laguna Hills teen grows up with AIDS virus. *Los Angeles Times*, pp. A1, 14, March 9.

CHAPTER 6

Andiman, W. (1995). Medical aspects of AIDS: What do children witness? Pp. 32–49 in S. Geballe, J. Gruendel, & W. Andiman (eds.), *Forgotten Children of the AIDS Epidemic*. New Haven, CT: Yale University Press.

Baines, C., Evans, P., & Neysmith, S. (eds.). (1991). Caring: Its impact on the lives of women. Pp. 11–35 in C. Baines, P. Evans, & S. Neysmith (eds.), *Women's Caring: Feminist Perspectives on Social Welfare*. Toronto: McClelland & Stewart.

Baker, L. S. (1992). The perspective of families. Pp. 147–161 in M. L. Stuber (ed.), *Children and AIDS*. Washington, DC: American Psychiatric Press.

Barlow, K. M., & Mok, J. Y. (1993). The challenge of AIDS in children. Pp. 113–124 in L. Sherr (ed.), *AIDS and the Heterosexual Population*. Chur, Switzerland: Harwood.

Bennett, L., Casey, K., & Austin, P. (1996). Issues for women as carers in HIV/AIDS. Pp. 177–190 in L. Sherr, C. Hankins, & L. Bennett (eds.), *AIDS as a Gender Issue: Psychological Perspectives*. London: Taylor & Francis.

Boland, M. G., Czarniecki, L., & Haiken, H. J. (1992). Coordinated care for children with HIV infection. Pp. 166–181 in M. L. Stuber (ed.), *Children and AIDS*. Washington, DC: American Psychiatric Press.

Bor, R. (1995). The family and HIV disease. Pp. 139–152 in L. Sherr (ed.), *AIDS and the Heterosexual Population*. Chur, Switzerland: Harwood.

Boyd-Franklin, N., & Boland, M. G. (1995). A multisystems approach to service delivery for HIV/AIDS families. Pp. 199–215 in N. Boyd-Franklin, G. L. Steiner, & M. G. Boland (eds.), *Children, Families, and HIV/AIDS: Psychosocial and Therapeutic Issues*. New York: Guilford Press.

Brown, S. T. (1991). The impact of AIDS on foster care: A family-centered approach to services in the United States. *Child Welfare*, 70, 193–209.

Cohen, M. H., & Kelly, P. (1995). HIV disease in the primary care setting. Pp. 9–18 in P. Kelly, S. Holman, R. Rothenberg, & S. P. Holzemer (eds.), *Primary Care of Women and Children with HIV Infection*. Boston: Jones & Bartlett.

Crystal, S., & Sambamoorthi, U. (1996). Care needs and access to care among women living with HIV. Pp. 191–196 in L. Sherr, C. Hankins, & L. Bennett (eds.), *AIDS as a Gender Issue: Psychological Perspectives*. London: Taylor & Francis.

Denenberg, R. (1995). Special concerns of women with HIV and AIDS. Pp.

References

115–135 in W. Odets & M. Shernoff (eds.), *The Second Decade of AIDS: A Mental Health Practice Handbook.* New York: Hatherleigh Press.

Forsyth, B. W. C. (1995). A pandemic out of control: The epidemiology of AIDS. Pp. 19–31 in S. Geballe, J. Gruendel, & W. Andiman (eds.), *Forgotten Children of the AIDS Epidemic.* New Haven, CT: Yale University Press.

Geballe, S., Gruendel, J., & Andiman, W. (1995). Pp. xiii–xiv in S. Geballe, J. Gruendel, & W. Andiman (eds.), *Forgotten Children of the AIDS Epidemic.* New Haven, CT: Yale University Press.

Gorna, R. (1996). *Vamps, Virgins, and Victims: How Can Women Fight AIDS?* New York: Cassell.

Greenblat, C. S. (1995). Women in families with hemophilia and HIV: Improving communication about sensitive issues. Pp. 124–138 in B. E. Schneider & N. E. Stoller (eds.), *Women Resisting AIDS: Feminist Strategies of Empowerment.* Philadelphia: Temple University Press.

Gross, J. (1987). The bleak and lonely lives of women who carry AIDS. *New York Times,* August 27.

Hammer, S. (1996). Personal communication.

Holzemer, S. P., Rothenberg, R., & Fish, C. A. (1995). Continuity of care. Pp. 195–205 in P. Kelly, S. Holman, R. Rothenberg, & S. P. Holzemer (eds.), *Primary Care of Women and Children with HIV Infection.* Boston: Jones & Bartlett.

Jones, P. (1995). Haemophilia and HIV infection: Some lessons learned. Pp. 192–204 in J. Q. Mok & M. L. Newell (eds.), *HIV Infection in Children: A Guide to Practical Management.* Cambridge: Cambridge University Press.

King, M. B. (1993). *AIDS, HIV, and Mental Health.* Cambridge: Cambridge University Press.

Kolata, G. (1988). Hemophilia and AIDS: Silent suffering. *New York Times,* Pp. A1, 13, May 16.

Kurth, A. (1993). An overview of women and HIV disease. Pp. 1–18 in A. Kurth (ed.), *Until the Cure: Caring for Women with HIV.* New Haven, CT: Yale University Press.

Levine, C. (1996). Children in mourning: Impact of the HIV/AIDS epidemic on mothers with AIDS and their families. Pp. 197–214 in L. Sherr, C. Hankins, & L. Bennett (eds.), *AIDS as a Gender Issue: Psychological Perspectives.* London: Taylor & Francis.

(1995). Today's challenges, tomorrow's dilemmas. Pp. 190–204 in S. Geballe, J. Gruendel, & W. Andiman (eds.), *Forgotten Children of the AIDS Epidemic.* New Haven, CT: Yale University Press.

Mellins, C. A., Ehrhardt, A. A., Newman, L., & Conrad, M. (1996). "Selective kin." Defining the caregivers and families of children with HIV disease. Pp. 123–149 in A. O'Leary & L. S. Jemmott (eds.), *Women and AIDS: Coping and Care*. New York: Plenum.

Miller, J. B. (1986). *Toward a New Psychology of Women*. Boston: Beacon Press.

Miller, R., Goldman, E., Bor, R., & Kernoff, P. (1989). AIDS and children: Some of the issues in haemophilia care and how to address them. *AIDS Care*, 1, 59–65.

Nehring, W., Malm, K., & Harris, D. (1993). Family and living issues for HIV-infected children. Pp. 211–227 in F. L. Cohen & J. P. Durham (eds.), *Women, Children, and HIV/AIDS*. New York: Springer.

Olson, R., Huszti, H., & Chaffin, M. (1992). Children and adolescents with hemophilia. Pp. 70–85 in M. L. Stuber (ed.), *Children and AIDS*. Washington, DC: American Psychiatric Press.

Richardson, D. (1988). *Women and AIDS*. New York: Methuen.

Rodriguez-Trias, H., & Marte, C. (1995). Challenges and possibilities: Women, HIV, and the health care system in the 1990s. Pp. 301–321 in B. E. Schneider & N. E. Stoller (eds.), *Women Resisting AIDS: Feminist Strategies of Empowerment*. Philadelphia: Temple University Press.

Rosenbaum, M. (1981). *Women on Heroin*. New Brunswick, NJ: Rutgers University Press.

Sherr, L. (1995). Psychological aspects of providing care for women with HIV infection. Pp. 107–123 in H. Minkoff, J. A. DeHovitz, & A. Duerr (eds.), *HIV Infection in Women*. New York: Raven Press.

Siegel, K., & Gorey, E. (1994). Childhood bereavement due to parental death from AIDS. *Developmental and Behavioral Pediatrics*, 15, S66–70.

Simpson, B. J., & Williams, A. (1993). Caregiving: A matriarchal tradition continues. Pp. 200–211 in A. Kurth (ed.), *Until the Cure: Caring for Women with HIV*. New Haven, CT: Yale University Press.

Smith, J. M. (1996). *AIDS and Society*. Upper Saddle River, NJ: Prentice-Hall.

Springer, E. (1992). Reflections on women and HIV/AIDS in New York City and the United States. Pp. 32–40 in J. Bury, V. Morrison, & S. McLachian (eds.), *Working with Women and AIDS*. London: Tavistock.

Stephens, P. C. (1989). U.S. women and HIV infection. Pp. 381–401 in P. O'Malley (ed.), *The AIDS Epidemic*. Boston: Beacon Press.

Stowe, A., Ross, M. W., Wodak, A., Thomas, G. V., & Larson, S. A. (1995). Significant relationships and social supports of injecting drug users and their implications for HIV/AIDS services. Pp. 129–140 in R. Bor & J. Elford (eds.), *The Family and HIV*. New York: Cassell.

Sunderland, A., & Holman, S. (1993). Optimizing the delivery of health and social services: Case study of a model. Pp. 212–227 in A. Kurth (ed.),

References

Until the Cure: Caring for Women with HIV. New Haven, CT: Yale University Press.

Tsiantis, J., Anastasopoulous, D., Meyer, M., Panitz, D., Ladis, V., Platokouki, H., Aroni, S., & Kattamis, C. (1995). A multilevel intervention approach for care of HIV-positive haemophiliac and thallassaemic patients and their families. Pp. 248–263 in R. Bor & J. Elford (eds.), *The Family and HIV.* New York: Cassell.

Valdiserri, R. O. (1989). *Preventing AIDS.* New Brunswick, NJ: Rutgers University Press.

Wardlaw, L. A. (1994). Sustaining informal caregivers for persons with AIDS. *Families in Society: The Journal of Contemporary Human Services,* 373–384, June.

Wicklund, B. M., & Jackson, M. A. (1992). Coping with AIDS in hemophilia. Pp. 255–268 in P. I. Ahmed (ed.), *Living and Dying with AIDS.* New York: Plenum.

Wilkie, P. (1990). Haemophilia, AIDS, and HIV: Some social and ethical considerations. Pp. 34–40 in B. Almond, (ed.), *AIDS – A Moral Issue.* New York: St. Martin's Press.

Williams, A., & O'Connor, P. G. (1995). Substance abuse issues. Pp. 217–238 in P. Kelly, S. Holman, R. Rothenberg, & S. P. Holzemer (eds.), *Primary Care of Women and Children with HIV Infection.* Boston: Jones & Bartlett.

Wilson, J. (1992). Women as carers. Pp. 117–122 in J. Bury, V. Morrison, & S. McLachian (eds.), *Working with Women and AIDS.* London: Tavistock.

Wissow, L., Hutton, N., & McGraw, D. C. (1996). Psychological issues in children born to HIV-infected mothers. Pp. 78–95 in R. P. Faden & N. E. Kass (eds.), *HIV, AIDS, and Childbearing.* New York: Oxford University Press.

CHAPTER 7

Alemán, J. del C., Kloser, P., Kreibick, T., Steiner, G. L., & Boyd-Franklin, N. (1995). Women and HIV/AIDS. Pp. 90–111 in N. Boyd-Franklin, G. L. Steiner, & M. G. Boland (eds.), *Children, Families, and HIV/AIDS: Psychsocial and Therapeutic Issues.* New York: Guilford Press.

Altman, D. (1994). *Power and Community: Organizational and Cultural Responses to AIDS.* London: Taylor & Francis.

Ankrah, E. M., Schwartz, M., & Miller, J. (1996). Care and support systems. Pp. 264–293 in L. D. Long & E. M. Ankrah (eds.), *Women's Experiences with HIV/AIDS: An International Perspective.* New York: Columbia University Press.

References

Baines, C. T. (1991). The professions and an ethic of care. Pp. 36–72 in C. Baines, P. Evans, & S. Neysmith (eds.), *Women's Caring: Feminist Perspectives on Social Welfare*. Toronto: McClelland & Stewart.

Baines, C., Evans, P., & Neysmith, S. (eds.) (1991). Caring: Its impact on the lives of women. Pp. 11–35 in C. Baines, P. Evans, & S. Neysmith (eds.), *Women's Caring: Feminist Perspectives on Social Welfare*. Toronto: McClelland & Stewart.

Baker, L. S. (1992). The perspective of families. Pp. 147–161 in M. L. Stuber (ed.), *Children and AIDS*. Washington, DC: American Psychiatric Press.

Barnhart, K. (1997). Adolescent underrepresentation in clinical AIDS research. Pp. 74–85 in N. Goldstein & J. L. Manlowe (eds.), *The Gender Politics of HIV/AIDS in Women*. New York: New York University Press.

Bennett, L., Casey, K., & Austin, P. (1996). Issues for women as carers in HIV/AIDS. Pp. 177–190 in L. Sherr, C. Hankins, & L. Bennett (eds.), *AIDS as a Gender Issue: Psychological Perspectives*. London: Taylor & Francis.

Bergman, J. L. (1997). Coercive testing and the demonization of mothers: HIV policy and politics in New York state. HIV testing and reproductive choices for HIV positive women, Session No. 225, National Conference on Women and HIV, Pasadena, CA.

Blum, R. (1993). Critical issues for the family research agenda and their use in policy formulation. Pp. 110–112 in G. E. Hendershot & F. B. LeClere (eds.), *Family Health: From Data to Policy*. Minneapolis, MN: National Council on Family Relations.

Brown, V. (1997). Substance abuse, women, and HIV prevention and policy implications, Session No. 117, National Conference on Women and HIV, Pasadena, CA.

Burkett, E. (1995). *The Gravest Show on Earth: America in the Age of AIDS*. Boston: Houghton Mifflin.

Callahan, J. C., & Powell, J. (1994). Nursing and AIDS: Some special challenges. Pp. 51–73 in E. D. Cohen & M. Davis (eds.), *AIDS: Crisis in Professional Ethics*. Philadelphia: Temple University Press.

Chavkin, W. (1995). Women and HIV/AIDS. *Journal of the American Medical Association*, 50, 72.

Cohn, J., & Futterman, D. (1995). Adolescents and HIV. Pp. 133–148 in P. Kelly, S. Holman, R. Rothenberg, & S. P. Holzemer (eds.), *Primary Care of Women and Children with HIV Infection*. Boston: Jones & Bartlett.

College of Public and Community Service & Multicultural AIDS Coalition (1992). Counseling: Issues unique to women at risk. Pp. 123–149 in *Searching for Women: A Literature Review on Women, HIV, and AIDS in the U.S.* Boston: University of Massachusetts.

237

References

Connors, M. (1996). Sex, drugs, and structural violence: Unraveling the epidemic among poor women in the United States. Pp. 91–123 in P. Farmer, M. Connors, & J. Simmons (eds.), *Women, Poverty, and AIDS: Sex, Drugs, and Structural Violence*. Monroe, ME: Common Courage Press.

Crystal, S., & Sambamoorthi, U. (1996). Care needs and access to care among women living with HIV. Pp. 191–196 in L. Sherr, C. Hankins, & L. Bennett (eds.), *AIDS as a Gender Issue: Psychological Perspectives*. London: Taylor & Francis.

Currie, E., & Skolnick, J. H. (1997). *America's Problems: Social Issues and Public Policy*. New York: Longman.

Denenberg, R. (1995). Special concerns of women with HIV and AIDS. Pp. 115–135 in W. Odets & M. Shernoff (eds.), *The Second Decade of AIDS: A Mental Health Practice Handbook*. New York: Hatherleigh Press.

Division of Adolescent Medicine, Children's Hospital, Los Angeles. (1996). An evaluation of HIV risk and prevention among adolescents in Los Angeles. Executive Report, 1–149, May.

Durham, J. D., & Douard, J. (1993). The challenge of AIDS for health care workers. Pp. 286–300 in F. L. Cohen & J. D. Durham (eds.), *Women, Children, and HIV/AIDS*. New York: Springer.

Ellis, V. (1996). Alcoholics, drug addicts to lose aid. *Los Angeles Times*, pp. A1, 37, October 29.

Fox, L. J., Williamson, N. E., Cates, W., & Dallabetta, G. (1995). Improving reproductive health: Integrating STD and contraceptive services. *Journal of the American Medical Association, 50,* 129–136.

Fox, R. C., Aiken, L. H., & Messikomer, C. M. (1991). The culture of caring: AIDS and the nursing profession. Pp. 119–149 in D. Nelkin, D. P. Willis, & S. V. Parris (eds.), *A Disease of Society: Cultural and Institutional Responses to AIDS*. New York: Cambridge University Press.

Fraser, M., & Jones, D. (1995). The role of nurses in the HIV epidemic. Pp. 286–297 in B. E. Schneider & N. E. Stoller (eds.), *Women Resisting AIDS: Feminist Strategies of Empowerment*. Philadelphia: Temple University Press.

Geballe, S. (1995). Towards a child-responsive legal system. Pp. 140–164 in S. Geballe, J. Gruendel, & W. Andiman (eds.), *Forgotten Children of the AIDS Epidemic*. New Haven, CT: Yale University Press.

Gillman, R. R. (1996). Women care providers in HIV: A strengths perspective. Pp. 33–53 in V. J. Lynch & P. A. Wilson (eds.), *Caring for the HIV/AIDS Caregiver*. Westport, CT: Auburn House.

Gorna, R. (1996). *Vamps, Virgins, and Victims: How Can Women Fight AIDS?* New York: Cassell.

References

Gruendel, J. M., & Anderson, G. R. (1995). Building child- and family-responsive support systems. Pp. 165–189 in S. Geballe, J. Gruendel, & W. Andiman (eds.), *Forgotten Children of the AIDS Epidemic*. New Haven, CT: Yale University Press.

Guinan, M. E., & Leviton, L. (1995). Prevention of HIV infection in women: Overcoming barriers. *Journal of the American Medical Association*, 50, 74–77.

Hansen, E. (1997). Mandatory HIV testing of childbearing women, Session No. 218, National Conference on Women and HIV, Pasadena, CA.

Harvey, D. C. (1995). HIV/AIDS and public policy. Pp. 311–324 in N. Boyd-Franklin, G. L. Steiner, & M. G. Boland (eds.), *Children, Families, and HIV/AIDS: Psychsocial and Therapeutic Issues*. New York: Guilford Press.

Hein, K., Blair, J. F., Ratzan, S. C., & Dyson, D. E. (1993). Adolescents and HIV: Two decades of denial. Pp. 215–232 in S. C. Ratzan (ed.), *AIDS: Effective Health Communication for the 90s*. Washington, DC: Taylor & Francis.

Jonson, A. R., & Stryker, J. (1993). *The Social Impact of AIDS in the United States*. Washington, DC: National Academy Press.

King, P. A. (1996). Reproductive choices of adolescent females with HIV/AIDS. Pp. 345–366 in R. R. Faden & N. E. Kass (eds.), *HIV, AIDS and Childbearing: Public Policy, Private Lives*. New York: Oxford University Press.

Kloser, P., & Craig, J. M. (1994). *The Woman's HIV Sourcebook: A Guide to Better Health and Well-Being*. Dallas: Taylor.

Land, H. (1996). The social and psychological contexts of HIV/AIDS caregiving. Pp. 1–32 in V. J. Lynch & P. A. Wilson (eds.), *Caring for the HIV/AIDS Caregiver*. Westport, CT: Auburn House.

Lester, B. (1989). *Women and AIDS: A Practical Guide for Those Who Help Others*. Lavergne, TN: Crossroads.

Levine, C. (1995). Today's challenges, tomorrow's dilemmas. Pp. 190–204 in S. Geballe, J. Gruendel, & W. Andiman (ed.)., *Forgotten Children of the AIDS Epidemic*. New Haven, CT: Yale University Press.

——— (1996). Children in mourning: Impact of the HIV/AIDS epidemic on mothers with AIDS and their families. Pp. 197–214 in L. Sherr, C. Hankins, & L. Bennett (eds.), *AIDS as a Gender Issue: Psychological Perspectives*, London: Taylor & Francis.

Males, M. A. (1996). *The Scapegoat Generation: America's War on Adolescents*. Monroe, ME: Common Courage Press.

Maslanka, H. (1993). Women volunteers at GMHC. Pp. 110–125 in C. Squire (ed.), *Women and AIDS: Psychological Perspectives*. London: Sage.

References

McCann, K., & Wadsworth, E. (1994). The role of informal carers in supporting gay men who have HIV-related illness: What do they do and what are their needs? Pp. 118–128 in R. Bor & J. Elford (eds.), *The Family and HIV.* New York: Cassell.

McGarrahan, P. (1994). *Transcending AIDS.* Philadelphia: University of Pennsylvania Press.

McGovern, T. (1997). Family welfare and guardianship. Policy Track, Session No. 302, National Conference on Women and HIV, Pasadena, CA.

Merkel-Holguin, L. A. (1994). *Because You Love Them: A Parent's Planning Guide.* Washington, DC: Child Welfare League of America.

Moffat, B. C. (1987). *When Someone You Love Has AIDS: A Book of Hope for Family and Friends.* New York: Penguin.

Monette, P. (1988). *Borrowed Time: An AIDS Memoir.* San Diego: Harcourt, Brace, Jovanovich.

National Conference on Women and HIV (1997). Pasadena, CA.

Nazario, S. (1993). Sex, drugs, and no place to go. *Los Angeles Times,* pp. A 1, 38–40, December 12.

Nehring, W., Malm, K., & Harris, D. (1993). Family and living issues for HIV-infected children. Pp. 211–227 in F. L. Cohen & J. P. Durham (eds.), *Women, Children, and HIV/AIDS.* New York: Springer.

Novick, A. (1995). Women and children in the time of plague in America. Pp. 247–149 in S. Geballe, J. Gruendel, & W. Andiman (eds.), *Forgotten Children of the AIDS Epidemic.* New Haven, CT: Yale University Press.

Omoto, A. M., & Crain, A. L. (1994). Coping, social support, and psychological distress in gay men whose partners have AIDS. Unpublished manuscript, University of Kansas.

Omoto, A. M., & Snyder, M. (1995). Sustained helping without obligation: Motivation, longevity of service, and perceived attitude change among AIDS volunteers. *Journal of Personality and Social Psychology,* **68,** 671–686.

Patton, C. (1994). *Last Served? Gendering the HIV Pandemic.* New York: Taylor & Francis.

Peabody, B. (1987). *The Screaming Room.* New York: Avon.

Rivera, C. (1996). Grandparents fear price of welfare cuts. *Los Angeles Times,* pp. A1, 35, November 24.

Roan, S. (1994). The street fighter. *Los Angeles Times,* pp. E 1–2, January 3.

Rodriguez-Trias, H. (1997). Welfare legislation and immigrant women. Session No. 202, National Conference on Women and HIV, Pasadena, CA.

Rodriguez-Trias, H., & Marte, C. (1995). Challenges and possibilities: Women, HIV, and the health care system in the 1990s. Pp. 301–321 in B. E. Schneider & N. E. Stoller (eds.), *Women Resisting AIDS: Feminist Strategies of Empowerment.* Philadelphia: Temple University Press.

References

Rogers, M. F. (1997). The challenges of implementing recommendations for prevention of HIV perinatal transmission: How have we done so far? Session No. 204, National Conference on Women and HIV, Pasadena, CA.

Rotheram-Borus, M. J. (1997a). HIV prevention challenges – realistic strategies and early detection programs (annotation). *American Journal of Public Health*, 87, 544–546.

(1997b). AIDS prevention with adolescents. HIV prevention programs: A spectrum of effective behavioral approaches, Session No. 110, National Conference on Women and HIV, Pasadena, CA.

Rotheram-Borus, M. J., Koopman, C., & Ehrhardt, A. (1991). Homeless youth and HIV infection. *American Psychologist*, 46, 1188–1197.

Rubin, G. (1996). Confronting obstacles (1996). Pp. 279–298 in P. Farmer, M. Connors, & J. Simmons (eds.), *Women, Poverty, and AIDS: Sex, Drugs, and Structural Violence*. Monroe, ME: Common Courage Press.

Schaffzin, T. (1997). Changing from within: Services for women at Gay Men's Health Crisis, Inc. Innovative Health Service Models, Session No. 223, National Conference on Women and HIV, Pasadena, CA.

Schiller, N. G. (1993). The invisible women: Caregiving and the construction of AIDS health services. *Culture, Medicine, and Psychiatry*, 17, 487–512.

Shelby, R. D. (1992). *If a Partner Has AIDS: Guide to Clinical Intervention for Relationships in Crisis*. New York: Harrington Park Press.

(1995). *People with HIV and Those Who Help Them*. Binghamton, NY: Haworth.

Sherr, L. (1995). Psychological aspects of providing care for women with HIV infection. Pp. 107–123 in H. Minkoff, J. A. DeHovitz, & A. Duerr (eds.), *HIV Infection in Women*. New York: Raven Press.

Simpson, B. J., & Williams, A. (1993). Caregiving: A matriarchal tradition continues. Pp. 200–211 in A. Kurth (ed.), *Until the Cure: Caring for Women with HIV*. New Haven, CT: Yale University Press.

Smith, D., Johnson, G., & O'Reilly, R. (1997). Aid recipients face battle for limited jobs. *Los Angeles Times*, pp. A1, 32–33, June 1.

Smith, J. M. (1996). *AIDS and Society*. Upper Saddle River, NJ: Prentice-Hall.

Sondheimer, D. L. (1992). HIV infection and disease among homeless adolescents. Pp. 71–85 in R. DiClemente (ed.), *Adolescents and AIDS: A Generation in Jeopardy*. Newbury Park, CA: Sage Publications.

Squire, C. (1993). Women providing AIDS-related services. Pp. 107–109 in C. Squire (ed.), *Women and AIDS: Psychological Perspectives*. London: Sage.

Stoller, N. S. (1995). Lesbian involvement in the AIDS epidemic: Changing roles and generational differences. Pp. 270–285 in B. E. Schneider & N. E. Stoller (eds.), *Women Resisting AIDS: Feminist Strategies of Empowerment*. Philadelphia: Temple University Press.

References

Taylor-Brown, S. (1998). Talking with parents about permanency planning. Pp. 349–359 in D. M. Aronstein & B. J. Thompson (eds.), *HIV and Social Work: A Practitioner's Guide*. New York: Harrington Park Press.

Ward, M. C. (1993). A different disease: HIV/AIDS and health care for women in poverty. *Culture, Medicine, and Psychiatry*, 17, 413–430.

Wilcox, B. L. (1990). Federal policy and adolescent AIDS. Pp. 61–70 in W. Gardner, S. G. Millstein, & B. L. Wilcox (eds.), *Adolescents in the AIDS Epidemic*. San Francisco: Jossey-Bass.

Williams, M. J. (1988). Gay men as "buddies" to persons living with AIDS and ARC. *Smith College Studies in Social Work*. 59, 38–52.

Wissow, L., Hutton, N., & McGraw, D. C. (1996). Psychological issues in children born to HIV-infected mothers. Pp. 78–95 in R. P. Faden & N. E. Kass (eds.), *HIV, AIDS, amd Childbearing*. New York: Oxford University Press.

SUGGESTED READING

ACE Program of the Bedford Hills Correctional Facility Staff. (1998). *Breaking the Walls of Silence: AIDS and Women in a New York State Maximum Security Prison*. New York: Overlook Press.

The ACT UP/New York Women & AIDS Book Group (1990). *Women, AIDS, and Activism*. Boston: South End Press.

Adam, B. D., & Sears, L. (1996). *Experiencing HIV: Personal, Family, and Work Relationships*. New York: Columbia University Press.

Berer, M., & Ray, S. (eds.). (1993). *Women and HIV/AIDS: An International Resource Book*. London: Pandora.

Bury, J., Morrison, V., & McLachian, S. (eds.). (1992). *Working with Women and AIDS: Medical, Social and Counselling Issues*. London: Tavistock.

Cohen, F. L., & Durham, J. D. (eds.). (1993). *Women, Children, and HIV/AIDS*. New York: Springer.

Corea, G. (1992). *The Invisible Epidemic: The Story of Women and AIDS*. New York: Harper Collins.

Dane, B. O., & Levine, C. (1994). *AIDS and the New Orphans: Coping with Death*. Westport, CT: Auburn House.

Dansky, S. (1997). *Nobody's Children: Orphans of the HIV Epidemic*. New York: Harrington Park Press.

Dorn, N., Henderson, S., & South, N. (eds.). (1992). *AIDS: Women, Drugs, and Social Care*. London: Falmer Press.

Doyal, L., Naidoo, J., & Wilton, T. (eds.). (1994). *AIDS: Setting a Feminist Agenda*. New York: Taylor & Francis.

Faden, R., Geller, G., & Powers, M. (eds.). (1991). *AIDS, Women, and the Next Generation: Towards a Morally Acceptable Public Policy for HIV Testing of Pregnant Women and Newborns*. New York: Oxford University Press.

Faden, R. R., & N. E. Kass (eds.). (1996). *HIV, AIDS and Childbearing*. New York: Oxford University Press.

Suggested Reading

Farmer, P., Connors, M., & Simmons, J. (eds.). (1996). *Women, Poverty, and AIDS: Sex, Drugs, and Structural Violence.* Monroe, ME: Common Courage Press.

Geballe, S., Gruendel, J., & Andiman, W. (eds.). (1995). *Forgotten Children of the AIDS Epidemic.* New Haven, CT: Yale University Press.

Goldstein, N., & Manlowe, J. L. (eds.). (1997). *The Gender Politics of HIV/AIDS in Women.* New York: New York University Press.

Gorna, R. (1996). *Vamps, Virgins, and Victims: How Can Women Fight AIDS?* New York: Cassell.

Huston, R., & Berridge, M. (1997). *A Positive Life: Portraits of Women: Living with HIV.* Philadelphia: Running Press.

Kelly, P., Holman, S., Rothenberg, R., & Holzemer, S. P. (1995). *Primary Care of Women and Children with HIV Infection.* Boston: Jones & Bartlett.

Klitzman, R. (1997). *Being Positive: The Lives of Men and Women with HIV.* Chicago: I. R. Dee.

Kloser, P., & Craig, J. M. (1994). *The Women's HIV Sourcebook: A Guide to Better Health and Well-Being.* Dallas: Taylor.

Kurth, A. (ed.). (1993). *Until the Cure: Caring for Women with HIV.* New Haven, CT: Yale University Press.

Lather, P., & Smithies, C. (1997). *Troubling the Angels: Women Living with HIV.* Boulder, CO: Westview.

Long, L. D., & Ankrah, E. M. (1996). *Women's Experiences with HIV/AIDS: An International Perspective.* New York: Columbia University Press.

Norwood, C. (1987). *Advice for Life: A Woman's Guide to AIDS Risks and Prevention.* New York: Pantheon Books.

O'Leary, A., & Jemmott, L. S. (eds.). (1995). *Women at Risk: Issues in the Primary Prevention of AIDS.* New York: Plenum.

(1996). *Women and AIDS: Coping and Care.* New York: Plenum.

O'Sullivan, S., & Thomson, K. (eds.). (1996). *Positively Women Living with AIDS.* New York: Harper Collins.

Patton, C. (1994). *Last Served? Gendering the HIV Pandemic.* New York: Taylor & Francis.

Pearlberg, G. (1991). *Women, AIDS, and Communities: A Guide for Action.* Lanham, MD: Scarecrow Press.

Peavy, F. (1990). *A Shallow Pool of Time: An HIV+ Woman Grapples with the AIDS Epidemic.* Philadelphia: New Society Publishers.

Reider, I., & Ruppelt, P. (eds.). (1988). *AIDS: The Women.* San Francisco: Cleis Press.

Richardson, D. (1988). *Women and AIDS.* New York: Methuen.

Roth, N. L., & Fuller, K. K. (eds.). (1998). *Women and AIDS: Negotiating Safer Practices, Care, and Representation.* New York: Haworth Press.

Rudd, A., & Taylor, D. (eds.). (1992). *Positive Women: Voices of Women Living with AIDS.* Toronto: Second Story Press.

Schneider, B. E., & Stoller, N. E. (eds.). (1995). *Women Resisting AIDS: Feminist Strategies of Empowerment.* Philadelphia: Temple University Press.

Sherr, L. (1991). *HIV and AIDS in Mothers and Babies.* Oxford: Blackwell.

Sherr, L. (ed.). (1994). *AIDS and the Heterosexual Population.* New York: Harwood Academic Publishers.

Sherr, L., Hankins, C., & Bennett, L. (eds.). (1996). *AIDS as a Gender Issue.* London: Taylor & Francis.

Sobo, E. J. (1995). *Choosing Unsafe Sex: AIDS Risk Denial among Disadvantaged Women.* Philadelphia: University of Pennsylvania Press.

Sonder, B. (1995). *Epidemic of Silence: The Facts about Women and AIDS.* New York: Franklin Watts.

Squire, C. (ed.). (1993). *Women and AIDS: Psychological Perspectives.* Newbury Park, CA: Sage.

Stein, T. J. (1998). *The Social Welfare of Women and Children with HIV and AIDS: Legal Protections, Policy, and Programs.* New York: Oxford University Press.

Stevens, S. J., Tortu, S., & Coyle, S. L. (1998). *Women, Drug Use, and HIV Infection.* New York: Haworth Medical Press.

Stoller, N. E. (1998). *Lessons from the Damned: Queers, Whores, and Junkies Respond to AIDS.* New York: Routledge.

Waldby, C. (1996). *AIDS and the Body Politics: Biomedicine and Sexual Difference.* New York: Routledge.

Walker, S. E. (1998). *Women with AIDS and their Children.* New York: Garland.

Whitmire, L. E. (1998). *Childhood Trauma and HIV: Women at Risk.* Philadelphia, PA: Brunner/Mazel.

Wyatt-Morley, C. (1997). *AIDS Memoir: Journal of an HIV-Positive Mother.* West Hartford, CT: Kumarian Press.

INDEX

t following a page number indicates *table*

Index

African Americans (*cont.*)
    statistics about, 11, 12
    women, 12, 18, 91–92, 99, 109
age
    of adolescence, 183
    and AIDS incidence, 32–33
    and caregiving, 144
    and clinical trials, 100
    factors related to, 9–11, 19–20
    and long-term survival, 33–34
AIDS: *see* more specific topic
AIDS Action Committee, 174
AIDS Clinical Trials Groups, 100–1
AIDS Coalition to Unleash Power, 103
AIDS Project Los Angeles, 172
AIDS Targeted Outreach Model (ATOM), 68
alcohol use, 32, 122
"America Responds to AIDS," 105–6
American Red Cross, 117
anal intercourse, 19, 21, 22*t*
antenatal care: *see* pregnancy, care during
antibody test, 3, 8, 56, 76
antiretroviral drugs, 44
antiseptics during childbirth, 43
artificial insemination, 21–22
athletes, 120
ATOM (AIDS Targeted Outreach Model), 68
aunts: *see* kinship care
AZT (zidovudine), 19, 22*t*, 29, 39, 99–101
    and perinatal transmission, 44–45

Baby Moms (San Francisco), 162
barriers to service: *see* health care, barriers to;
    social services, barriers to
behavior: *see* risk behavior; sexual behavior
bereavement, 147–51, 189–90
birth control: *see* contraception
bisexual men, 124–27; *see also* homosexual men
    in prison, 123
    and sex partners, 15, 17*t*, 31*t*, 126
bisexual transmission, 9*t*
bisexual women, 25; *see also* lesbians
Blacks: *see* African Americans
blood, 23, 60, 125, 128, 129; *see also* factor VIII
    concentrate; hemophilia
    transfusions, 9*t*, 17*t*, 23, 24, 30, 30*t*, 31*t*
"boarder babies," 154
breastfeeding, 42–43
brothels, 75–76, 133

Caesarian delivery, 39, 41–42, 101; *see also*
    childbirth
candida vulvovaginitis, 26
CARE Program (Long Beach), ix, 177
caregiving
    for elders, 144
    as female responsibility, 5, 151–52
    and health care system, 114
    by men, 162, 170
    and poverty, 173
    professional, 167–70
    and respite services, 162
    social services for, 174
    and socioeconomic differences, 173
    by volunteers, 170–72
    by women, 104, 109, 144–48, 171
    by younger generation, 151
Caribbean, 74
causes of AIDS: *see* epidemiology
CD4+ lymphocyte counts, 26
Center for Disease Control, 72–74, 94–95,
    96–97, 105–6
cervical diseases, 19–20, 22*t*, 26–28, 95, 100
Chamberlain, Wilt, 120
Chicanas, 12, 89–90, 109
child welfare agencies, 162, 163, 180–82
childbirth, 39, 41–42, 43; *see also* Caesarian
    delivery
children: *see also* child welfare agencies; cus-
    tody; infants; pediatric AIDS
    and AIDS education, 189
    and bereavement, 147–51
    care of, 57, 145, 147–51; *see also* kinship care
    and chronic illness, 141–43
    desire for, 22, 53, 55, 128; *see also* father-
    hood; motherhood
    and drug abuse, 66–67, 69, 152–54
    epidemiology, 29–30
    with hemophilia, 155, 156–57
    of HIV mothers, 144
    homes of, 148–49
    long-term survival, 33
    mortality, 31
    neglect of, 181
    in poverty, 184
    seroprevalence, 30
    social services to, 180–82
    transmission categories, 30*t*
circumcision, 21

Index

Index

Index

Index